Professor Klonowski has produced an impressive and well-documented, easy to read book that serves as an excellent after action report of the devastating fall-out from the extraordinary measures imposed by federal government agencies world-wide to confront a highly overblown COVID-19 threat. His book demonstrates that the SARS-CoV-2 virus was far from being as deadly as originally portrayed, and chronicles the ineffectiveness of quarantining, lockdowns, masking, COVID-19 vaccines and other measures that assaulted human rights and freedoms. In particular, his book does a superb job of analyzing the extensive collateral damage of these measures that divided families and friends, took a terrible toll on the physical and mental health, and economic security of children through to the most elderly, and particularly targeted the most marginalized in our society. The information provided in this book should serve as a powerful wake up call to citizens and politicians that do not want to repeat the costly mistakes of the COVID-19 pandemic.

– STEVEN PELECH, Ph.D., Professor of Medicine, University of British Columbia, vice-president, Canadian Citizens Care Alliance, editor and author of "Down the COVID-19 Rabbit Hole" and "COVID-19 Pandemonium"

This book was a worthy read, giving an account of the COVID-19 pandemic. It provides an opportunity for introspection of the events that unfolded, policy paths that were taken and those that were not, and some lessons to be learned.

– CARLOS ALEGRIA, Ph.D., CEO of Phinance Technologies

Darek Klonowski is Professor of Business Administration at Brandon University in Canada. Prior to joining academia, he worked in the venture capital and private equity industry.

Blessed be the Lord, my rock
Psalm 144

The Covid-19 Wreckage

How COVID-19 Response Impacted the Family, Small Business, and Religious Life

Darek Klonowski

Connor Court Publishing

Table of Contents

— - -

Tables

Figures

Preface

On March 11, 2020, the World Health Organization (WHO) announced to the world the existence of novel coronavirus, which was given the abbreviation SARS-CoV-2. Specialists from Imperial College London subsequently released an epidemiological model that estimated that in the absence of strong interventions, the novel SARS-CoV-2 coronavirus would result in 7 billion infections and 40 million deaths globally in 2020 alone. As a result, governments around the world implemented wide-ranging restrictive measures to "flatten the curve" and allegedly avoid overwhelming the healthcare system. However, these short-term restrictions were continually extended and remained in place for nearly 2 years.

These restrictions did not occur in a vacuum, so it is possible to trace both direct and indirect impacts on socioeconomic instability experienced by the population and the economy because of public policy and decisions taken by governments and their associated stakeholders; I term these decisions and subsequent actions as COVID-19 response. In other words, what individuals, families, small businesses, the clergy, and others experienced was due to the choices made by governments. Viruses have historically been a regular part of human existence, and, like the current coronavirus, cause sickness, mutate, expand, and unfortunately, result in human deaths despite normal precautions and vaccinations. What was atypical in the case of novel coronaviruses was the response of public authorities and their stakeholders.

This book is an interdisciplinary project with a focus on socioeconomics, public health, and public accountability. It is predominantly about the harm and damage that arose from lockdowns due to COVID-19 response. Some aspects of this harm can be quantified in terms of excess deaths, the number of small businesses closed, the volume of consumers forced to declare bankruptcy, and the total people who were unemployed. Other estimates of damage include that about "300 million humans fell into poverty ... 10,000 children died each month due to virus-linked hunger from global lockdowns ... [and] 500,000 children per month experienced wasting and stunting from malnutrition."[1] However, there are other metrics that may be impossible to calculate, so "we have no way of knowing how many people died from isolation, unemployment, deferred medical care, depression, mental illness, obesity, stress, overdoes, suicide, addiction, alcoholism, and the accidents that so often accompany despair."[2] Thus, the consequences of COVID-19 response were unprecedented and nearly incalculable.

People may view this book from different perspectives. There will be individuals who have closely scrutinized the developments around lockdowns, restrictions, COVID-19 vaccines, and alternative treatments, and will be unsurprised by most of this book's contents. However, this book may represent a more complex read for those that followed the behavioural cues prescribed by various governments and their associated stakeholders and experts. For this latter group, the book may raise multiple questions and concerns in addition to invoking negative feelings.

The material for this book project was collected over a period of about 4 years since the onset of the pandemic. This book relies on a wide variety of sources, including academic studies and reviews, commentaries, books, public and private datasets, open letters, public disclosures, and articles from mainstream media. Particularly important were alternative sources of information due to the mass censorship in mainstream and social media, which in lockstep action aimed to protect the integrity of the main governmental narrative of lockdowns and mass vaccinations. Thus, this book relies on important material from legal cases, inquiries, discoveries, legal agreements and testimonies that often did not make it into the public domain. This book also includes many direct quotes, especially from medical and scientific studies, to avoid any confusion or misinterpretation and to allow readers to construct their own conclusions and judgements.

While the pandemic itself seems to have subsided, the story of COVID-19 response is far from over. Even four years later, there are still new observations, commentaries, analyses, investigations, formal inquiries and hearings, and academic studies that contradict the efficacy and validity of lockdowns and mass vaccinations. For example, many interesting disclosures came from the testimony given at the House Select Subcommittee on the Coronavirus Pandemic in the United States. One may have some doubts whether this and other such inquiries are likely to lead to any sort of accountability for public and unelected officials. Most importantly, it is unclear whether any proper lessons were derived from these experiences. The lack of any final conclusions in this respect means that this book is inherently incomplete. However, it could be conjectured that an analysis of the historical record of the COVID-19 pandemic may not be kind to those who instigated COVID-19 response.

Book structure

This book is comprised of four sections and eight chapters. Each section consists of one to three chapters of varying length. There are 18 figures and tables to illustrate and provide further support for key observations, discussions, analyses, and hypotheses.

The introductory section of the book includes one chapter that is predominantly dedicated to describing one of the central narratives of the COVID-19 pandemic, namely vaccines, which have traditionally played an important role in public health. While the official public narrative was overwhelmingly positive about these novel treatments, the main objective in this part of the book is to present information that mainstream and social media avoided, downplayed, ignored, or even outright censored. In other words, the chapter focuses on the debate we did not but should have had. The chapter specifically identifies fatality rates from SARS-CoV-2, concepts of relative risk reduction (RRR) and absolute risk reduction (ARR), and herd immunity. It outlines the problems potentially associated with COVID-19 vaccines, highlights safety signals generated through official data sets designed to catch such signals and provides a short overview of academic studies related to vaccine-associated issues. The chapter discusses some challenges related to vaccine manufacturers. Pfizer, for example, was reprimanded by the Prescription Medicines Code of Practice Authority (PMCPA) in the United Kingdom. AstraZeneca only acknowledged that its vaccine products can possibly cause a rare side effect when under legal pressure, and consequently withdrew its vaccines from the market.

This book's second section is titled "The characteristics of COVID-19 response" and is comprised of two chapters. The first chapter of this section, or the second chapter of the book, outlines the range of society-wide restrictive measures seen during COVID-19 response. One of the most predominant of these measures was mass testing with the use of the polymerase chain reaction (PCR) testing method. The chapter also focuses on lockdowns, which represented a combination of severe, consequential, and lasting restrictions, including stay-at-home orders, stoppage of economic activities, closure of businesses, termination of various social activities, masking, and social distancing. This chapter is closed with a brief discussion of social distancing and its non-scientific basis. This chapter would not be complete without a brief look at the case of Sweden, which challenged the conventional approach to lockdowns because the local government allowed its society and economy to remain open. In consequence, the country scored better on many quantitative and non-quantitative measures compared to other countries that implemented heavy-handed and draconian COVID-19 response measures.

The third chapter of this book focuses on other components of what were termed COVID-19 response, including political decisions made at the federal, provincial, state, or municipal levels. It is noted how these political decisions were influenced by non-elected individuals, some specialists and experts, and institutions. The chapter also discusses how COVID-19 response contributed to macroeconomic damage, the centralization of political power, censorship, the oppression of medical professionals, public communications, so-called COVID-19 scientism, and division among people.

The third section of the book, titled "The main areas of impact of COVID-19 response," highlights three distinct consequences of COVID-19 response. The fourth chapter of this book focuses on how COVID-19 restrictions impacted the family by illuminating that the pandemic and COVID-19 response were driven by fear and division. Most importantly, the lockdowns, quarantines, stay-at-home orders, and other restrictions resulted in changes to normal patterns of family life by causing home to become the centre of gravity for the entire family. An inability to leave one's home thus created tension and caused problems in the areas of familial relations, family economics, and mental health. Family economic problems were quantifiably visible in raising credit card debt, credit card delinquencies, and consumer insolvencies. In terms of mental health issues, the most affected groups were children, adolescents, and the elderly.

The fifth chapter of this book focuses on the negative impact of COVID-19 response on religious faith and practice. This chapter argues that COVID-19 response caused a severe curtailment of religious freedom, conscience, faith, and expression. Restrictions not only negatively affected traditional faith-based practices, but other aspects of religious life as well. The religious clergy were also severely impacted and suffered from mental and physical health problems as a result. Most worryingly, however, was the manifestation of political power against religious freedoms exhibited when Canadian pastors were jailed due to alleged violations of COVID-19 restrictions.

The sixth chapter details the assault on small businesses, which came through the actions of various levels of the state (i.e., municipal, local, and federal), public health, and even law enforcement. The severe disruption of small business operations due to COVID-19 response led to a rapid revenue decline, cash flow issues, an inability for small firms to cover fixed cost obligations, and a disruption of existing business models. Damage in this area has been further reflected in insolvencies and bankruptcies for existing businesses and limited new business formations. Small business owners also suffered from mental health issues that are likely to impact their propensity to engage in entrepreneurial activities in the future.

Chapter seven examines excess deaths, which are defined as the number of deaths by any cause that arise during a particular situation or circumstance and are above what could reasonably be expected under normal conditions. The special circumstance in this case pertains to the COVID-19 pandemic, which is a special event of interest. It is also examined where these excess deaths came from, as they are now well documented across many countries. Although the chapter engages in a broader international analysis of excess deaths, it focuses specifically on excess deaths in the United Kingdom and Canada.

The fourth and concluding section of this book discusses arguably the most difficult topic, namely public accountability and trust. If harm and damage were caused by COVID-19 response public policy, there must be public accountability. The concept of public accountability for COVID-19 response is analysed in accordance with selected criteria that are applied to different countries around the world. The decisions made by the state are also evaluated in the context of strategic management and outline key areas of public policy failure. Moreover, the chapter assesses COVID-19 related public policy in relation to the key stakeholders of the lockdown operations and vaccine campaigns, namely the elected and unelected decision makers, and identifies the disproportionally influential role of unelected public officials in the pandemic.

Contributions of this book

In the last few years, there have been numerous books written from a perspective that challenges the official public narrative of COVID-19. These books include *The Real Anthony Fauci* and *The Wuhan Cover-up* by Robert F Kennedy Jr., *Lies My Gov't Told Me* by Robert Malone, *Fisman's Fraud* by Regina Watteel, *Deception: The Great Cover-up* by Rand Paul, *The War on Ivermectin* by Pierre Kory and Jenna McCarthy, and *Cause Unknown: The Epidemic of Sudden Deaths in 2021 & 2022 & 2023* by Ed Dowd, just to name a few. No doubt more books will be written as new information and evidence comes to light.

This book seeks to complement those already written by further extending their contemplations in several unique areas. Firstly, this book provides readers with an analysis of the harm and damage generated by COVID-19 response to small businesses. As it is argued throughout this book, COVID-19 response represented a direct attack on entrepreneurship and the middle class. Moreover, this book identifies the impact of COVID-19 response on the family and religious life, two concepts which are critical to the fabric and foundations of society and were unduly targeted. This book also questions how the public's trust was broken.

Acknowledgments

While preparing the initial manuscript, I benefited from informal discussions and exchanges with medical doctors, scientists, academics, and work colleagues. These informal interactions were critical in shaping this book. I would also like to sincerely thank Douglas Allen (Simon Fraser University), Mikolaj Raszek (Merogenomics), Jens Zimmermann (Regent College), Hamid Mumin (Brandon University), Marco Cosentino (University of Insurbia), Mark Mercure, Reverend John Okosun (Archdiocese of Winnipeg), Meryl Nass, George Farrow (McGill University), Casey Mulligan (University of Chicago), Ambarish Chandra (University of Toronto), Reverend Derek Remus (Diocese of Calgary), Michael Thoene (University of Warmia and Mazury in Olsztyn), Richard Bliss (Babson College), Steven Pelech (University of British Columbia [UBC] and Canadian Citizens Care Alliance [CCCA]), and Nicolas Hulscher for providing insightful and detailed feedback and comments on different parts of the manuscript. Thank you also for your encouragement. I would also like to thank Jeffrey Tucker (Brownstone Institute), Steven Pelech (UBC and CCCA), Carlos Alegria (Phinance Technologies), Pierre Kory (Rebuild Medicine and Leading Edge Clinic), Allison Pejovic (Charter Advocates Canada) and Nicholas Hulscher

(McCullough Foundation) for providing book quotes.

I would like to thank Marissa Stelmack, who provided careful, detail oriented, and invaluable editorial assistance. Marissa made numerous corrections to the manuscript and caught many of my omissions and errors.

I would also like to thank Anthony Cappello for providing an opportunity to publish with Connor Court Publishing. This is my first book with Connor Court. Also, I would like to thank individuals, who were involved in copyediting and production of the book, namely Julie Cappello, Maria Giordano and Michael Gilchrist.

It is important to state the obvious, namely that opinions expressed in this book are my personal thoughts, reflections, and opinions and they do not represent and reflect the opinions of any public or private institutions I am affiliated with.

Darek Klonowski

Brandon, December 2, 2024

PART I: INTRODUCTION

1

The COVID-19 pandemic narrative: A debate we didn't have

Global narrative on COVID-19 vaccines

In early March of 2020, the World Health Organization (WHO) announced to the world the existence of novel coronavirus. Subsequently, academics from Imperial College London released an epidemiological model that estimated that in the absence of strong interventions, the novel SARS-CoV-2 coronavirus would result in 7 billion infections and millions of deaths globally in 2020 alone. The disease arising from SARS-CoV-2 was termed COVID-19.

Although COVID-19 can be deadly, "the vast majority of all persons infected with COVID-19 recover after minor, often uncharacteristic illness."[3] For example, there were 15,651 COVID-19 deaths in Canada in 2020, resulting in a crude mortality rate (CMR, which reflects the fraction of deaths in the overall population, regardless of infection status)[4] of 0.041 percent (i.e., 15,651 deaths divided by 38,005,238 individuals).[5,6] There were 14,668 deaths in 2021, which is equal to a crude mortality rate of 0.039 percent.[7] The CMR from seasonal influenza and pneumonia (two illnesses combined by the Canadian government in its statistical reporting) was equal to about 0.02 percent.[8] While the CMR from SARS-CoV-2 may be seen as twice the rate from seasonal influenza and pneumonia combined, it represents an incremental increase of two 2 deaths per 10,000 people. And yet, researchers in other studies have still claimed that "COVID-19 absolute mortality levels are several times higher" than mortality from pneumonia and influenza.[9] In practical terms, even if the CMR related to COVID-19 in Canada was 5 times higher compared to influenza and pneumonia, it would still only be equal to 0.1 percent.

The case fatality rate (CFR, defined as the number of deaths from the disease expressed as a percent of confirmed cases)[10] was equal to 2.69 percent in Canada in 2020 (i.e., 15,651 deaths divided by 581,382 confirmed cases), meaning the associated survival rate was 97.31 percent. In 2021 the CFR declined and was equal to 0.91 percent (i.e., 14,668/1,606,663) and the survival rate was 99.09 percent.[11] It is likely that the number of COVID-19 cases were significantly higher, as most children and about 40 percent of adults were asymptomatic. Also, many people were not tested for COVID-19 since tests were not widely available early in the pandemic. In practice, this means that the actual CFR was likely much lower.

At the regional level and using one of the provinces in Canada (i.e., Manitoba) as an example, there were 667 deaths from COVID-19 in 2020 and 725 deaths in 2021, which equates to a CFR of 2.7 percent (i.e., 667/24,700) and 1.3 percent (i.e., 725/55,394), respectively.[12] Deaths associated with COVID-19 represented only about 7 percent of total deaths in the province in both years, meaning that around 93 percent of individuals died from other causes. Of those who died from COVID-19, 73 percent of deaths occurred in the population above 70 years old (data as of October 7, 2021). Since the onset of COVID-19 until October 2021, there were 3 total deaths in Manitoba associated with COVID-19 in the population between 0 and 19 years old. There were also only 38 total deaths from COVID-19 in the population between 20 and 39 years of age over the same period.[13] It has become evident that COVID-19 more severely impacted vulnerable individuals with pre-existing comorbidities and the elderly. Similarly, the Justice Center for Constitutional Freedoms (JCCF) reported in August 2021 that the average age of an individual who died with COVID-19 in another Canadian province (i.e., Alberta) was equal to 80 years while the average life expectancy was equal to 81.6 years.

Comparable statistics have also been obtained from international observations. For example, researchers Axfors and Ioannidis estimated infection fatality rates (IFR, defined as a total number of deaths divided by a total number of estimated infections, including undiagnosed and asymptomatic cases)[14] on the basis of meta-analysis to be as follows: age 0-19 IFR equal to 0.0013 percent, age 20-29 IFR equal to 0.0088 percent, age 30-39 IFR equal to 0.021 percent, age 40-49 IFR equal to 0.042 percent, age 50-59 equal to 0.14 percent, and age 60-69 equal to 0.65 percent.[15] The highest estimation by the authors were for deaths of the elderly (above 70) at about 2.9 percent. In another study, Ioannidis, Axfors and Contopoulos-Ioannidis concluded that "people <65 years old have very small risks of COVID-19 death even in pandemic epicenters and deaths for people <65 years without underlying predisposing conditions are remarkably uncommon."[16] Lastly, it is reasonable to assume that IFRs were not static throughout the pandemic but changed as the virus evolved, the population acquired immunity, and some individuals were vaccinated.

Confirmation of the CFRs came early in the form of two events that affected individuals from different demographic groups, namely the cases of SARS-CoV-2 at sea. The first instance relates to the Diamond Princess cruise ship, a luxury cruise ship, with 2,666 passengers and 1,054 crew members on board.[17] This setting facilitated what was perhaps one of the first natural experiments regarding the spread of SARS-CoV-2, its infectivity, and mortality, especially in relation to a more mature population (passengers onboard had "a median age of 60 to 69 years old, and another 14 percent of passengers" were above 70).[18] Without going into details here, in spite of imperfect emergency preparedness, difficult operating conditions, and a potentially more vulnerable population, there were only three deaths. The CFR among all the individuals on board was equal to 0.23 percent (3 deaths/1,300 confirmed cases).[19] In another example, there was an outbreak of SARS-CoV-2 on board the U.S. aircraft carrier U.S.S. Theodore Roosevelt, which maintained a crew of 4,779 with a mean age of 27 years.[20] In this case there was one death, resulting in a CFR equal to 0.08 percent (1/1,271 confirmed cases).[21] Of those with positive tests, 76.9 percent had no symptoms, 23 individuals were hospitalized, and 4 ended up in the ICU.[22] Among symptomatic individuals, 59.5 percent experienced a cough, 43.8 percent noted nasal or sinus congestion, 42.3 percent reported an altered sense of taste/smell, and 31.0 percent suffered a headache.[23] It is important to note that while 970 asymptomatic passengers were disembarking from the Diamond Princess in late February 2020 with negative test results,[24] the modellers from Imperial College London compared the potential impact of SARS-CoV-2 to the devastation caused by the Spanish flu.[25] Did the modellers know about these important data points? Did they take them into account when forecasting the "doom and gloom" scenario for the world?

Despite a lack of evidence of high COVID-19 deaths and potential misattribution of deaths to COVID-19 (which could make the IFR appear high), and following a period of lockdowns and severe restrictions, a single narrative emerged or was imposed that the only viable choice for resolving the pandemic was a safe and effective vaccine (despite the suggestion by others that natural population immunity would solve the problem). Furthermore, the vaccine was presented as the proverbial magic bullet that would end the pandemic. While vaccines can be an important component for the eradication of some diseases, epidemiologic evidence suggests that a proper strategy to minimize or outright eradicate disease normally includes a wide range of strategies, tactics, and plans. It is also difficult to know if vaccines are efficacious for new and emerging diseases. However, the single-minded narrative around the vaccine's essentiality was promoted by the state and its associated stakeholders everywhere (i.e., the mainstream media, social media, unelected public health officers, medical establishments, academia, and elsewhere). Messaging that genuinely attempted to provide alternative points of view to the main narrative was often suppressed and censored. However, COVID-19 vaccines were still in clinical trials when they were rolled out, meaning that injections could be regarded as "experimental" or "investigational". Vaccines also first emerged under the Emergency Use Authorization (EUA). The 21 U.S. Code § 360bbb-3 (e)(1)(A)(i)(II) states that the authorization of medical product usage in the U.S. requires that individuals are informed "of significant and potential benefits and risks of such use, and of the extent to which such benefits and risks are unknown."[26] Under the terms of the EUA, any party involved in the vaccination process and program, including manufacturers and administrators, obtained a broad liability shield against any potential lawsuits.

Under normal circumstances, vaccine development takes about 10 years to complete (this timeline is variable), which includes numerous safety testing protocols, toxicology studies, long periods of observation, surveillance of adverse events, and other regulatory requirements. It is also important to note that in previous outbreaks, some vaccination programs were suspended when even minimal deaths were associated with the vaccine. For example, the 1976 swine vaccination program in the United States (U.S.) was suspended when only 10 deaths occurred as a direct result of the vaccine. Now, the 1976 vaccine is associated with between 25-40 deaths in addition to about 400 reported cases of Guillain-Barré syndrome (GBS).

While the main narrative encompassed the importance of vaccination, the public messaging shifted over time.[27] The primary narrative was that emergent and experimental vaccines are "safe and effective", hence all should seek to be vaccinated for the "greater good." A small technicality to note here is that the term "safe and effective" is normally only used by the FDA in the case of licensed drugs. When it was clear that breakthrough infections occurred despite high vaccination rates, studies emerged confirming that COVID-19 vaccines cannot prevent transmission. Despite the appearance of safety concerns with the vaccines, the narrative switched again to emphasize their effectiveness in preventing severe disease and death. By the time the vaccinated accounted for a higher proportion of hospitalizations and deaths due to COVID-19, official reporting of cases often stopped, and the narrative again shifted to encourage people to remain up-to-date and current with their COVID-19 vaccinations. Thus, it is evident that governments around the world engaged in and executed a mass global vaccination campaign. According to Our World in Data, 70.6 percent of the global population received at least a single dose of the COVID-19 vaccine that was developed at a "warp speed", which is equivalent to over 13 billion doses.[28] Our World in Data also reports that, at the peak of COVID-19 vaccination (June, August, and September of 2021), there were over 40 million doses of the vaccine administered daily. However, peak vaccination periods may have occurred at different times globally.

It is important to note that mRNA-based COVID-19 vaccines are not the same as traditional vaccines that have been given to populations for decades. Traditional vaccines operate based on inserting attenuated, inactive, or parts of a virus into the human body, subsequently triggering an immune response to the microbe that ensures protection against future infections. Contrarily, mRNA vaccines work much differently by injecting a synthetic sequence RNA (based on a known spike protein sequence but with certain changes) encapsulated in a lipid nanoparticle (LNP) into a deltoid muscle. Once inside the cell, the package releases the mRNA, which is processed by the ribosome and creates a spike protein. Also, due to the use of artificial nucleotides in the RNA (i.e., replacement of "all uridine nitrogen bases" with N1-methyl-pseudouridine, m1Ψ),[29] the mRNA becomes stabilized and "immune evasion" enhanced.[30,31] As a result, a much greater number of spike protein molecules may potentially be generated from a single mRNA molecule. It is also worthwhile to add that the use of m1Ψ in mRNA vaccines may possibly be problematic for the production of highly mutated forms of the spike protein due to phenomenon known as "ribosomal frameshifting" (see, for example, a review paper by Rubio-Casillas et al.).[32] At the end, in a nutshell, the spike protein activates the immune system.

Medical treatments, drugs, and vaccines are all interventions that implicitly carry certain levels of risk, and the COVID-19 vaccine was no different. In a more than 30-page version of its COVID-19 vaccine factsheet dated April 6, 2021, Pfizer-BioNTech confirmed that its vaccine was not an FDA-approved product (p. 1, 8) and it may not protect all vaccine recipients (p. 7).[33] The factsheet also stated that serious adverse reactions to the vaccine may include death, life-threatening events, birth defects, miscarriages, multisystem inflammatory disease, and other illnesses requiring medical intervention (p. 1, 8, 26). Pfizer specifically cautioned about complications causing Bell's palsy as well as neurologic, inflammatory, and thrombotic (clotting) events (p. 24). It further warned that test recipients were only observed for a short period of about 2 months (p. 19). Of course, it is difficult to quantify how many individuals saw this factsheet, read it, or were otherwise advised about potential adverse medical events. Importantly, in their shorter 7-page version of the fact sheet, Pfizer-BioNTech does not mention these more severe adverse events, and only includes less severe events such as allergic reactions, pain at the injection site, tiredness, and headache.[34] The possibility of death is notably absent in the shorter version of the factsheet.

Furthermore, sections Annex I: Vaccine Order Form, Article I, and section 4 of the Advance Purchase Agreement (APA) between the European Commission, Pfizer Inc., and BioNTech Manufacturing GmbH signed on November 20, 2020, provides additional information regarding the vaccine's risk. This document, which was hidden from the public for a considerable period and was subsequently only available in a heavily redacted format, stated the following (p. 48-49; note that this paragraph was redacted in the document's original release to the public):[35]

> The Participating Member States acknowledge that the Vaccine and materials related to the Vaccine, and their components and constituent materials are being rapidly developed due to the emergency circumstances of the COVID-19 pandemic and will continue to be studied after provision of the Vaccine to the Participating Member States under the APA. The Participating Member State further acknowledges that the long-term effects and efficacy of the Vaccine are not currently known and that there may be adverse effects of the Vaccine that are not currently known.[36]

It is important to highlight some significant discrepancies between the wording found in the European vaccine agreement (i.e., "long-term effects and efficacy of the Vaccine are not currently known") and the narrative offered in the mainstream and social media. In just one example, CNN observed on November 9, 2020 that "Pfizer said that the vaccine, made with German partner BioNTech, had an efficacy rate higher than 90% at seven days after the second dose, which means protection is achieved 28 days after a person begins vaccination."[37] The date of this communication from CNN is only a few days prior to the date of the signed agreement, which notably does not include such claims. In another article posted November 18, 2020, CNN held that "a final analysis of the Phase 3 trial of Pfizer's coronavirus vaccine shows it was 95% effective in preventing infections, even in older adults, and caused no serious safety concerns"[38] despite Pfizer and BioNTech's explicit acknowledgement in their contract with the European Commission that "there may be adverse effects of the Vaccine."[39] While it was reasonable as a matter of course for Pfizer and BioNTech to forewarn about potential long-term side effects related to its vaccine, and for the European Commission to acknowledge the risk, the key concern was different, namely that Pfizer's safety declarations were made on the basis of short-term studies. And in fact, complications and adverse events potentially associated with COVID-19 vaccines did emerge.

Less than two years later, in a form 20-F submitted to the Securities and Exchange Commission on 30 March 2022, BioNTech SE admitted in its risk factors section that "we may not be able to demonstrate sufficient efficacy and safety of our COVID-19 vaccine and/or variant specific formations to obtain permanent regulatory approval" and that "significant adverse events may occur during our clinical trials or even after receiving regulatory approval."[40]

Relative risk reduction (RRR) versus absolute risk reduction (ARR)

It is generally understood that vaccine efficiency can be reported in multiple ways. One of the most common methods is a relative risk reduction (RRR) ratio, which represents the relative decrease in the level of risk of a negative event or case occurring in a treatment group (i.e., experimental group receiving a vaccine) in comparison to a placebo group (i.e., control group not receiving a vaccine). In formulaic terms, the RRR is calculated as a ratio of the difference between the number of cases in the placebo group and the number of cases in the experimental group divided by the number of cases in the placebo group.

In terms of COVID-19, it has been widely reported by the media, politicians, public health officials, medical doctors, and experts that vaccine efficacy was equal to 95 percent for Pfizer-BioNTech, 94 percent for Moderna, and 67 percent for AstraZeneca. These higher numbers gave the impression that COVID-19 vaccines could end the pandemic, prevent illness, and stop deaths. The interpretation of this data by uninformed, naïve individuals was perhaps that out of 100 individuals who received the vaccine, 95 of them would be protected. If this was the prevailing understanding, taking the vaccine was indeed a no-brainer to the unsuspecting public, particularly in light of the fact that headlines reporting this purported vaccine efficacy data appeared everywhere.[41] *Forbes*, for example, noted that "Pfizer-BioNTech Says Covid-19 Vaccine is 95% Effective,"[42] which CNN seconded with their headline that "Pfizer and BioNTech say final analysis shows coronavirus vaccine is 95% effective with no safety concerns."[43] CNN was particularly adamant about the vaccination of the young, even going so far as to publish an article titled "10 reasons why young, healthy people should get vaccinated" and warned that "if young people don't get vaccinated, it could leave everyone vulnerable."[44] In addition to its acceptance in the mainstream media, Pfizer employees engaged in self-promotion on social media, including X (formerly Twitter), a case discussed below.

Of course, the statements claiming the vaccine's 95% efficacy were problematic, which can be understood by a practical examination of relative risk reduction using data from Pfizer and BioNTech. In its first report, Pfizer-BioNTech reported that 43,448 participants were enrolled in a randomized study of individuals receiving injections. The experimental vaccine was delivered to about 21,720 volunteers while the remaining 21,728 received a placebo. Pfizer-BioNTech recorded 170 cases of COVID-19 between the two groups, including 8 cases in the vaccinated group and 162 cases in the placebo group. Hence, the relative reduction in the cases was 154 (162–8) and the relative risk reduction in percentage terms was equal to 95 percent ([162–8]/162 = 0.9505 or 95%). It seemed impressive, but such claims are misleading without a proper understanding and contextualization of other important measures. However, one would be hard pressed to find any clarification of what these efficacy numbers related to the RRR meant in practice. Politicians, governments, public health officers, epidemiologists, medical doctors, and experts certainly did not clarify this nuance. It is possible that some of them did not know. But, the U.S. Food and Drug Administration (FDA) has warned about the dangers of using the RRR for years. Stadel and colleagues have similarly observed that "risk ratios are widely misused in ways that exaggerate both the benefits and harms of drugs. This is especially true when a risk ratio is called 'relative risk'."[45] As a result, the FDA has advised pharmaceutical firms to "provide absolute risks, not just relative risks. Patients are unduly influenced when risk information is presented using a relative risk approach."[46] This was good advice which the FDA itself seems to have ignored when it came to COVID-19 vaccines.

In addition to past warnings from the FDA, there have been other concerns about Pfizer's trial data. For example, Peter Doshi, associate editor of the *British Journal of Medicine*, raised the issue of "'suspected COVID-19 cases'– those with symptomatic COVID-19 that were not PCR confirmed."[47] The total number of suspected but unconfirmed COVID-19 cases was equal to 3,410 cases, of which 1,594 were in the vaccine group and 1,816 in the placebo group. As Doshi noted, "a rough estimate of vaccine efficacy against developing COVID-19 symptoms, with or without a positive PCR test, would be a relative risk reduction of 19% … far below the 50% effectiveness threshold set by regulators."[48] He also added that "if many or most of these suspected cases were in people who had a false negative PCR test result, this would dramatically decrease vaccine efficacy."[49] Furthermore, Doshi raised concerns about individuals excluded from Pfizer vaccine analysis and unblinding the study. These and other concerns were also noted by additional researchers later in the pandemic. For example, Sin Hang Lee, medical doctor and director of Milford Molecular Diagnostics Laboratory, advocated that "until an accurate count of COVID-19 cases in the vaccinated and placebo groups has been determined for vaccine efficacy evaluation, we are asking the FDA to stay its decision regarding the emergency use authorization for this vaccine."[50]

Another important measure of the success of a medical treatment is absolute risk reduction (ARR), which in this case represents the risk of "being infected and becoming ill with COVID-19 ... [and] the difference between attack rates with and without the vaccine" for the whole population.[51] Needless to say, the ARR rates were not freely disclosed in the media as these numbers were clearly less impressive compared to the RRR rates. In practice, the ARR rates were reported to be equal to less than 1 percent for Pfizer-BioNTech, 1 to 3 percent for AstraZeneca, and between 1 and 2 percent for Moderna. Using the previous study data from Pfizer-BioNTech, less than one percent ($162/21,728 = 0.00746$ or 0.75%) of the placebo group got COVID-19. It can therefore be argued that less than one percent of individuals included in the experimental group could eventually be protected by the vaccine.

Similarly overstated efficacy arguments have been made with respect to the vaccination of adolescents aged 12 to 15 years. In this case, Pfizer-BioNTech claimed that its vaccine "demonstrated 100% efficacy and robust antibody response."[52] This vaccination trial involved 2,260 participants in the U.S. who were divided into the placebo arm (1,129 individuals) and the vaccinated arm (1,131 individuals). Since there were zero cases in the vaccinated (experimental) group and 18 cases in the placebo group, Pfizer-BioNTech claimed 100 percent efficacy for this age bracket ($[18-0]/18 = 1.0$ or 100%) and an absolute risk reduction (ARR) equal to 1.59 percent ($18/1,129 = 0.0159$). Of course, Pfizer-BioNTech did not mention that adolescents have an extremely low risk of death from COVID-19. In its news release document, Pfizer-BioNTech also omitted the possibility of adverse events such as heart complications (discussed below) that predominantly affects adolescents and young adults. Lastly, it should also be noted that despite 18 cases of coronavirus in the placebo group, there were no deaths in either the experimental or placebo group.

Another measure of efficacy to consider is the "number needed to vaccinate" (NNV), which represents the number of people needed to be vaccinated to prevent one case of COVID-19. This indicator can also be calculated in terms of preventing one hospitalization or one death. For example, Bardosh et al. estimated that in a university setting, between 20,000 and 30,000 "uninfected adults aged 18-29 must be boosted with an mRNA vaccine to prevent one COVID-19 hospitalization."[53] The authors also concluded that they expected 18 to 98 serious adverse events as a result of such a vaccination campaign, including 1.7 to 3.0 cases of booster-related myocarditis and a significant number of illnesses that would interfere with daily activities. In another example, the U.K.'s Joint Committee on Vaccination and Immunization (JCVI) estimated that to prevent one case of intensive care unit (ICU) admission among 5- to 11-year-olds, 3.8 million doses would need to be administered.[54] At the same time, JCVI admits to less than 2 cases of myocarditis per 1 million doses, based on data from the U.S. In other words, to prevent one ICU admission, there was an expectation of about 4 cases of myocarditis that could also result in hospital admission.

Furthermore, there have also been problems with the proper disclosure of information. In one significant example, the Centers for Disease Control and Prevention (CDC) "withheld vast swaths of the information it holds about the impact of COVID-19, leading to anger from the scientific community."[55] A call from one epidemiologist was simple: "Tell the truth, present the data."[56] Early in the pandemic, Peter Doshi also called for the release of data, noting that "addressing the many open questions about these trials requires access to the raw trial data. But no company seems to have shared data with any third party at this point."[57]

A reprimand to Pfizer and Moderna in the United Kingdom

Considering the bold efficacy claims made regarding COVID-19 vaccines, Pfizer did face consequences. A pharmaceutical regulator in the United Kingdom (U.K.) called the Prescription Medicines Code of Practice Authority (PMCPA) found Pfizer in breach of its regulatory code on five occasions in relation to a re-tweet of a post by a senior Pfizer employee in the U.K. which was originally posted on X by medical director Berkeley Phillips in the U.S.[58] The tweet claimed:

> Our vaccine candidate is 95 percent effective in preventing Covid-19, and 94 percent effective in people over 65 years old. We will file all of our data with health authorities within days. Thank you to every volunteer in our trial, and to all who are tirelessly fighting this pandemic.[59]

The complainant in this case alleged that Pfizer's tweet misled the public by including the relative risk reduction data but failing to note any information about the absolute risk reduction. They also claimed that Pfizer's post did not include any safety data or information about adverse medical events, thus illegally promoting its candidate COVID-19 vaccine. According to the PMCPA's verdict dated March 1, 2024 related to Pfizer's violation of the ABPI Code of Practice[60], they concluded that Pfizer did breach Clause 2 ("bringing discredit upon, and reducing confidence in, the pharmaceutical industry"), Clause 3.1 ("promoting an unlicensed medicine"), Clause 7.2 ("making a misleading claim"), Clause 7.9 ("making claims that did not reflect the available evidence regarding possible adverse reactions"), and Clause 9.1 ("failing to maintain high standards").[61] Pfizer's U.K. spokesperson stated that Pfizer "fully recognizes and accepts the issues highlighted by this PMCPA ruling" and added that they were "deeply sorry."[62] The re-tweets were regarded by Pfizer's medical director Philips as "accidental and unintentional."[63] The PMCPA's Panel reminded Pfizer that "the tweet contained limited information regarding the efficacy of the vaccine candidate with no safety information." [64]

This was not the first time Pfizer was reprimanded by the PMCPA in relation to COVID-19 vaccines, as the company has been noted for other previous incidents. The most serious reprimand previously issued by the PMCPA related to information shared by Pfizer CEO Albert Bourla's statement regarding COVID-19 vaccination for adolescents in which he stated: "I believe it [vaccinating 5- to 11-year-olds] is a very good idea" and "there is no doubt in my mind about the benefits completely are in favour of doing it."[65] The PMCPA panel found that the implication of Bourla's statements was "misleading and incapable of substantiation. The Appeal Board therefore upheld the Panels rulings of breaches of Clauses 6.1, 6.2 and 26.2."[66] These clauses refer to the fact that "any information, claim or comparison must be capable of substantiation" (Clause 6.2) and "information about prescription only medicines which is made available to the public either directly or indirectly must be factual and presented in a balanced way. It must not raise unfounded hopes of successful treatment or be misleading with respect to the safety of the product."[67]

Moderna was similarly reprimanded by the PMCPA in a case that involves inviting "those aged between 12 and 18 years old to enrol in the NextCove trial, which was examining the efficacy of Moderna's booster jab."[68] This offer, which was eventually not paid, was made by a "paediatrician from an unnamed HHS [National Health Services] trust."[69] In its final decision, the PMCPA's panel noted the following:

> The Medicines for Human Use (Clinical Trials) Regulations (2004) state that "No incentives or financial inducements" may be given to a "minor" (a person under the age of 16 years) or "to a person with parental responsibility for that minor or, as the case may be, the minor's legal representative". The Panel noted that the WhatsApp message was specifically aiming to recruit "children aged 12–18 years" and that it implied that participants would receive £1,500 on completion of the study. The Panel considered that the level of payment represented an offer of a financial incentive.[70]

The PMCPA also noted that "the Panel considered that this brought discredit upon and reduced confidence in the pharmaceutical industry.

A breach of Clause 2 was ruled."[71] As a result, Moderna was ordered to pay a fine in the amount of £14,000. Esther McVey, Member of Parliament in the U.K., noted that "a £14,000 charge is a paltry sum indeed for a company that enjoyed revenue of $6.8 billion last year."[72] She also reconfirmed that "it has been well known for years that healthy children are, mercifully, at a vanishing low risk of serious ill health from Covid-19."[73]

Following the completion of another case by the PMCPA in August of 2024, Moderna was found in breach of Clause 11.2 by "promoting a medicine in a manner that was inconsistent with its SPC" (summary of product characteristics).[74] This related to the firm's promotion of its Spikevax COVID-19 vaccine at the European Congress of Clinical Microbiology and Infectious Diseases in April 2022. The PMCPA concluded that "the presentation could not be seen as anything other than promotion of Spikevax."[75]

Natural immunity versus vaccination

For years scientific studies have confirmed the value of acquired immunity through prior infection. While academic studies have also confirmed the relevancy of acquired immunity in the case of COVID-19, the mainstream media and others downplayed its protections. For example, in a comparison between individuals with naturally acquired immunity and individuals injected with two doses of COVID-19 vaccines, Gazit et al. concluded that "naturally acquired immunity confers stronger protection against infection and symptomatic disease caused by the Delta variant of SARS-CoV-2, compared to the BNT162b 2-dose vaccine-induced immunity."[76] They further observed that "SARS-CoV-2 naïve vaccinees had a 13.06-fold (95% confidence interval [CI], 8.08–21.11] increased risk for breakthrough infection with the Delta variant compared to the unvaccinated-previously-infected individuals."[77] In other words, individuals whose immune system was prompted by the vaccine were at a 13-times higher risk of being infected with SARS-CoV-2.

Other studies have found similar results, such as the so-called Cleveland Clinic study among 51,011 employees that made it clear the "risk of COVID-19 increased with the time since the most recent prior COVID-19 episode and the number of vaccine doses previously received."[78] Put simply, individuals who had the most doses were most likely to get COVID-19. This is corroborated by the everyday experiences of ordinary people who caught COVID-19 (even multiple times) after receiving the vaccine. Another study by Chemaitelly et al. found that "protection of natural infection against reinfection wanes and may diminish within a few years" but added that "protection against severe reinfection remains strong, with no evidence of waning."[79] In a different study, Shrestha et al. confirmed that the "vaccination of previously infected individuals does not provide additional protection against COVID-19 for several months, but after that provides significant protection at least against symptomatic COVID-19."[80] There are also instances in which individuals have been observed with relevant antibodies against COVID-19 spike proteins. For example, it was confirmed that about 60 percent of individuals in British Columbia had the relevant antibodies. More specifically, in a study of 276 healthy adults in British Columbia in the middle of 2020, "more than 90% of uninfected adults showed antibody reactivity against the spike protein."[81] Therefore, a large portion of the population already exhibited natural immunity which could be assumed to convey at least partial protection against SARS-CoV-2 and, consequently, there may have been limited need to seek vaccination, especially in less vulnerable segments of the population.

Medical staff and COVID-19 injections

Many medical doctors and other healthcare professionals received the vaccine, no questions asked. While some medical doctors and professionals had questions but were ultimately convinced, others were not. There are many instances in which frontline health workers, firefighter, paramedics, police officers, and others were placed under considerable pressure from administrators to receive the vaccine to maintain employment. Many maintained their stance without severe consequences; others were simply dismissed. Such employees went from "hero-to-zero" after having worked through perhaps the most difficult period in their professional careers (i.e., the onset of the COVID-19 pandemic).

There is evidence to support the large number of frontline workers who refused the injection. In California, for example, it was estimated that about 50 percent of workers did not take the vaccination at one hospital, while in other medical facilities around the state between 20 and 50 percent refused, which allegedly surprised researchers.[82] In another example, it was estimated that about 60 percent of nursing employees in Ohio were expected to refuse the injection.[83] The University of Pittsburgh Medical Centre did not require its health care staff to receive the COVID-19 vaccine, citing that the "reasons for hesitancy include concerns about safety and efficacy, mistrust of government and institutions, waiting for more data, and feeling that personal rights are being infringed upon."[84] According to one Kaiser report, about 29 percent of healthcare workers in the U.S. and as many as 40 percent in the U.K. were hesitant about accepting the vaccine.[85]

Early signals potentially associated with COVID-19 vaccines

As public messaging and narrative have changed over time, so too has the assessment of risks potentially associated with COVID-19 vaccines. As noted by Michael Thoene, academic views about the potential risks associated with COVID-19 vaccine has evolved over time.[86] For example, Thoene has distinguished three phases of the narrative regarding COVID-19 vaccines, including periods between November 2020 and the end of 2021, January 2022 and August 2022, and September 2022 and April 2024. In the first phase, as noted by the author, the narrative in the academic literature was "very positive" since adverse events were either ignored, not reported, or reported as "the same as placebo group", or "abnormally low" (see table 3 in the paper).[87] In fact, "in the period from 2020 to the end of 2021, the scientific literature claimed there were absolutely no serious adverse events (SAEs) whatsoever."[88] Many individuals undoubtedly acted on these claims. Scientists and physicians who raised concerns about COVID-19 vaccines during this time were publicly discredited, silenced, or called names. In the second phase, the narrative continued to be positive, although the reported adverse events were considered as "rare", "very rare", "miniscule", and "only coincidental not causal."[89] As the article notes, "mRNA vaccines were a miracle drug."[90] Despite these claims, many individuals discovered that they became sick with COVID-19 after receiving a vaccine which they believed was supposed to protect them against the disease. In the third phase, after most populations in the world were vaccinated, mainstream academic studies began to acknowledge adverse events and became increasingly critical of mRNA technologies. In other words, the existence of potential risks related to the vaccine became undeniable.

There were early warning signals about COVID-19 vaccines in addition to important signs pointing to their insufficient on-the-ground effectiveness. Many of these signals came from official manufacturers' studies, public databases, and academic research, as well as warnings stemming from quasi-public institutions and various levels of government. For example, in Canada, provincial public health officials in Ontario acknowledged that COVID-19 injections have potentially led to blood clots (in a now deleted post titled "COVID-19 viral vector vaccines and rare blood clots–Vaccine safety surveillance in action")[91] and heart inflammation (see post titled "myocarditis and pericarditis after COVID-19 mRNA vaccines").[92] A more complete analysis of serious health events caused by COVID-19 injections can be found in other publications by Public Health Ontario.[93]

In view of repeated calls for "booster" vaccinations, there were also national signals about vaccine effectiveness. For example, a continued program of vaccination against COVID-19 did not yield the desired effects in many instances. The best-case evidence of this failure is Israel, which experienced significant surges in the number of COVID-19 cases and deaths despite its booster program being implemented in August and September of 2021. The U.S. approved boosters in August 2021.

Biodistribution studies

In support of its application for the approval of its COVID-19 mRNA-based vaccine, Pfizer provided local licensing bodies with biodistribution studies that describe the transfer or transport of chemical compounds from one location in the body to another.[94] More specifically, these studies focus on pharmacokinetics and pharmacodynamics. Pharmacokinetics refers to how a subject's body may interact with drug products in terms of absorption, distribution, metabolism, and excretion, or more simply, what the body does to the drug. It is concerned with how the drug moves throughout the body over time (i.e., changes in drug quantity in the body over time), from absorption, through distribution, and up to elimination, thus helping to establish suitable concentrations aimed at maximizing drug efficacy and minimizing toxicity. Pharmacodynamics, on the other hand, focuses on what the drug does to the body, such as the relationship between certain levels of drug concentrations, the intensity of drug-induced responses, and the resulting patient outcomes, including the effectiveness of the drug and adverse events. In the specific context of mRNA vaccines, studying these themes is important since "detailed knowledge of biodistribution and disposition of vaccine-induced S [spike] protein would allow integration of its pharmacokinetics and pharmacodynamics, thus allowing the description of the time course of its effects in individual subjects", especially since (as Cosentino and Marino suggest) mRNA vaccines and their underlying technologies should be treated as "pharmaceutical drugs".[95] And yet, "there are still many gaps in our understanding of the biology of mRNA vaccines formulated with lipid nanoparticles."[96] In other words, there are many unknowns. Interestingly, professor Byram Bridle, who obtained and analysed data related to Pfizer's biodistribution studies from the Japanese Pharmaceuticals and Medical Devices Agency through a freedom of information request in 2021, raised such concerns, for which he was heavily targeted and ridiculed in the mainstream media.

However, it needs to be highlighted up front that early vaccine biodistribution studies reported by pharmaceutical firms were not completed on human subjects since these types of studies are not normally requested for regulatory purposes for conventional vaccines. Hence, biodistribution studies were completed on rodents (i.e., rats, mice, etc.) and nonhuman primates so the results may not be freely generalizable to humans. Having said this, it is well accepted that in pre-clinical drug trials "mice and rats have long served as the preferred species for biomedical research animal models due to their anatomical, physiological, and genetic similarity to humans"[97] and that rodents generally "have similar biological properties to humans."[98] Therefore, it was reasonable to draw at least some conclusions from these rodent-based studies as potentially pertinent to humans.

Firstly, Pfizer confirmed that its mRNA vaccine relies on "lipid nanoparticle (LNP) delivery systems to enable messenger RNA (mRNA)-based therapeutics."[99] It was viewed that LNPs could offer an ideal delivery system since LNPs "encapsulate mRNA, protecting it from degradation and allowing for transport from the injection site to target tissues. Once at the intended tissue, LNPs facilitate rapid cellular uptake and endosomal escape, enabling the entry of mRNA into the cytosol, where it can engage with ribosomes and be translated into protein."[100] A pre-clinical biodistribution study from Pfizer (based on rodents) obtained in the U.S. under the Freedom of Information Act (FOIA) by Judicial Watch, Inc. confirmed that "over 48 hours, the LNP distributed mainly to liver, adrenal glands, spleen and ovaries, with maximum concentrations observed at 8-48 hours post-dose."[101] It has to be considered that the 48 hour-time period was the last time point in the study, and the LNP may not have reached its peak concentration in organs by that time.

Early in the pandemic, in addition to studies provided by pharmaceutical manufacturers, there were also review papers that hypothesized and conjectured about the potential outcomes related to mRNA technologies and their application for treating COVID-19. Researchers raised multiple concerns at this time, noting that "we essentially do not know for how long and at what concentration the LNPs and the antigen(s) remain in human tissues or the circulation of poor vaccine responders, the elderly, or children ... and given the fact that cellular immunity likely persists despite reduced in vitro neutralizing titers, boosting doses should be delivered only where the benefit–risk profile is clearly established."[102] Najahi-Missaoui et al. conjectured that "once they reach the blood circulation, NPs [nano particles] can be distributed and can accumulate in different organs such as the liver, spleen, lungs and kidneys. Some studies suggest that NPs may also accumulate in the brain if they are small enough (<10 nm) and/or the blood brain barrier is not intact."[103] The authors also noted that "despite the potential for clinical application, some studies have suggested that NPs [nanoparticles] can be toxic. These studies have demonstrated the ability of NPs to accumulate in cells and induce organ-specific toxicity."[104] Hulscher et al. speculated that "SARS-CoV-2 Spike protein is the likely determinantal agent through which COVID-19 vaccines cause biological harm."[105] Parry et al. similarly concluded that "spike protein pathogenicity, termed 'spikeopathy', whether from the SARS-CoV-2 virus or produced by vaccine gene codes" may be able to "affect many organs."[106] The authors further stated that "the inflammatory properties of the nanoparticles used to ferry mRNA; N1-methyl-pseudouridine employed to prolong synthetic mRNA function; the widespread distribution of the mRNA and DNA codes and translated spike proteins, and autoimmunity via human production of foreign proteins, can contribute to harmful effects."[107] Cosentino and Marino identified a "possibility that COVID-19 mRNA vaccines under some circumstances induce high and possibly toxic amounts of S [spike] protein in organs and tissues, in turn leaking into the circulation."[108] Lastly, Emeritus Professor Robert Tindle more broadly estimated that "mRNA vaccines can result in spike protein expression in muscle tissue, the lymphatic system, cardiomyocytes and other cells after entry into the circulation."[109]

As noted by Cosentino, the "systematic bioavailability of COVID-19 mRNA vaccines has been excluded until May 2021"[110] when biodistribution studies on human subjects began to emerge, which occurred after a few rounds of COVID-19 vaccines and boosters. Most importantly and contrary to what has been believed by the public (but is now well confirmed), the mRNA vaccine does not stay at the injection site (i.e., the deltoid muscle) and can systemically spread around the body. As Cosentino and Marino observed

> The public was explicitly reassured by influential blogs ... as well as by academic institutional web pages ... that these products were not expected to exhibit any relevant systemic disposition and that the resulting S [spike] protein would remain attached to the surface of the cells and would not be released in the bloodstream and tissues to encounter ACE2 receptors and eventually induce organ damage. Step by step, however, it became clear that this was not the case.[111]

Moreover, "recent studies have shown that as soon as 1 day after the administration of an mRNA vaccine encoding the SARS-CoV-2 spike protein, S-protein can be detected in the blood of vaccinated people" [112] (for example, see study by Ogata et al.).[113] Research evidence also suggested an accumulation of "LNPs, mRNA, and protein products of mRNA vaccines" in many organs, including the heart, brain, lungs, ovaries, and so on.[114]

Furthermore, Pateev et al. have confirmed that "studies on humans show the detection of the antigen encoded by mRNA vaccines in blood plasma, lymph nodes, and skin at various times points."[115] More specifically, based on the analysis of human tissues obtained from autopsies, Krauson et al. concluded that "SARS-CoV-2 mRNA vaccines persist up to 30 days from vaccination and can be detected in the heart", although the "vaccine was not detected in the mediastinal lymph nodes, spleen, or liver."[116] Castruita et al. found that "in 10 of 108 HCV patient samples, full-length or traces of SARS-CoV-2 spike mRNA vaccine sequences were found in blood up to 28 days after COVID-19 vaccination."[117] Other studies also confirmed persistence (or circulation in the body) from 30 to 120 days, and perhaps even longer.[118] For example, based on biological samples from human subjects and the application of mass spectrometry techniques, Brogna et al. established that "the minimum and maximum time at which PP-Spike [recombinant spike protein] was detected after vaccination was 69 and

187 days, respectively."[119] In other words, spike protein could potentially remain in the body "for much longer than predicted in early studies" or hypothesized by researchers.[120]

There is also an ongoing debate about whether mRNA vaccines can impact newborns. In a study by Hanna et al., "of 11 lactating individuals enrolled, trace amounts of BNT162b2 and mRNA-1273 COVID-19 mRNA vaccines were detected in 7 samples from 5 different participants at various times up to 45 hours postvaccination." [121] The researchers concluded that "the sporadic presence and trace quantities of COVID-19 vaccine mRNA detected in EBM [expressed breast milk] suggest that breastfeeding after COVID-19 mRNA vaccination is safe" and they "believe it safe to breastfeed after maternal vaccination against COVID-19."[122,123] Another study by Hanna et al. confirmed that "of 13 lactating women receiving vaccine (20 exposures), trace mRNA amounts were detected in 10 exposures up to 45 h[ours] post vaccination."[124] The authors again claimed that "we believe breastfeeding post-vaccination is safe" but hypothetically (without any evidence) noted that "it is unlikely that intact LNPs will pass the blood-milk barrier." [125] However, in spite of these assurances, there are multiple outstanding concerns that require further investigation and confirmation (see, for example, a list of concerns posted by Cosentino on Substack).[126] Lastly, in terms of possible placental-based transfer, a study by Lin et al. suggests that the mRNA from the COVID-19 vaccine "can spread systemically to the placenta and umbilical cord blood."[127] Thus, the related topic of vaccinated pregnant women also needs scrutiny, especially in view of Pfizer's "5.3.6. Cumulative analysis of post-authorization adverse event reports of PF-0702048 (BNT162B2) received through 28-Feb-2021" (see table 6, for example).[128] To this end, the U.K. government has even admitted that "there is limited experience with use of the COVID-19 mRNA Vaccine BNT162b2 in pregnant women" and that "it is unknown whether the COVID-19 mRNA Vaccine BNT162b2 is excreted in human milk."[129]

The connection between LNPs preferentially accumulating in specific organs and spike protein toxicity could be important in determining potential mechanisms of pathogenicity, which may potentially be associated with COVID-19 vaccines, whether now or in the future. In a pharmacovigilance study focused on Korea and based on data from VigiBase (a global case safety report database from the World Health Organization), Kim et al. concluded that "there were disproportionate [greater than expected] reporting of immune-related AEs [adverse events] following COVID-19 vaccination. While awaiting definitive evidence, there is a need to closely monitor for any signs of immune-related AEs following COVID-19 vaccination among adolescents."[130]

Palmer et al. raised another important concern, namely that the European Medicines Agency (EMA) confirmed that there were no studies related to the interaction of COVID-19 vaccines with other pharmaceutical products, which in their view, created opportunities for adverse drug interactions. Similarly, and as corroborated by the EMA, no genotoxicity studies related to the damage of human genetic matter were conducted. With specific reference to lipids used in the Pfizer vaccine, Palmer et al. were concerned because "the cationic lipids ALC-0315 and the PEGylated lipids ALC-0159, which account for 30-50% and for 2-6% respectively, of the total lipid content–had not previously been approved for use in humans."[131] As Palmer et al. noted, this is not an idle threat, since LNPs can create problems when cationic lipids interrupt mitochondrial activities and possibly produce oxidative stress, leading to DNA damage and autoimmune disease, for example.

What is the significance of these biodistribution studies? What are the underlying concerns? Firstly, there are gaps in knowledge and a limited understanding of biodistribution in relation to COVID-19 vaccines. Secondly, there are concerns about the longevity of COVID-19 vaccine components, the spike protein, and the safety of these vaccine components. Thirdly, there is a potential cause for alarm regarding distribution from the point of view of tissue damage by the immune system, which is recognizing spike protein.

Antibody-dependent enhancement (ADE)

It is also important to briefly discuss antibody-dependent enhancement (ADE), which occurs when poorly neutralizing antibodies weakly bind the virus and allow its escape once the virus-antibody complex is internalized by specialized immune cells meant to destroy the virus. In other words, the treatment could strengthen the disease. Palmer et al. noted that ADE "can cause a hyperinflammatory response (a 'cytokine storm') that will amplify the damage to our lungs, liver and other organs of our body."[132] The authors also observed that "ADE can occur both after natural infection and after vaccination, and it has been observed with several virus families."[133] Palmer et al. warned about ADE in the context of studies conducted in the past where vaccinated animals developed antibodies after vaccination but became severely ill and often died upon exposure to the actual virus. In other papers, researchers outline similar risks related to ADE.[134] As one example, a study by Tseng et al. warned that "this combined expertise provides concern for trials with SARS-CoV vaccines in humans … The concern arising from the present report is for an immunopathologic reaction occurring among vaccinated individuals upon exposure to infectious SARS-CoV."[135]

Pfizer-BioNTech and its post-authorization documentation

In April 2021, Pfizer released its post-authorization document to the U.S. authorities; the document gained limited coverage in the mainstream and social media. Table 1 of the "5.3.6. Cumulative analysis of post-authorization adverse event reports of PF-0702048 (BNT162B2) received through 28-Feb-2021" outlines that in the period between December 1, 2020 and February 28, 2021, Pfizer reported 42,086 adverse cases related to its vaccine, of which 11,361 had not recovered, 520 recovered but experienced a lingering medical problem (i.e., sequelae), and 1,223 were fatal. [136] There were also 9,400 cases with unknown outcomes. These serious adverse events accounts for 31.1 percent of the total adverse events reported. Moreover, table 6 of the document reported 34 cases related to children (less than 12 years old), of which 24 children, 13 of whom had not recovered by the time of the report, experienced serious adverse events.

The Vaccine Adverse Events Reporting System (VAERS)

Prior to discussing the Vaccine Adverse Events Reporting System (VAERS), it is important to preface this section by stating that many studies examined below (including data from VAERS) refer to temporal association between an adverse event and COVID-19 vaccination. In other words, temporal association of an adverse health event with vaccination does not demonstrate causation. While some studies offer possible explanations, others infer causation due to a short time span between the onset of an adverse event and injection. To discern problems related to association and causation, one could also apply a list of so-called Bradford Hill criteria, which help to establish a causal relationship between a purported cause and an observable effect. These criteria (which include parameters such as consistency, strength, specificity, and plausibility) can be effectively applied to medicine (see for example, a study by Nowinski et al.).[137] There are also Koch's postulations, which were used in the past for "determining whether a microorganism is the cause of the disease."[138] One could also use the Granger causality test.

The Vaccine Adverse Event Reporting System (VAERS) was established in 1990 as an early warning system designed to capture any problems related to biological products, including vaccines. The CDC describes VAERS as "the nation's early warning system that monitors the safety of FDA-approved vaccines and vaccines authorized for use for public health emergencies."[139] The CDC also clarifies that "a VAERS report alone does not indicate whether a vaccine caused or contributed to an adverse event. Only scientists and public health professionals can make this determination after thorough investigation."[140] And yet, as reported by Harvard Pilgrim Healthcare, Inc., it is widely accepted that there is significant under-reporting of vaccine adverse reactions or injury to VAERS;[141] only between 1 and 13 percent of adverse events from vaccines are reported. Other researchers have even estimated that the underreporting factor could be equal to between 20 and 30, meaning that actual numbers of adverse events may be 20 or 30 times higher than reported. Lastly, it is worthwhile to note here that reporting is a function of severity of the side effects and public knowledge of a potential vaccine-side effect relationship and varies by side effect; the rate may be higher for serious reactions and adverse events.

VAERS is a passive system of surveillance for adverse events to biological products and has multiple limitations (i.e., possible multiple entries, entries by non-health professionals that need to be vetted, deleted reports, problems with causation, delayed entry of reports, redefinition or recoding of entries, and so on). However, it may help to generate important safety signals.[142] Prior to the pandemic, researchers freely used VAERS to investigate associations and safety signals of biological products. To provide one example, Goldman and Miller, who investigated the impact of vaccines on infants, noted that "our findings show a positive correlation between the number of vaccine doses administered and the percentage of hospitalizations and deaths."[143] The authors thus conclude that "since vaccines are given to millions of infants annually, it is imperative that health authorities have scientific data from synergistic toxicity studies on all combinations of vaccines that infants might receive. Finding ways to increase vaccine safety should be the highest priority."[144]

As of April 18, 2024, there were over 1.6 million vaccine adverse event reports registered in VAERS potentially associated with COVID-19 injections. VAERS recorded 22,264 deaths in 2021, 12,445 deaths in 2022, and 3,690 deaths in 2023 (see figure 1.1 below). This is striking considering that there was an average of only 289 deaths associated with a single vaccine per year in the prior 30 years (in the most recent years prior to the pandemic, VAERS recorded 603 deaths in 2019, and 534 deaths in 2018). There were also 15,701 reports of myocarditis and pericarditis in 2021, 10,590 in 2022, and 2,062 in 2023 (the average annual number of various forms of heart inflammation in previous years was equal to about 50 cases). The cumulative impact of serious adverse events since the onset of COVID-19 resulted in 70,361 cases of permanent disability, 21,616 cases of heart attacks, 9,176 cases of thrombocytopenia / low platelets, and 5,127 cases of miscarriages, to name only a few.[145]

Figure 1.1: Deaths reported to VAERS potentially associated with COVID-19 vaccines

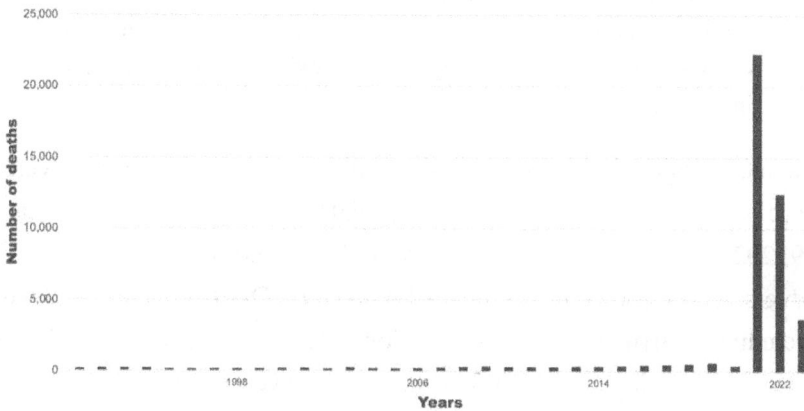

Source: www.openvaers.com

While one can debate issues related to potential causation, correlation, observation, association, and interconnection, it is difficult to ignore the sheer number of deaths that were reported to VAERS in 2021 and 2022. Reported deaths increased by a factor of 52 times (i.e., 5,201 percent) between 2020 and 2021 and 77.1 times (i.e., 7,710 percent) between 2021 and 2022 in comparison to an annual average of a 4.6 percent increase between 1991 and 2020. From another perspective, the number of deaths in 2021 alone exceeded the total sum of all deaths reported in VAERS in the last 30 years by a factor of 2.5 times. It is easily visible when inspecting figure 1.1 that there is a significant issue here. In statistical terms, the number of deaths from 2021 and 2022 was a multi-sigma event that normally does not occur. For example, the level of deaths in 2021 exceeded one standard deviation from the mean in the last 30 years equal to 115.7 by a factor of 192.4 times (22,264/115.7 = 192.4). In his letter to the commission of the U.S. FDA and CDC dated May 10, 2023, Joesph A Ladapo, State Surgeon in Florida, also drew upon this evidence when stating:

> Data are unequivocal: After the COVID-19 vaccine rollout, the Vaccine Adverse Events Reporting System (VAERS) reporting increased by 1,700%, including a 4,400% increase in life-threatening conditions. We are not the first to observe such a trend. Dismissing this pronounced increase as being solely due to reporting trends is a callous denial of corroborating scientific evidence also pointing to increased risk and a poor safety profile.[146]

Canada does not have a system like VAERS, but it does record adverse vaccine events as Adverse Events of Special Interest (AESI). As of January 19, 2024, the Government of Canada website reported a total of 58,712 adverse cases potentially associated with COVID-19 vaccine injections, including 47,010 considered non-serious and 11,702 as serious.[147] These serious events include death, life-threatening events (i.e., risk of death), hospitalization (including long-term hospital stays), persistent disability or incapacity, and so on. These numbers are small compared to the total number of COVID-19 injections but are meaningful to those who were presumably injured by these vaccinations. In terms of specific adverse events after COVID-19 injections, the Government of Canada's website reported 1,231 cases of myocarditis or pericarditis, 216 cases of Bells' palsy, 589 cases of pulmonary embolism, 380 cases of thrombosis (blood clots), 411 cases of deep vein thrombosis (DVT), 24 cases of GBS, 160 cases of heart attacks, 96 cases of spontaneous miscarriages, and 24 cases of MIS (Multisystem Inflammatory Syndrome).[148] Their site also reports 488 deaths, although it clarifies that while "these deaths occurred after being vaccinated with a COVID-19 vaccine, they are not necessarily related to the vaccine."[149] If one assumes that the incidence of vaccine injury reporting is similar to that in the U.S., actual numbers of adverse events in Canada are likely significantly higher. Notably, the Government of Canada has allocated some funds in its budget for vaccine injury, to the amount of $19 million for its fiscal year 2024/2025 and $17 million for

2025/2026, although the budget line does not clarify what type of vaccine harm these fiscal expenditures are intended to cover.[150]

The European Union operates a different adverse vaccine event system called EudraVigilance, which is operated by the European Medicines Agency (EMA). In its report from February 2022, the EMA reported adverse events potentially related to different types of COVID-19 injections. The agency reported 582,074 cases of suspected adverse events with 7,023 deaths potentially associated with Pfizer's Comirnaty (570 million doses administered), 40,766 cases with 279 deaths due to Janssen vaccine (19 million doses), and 150,807 cases with 834 deaths caused by Spikevax (139 million doses).[151]

Information from the CDC's V-safe program

The U.S. has another COVID-19 vaccine safety and warning database called V-safe that launched at the end of 2020 (i.e., beginning of the vaccine rollout program), which, as described by the CDC, allows individuals to share how they "feel after vaccination."[152] The V-safe program is accessible through a computer or smartphone and permits individuals to record their own information after receiving the COVID-19 vaccine. After a series of formal requests under the Freedom of Information Act (FOIA) and two subsequent lawsuits filed on behalf of the Informed Consent Action Network (ICAN), the CDC was ordered to release its data from the V-safe program.[153] What does the CDC's collected data reveal? Without delving too deep into the information, Siri and Glimstad, a law firm representing ICAN, summarized the data collected: "out of the approximate 10 million v-safe users, 782,913 individuals, or over 7.7% of v-safe users, had a health event requiring medical attention, emergency room intervention, and/or hospitalization."[154] ICAN further notes that over 3.3 million individuals of the total 10.1 million V-save users were impacted by joint pain (to varying degrees of severity), fatigue, headaches, and sleepiness, after receiving a COVID-19 vaccine.

Potential complications with COVID-19 injections: A brief review of research

It is important to preliminarily note that the FDA seemed to have been aware of possible and potential problems with COVID-19 vaccines from the outset. In his presentation at the FDA's Vaccine and Related Biological Products Advisory Committee, Director of the Office of Biostatistics and Epidemiology at the FDA Steve Anderson included a PowerPoint slide (shown for a brief moment) titled "FDA Safety Surveillance of COVID-19 Vaccines, <u>DRAFT</u> Working list of possible adverse outcomes ***Subject to change***."[155] The list of adverse events from this slide included a list of "possible" negative events such as Guillain–Barre Syndrome (GBS; ascending paralysis), stroke, anaphylaxis, myocarditis and pericarditis, thrombocytopenia, Multisystem Inflammatory Syndrome in children, and death. Notably, a few actual adverse events found in the FDA's preliminary list are somewhat congruent with Pfizer's list included in its fact sheet (i.e., GBS and death). Researchers have also confirmed a long list of potential complications associated with COVID-19 vaccines, which may include acute haemorrhagic leukoencephalitis (i.e., inflammation of the brain),[156] GBS,[157] deep vein thrombosis (DVT),[158] severe autoimmune hepatitis,[159] thrombocytopenia (i.e., low blood platelet count),[160] multisystem inflammatory syndrome in children (MIS-C),[161] and abnormal menstrual cycles.[162] There is also reference to the potential for strokes, including ischemic stroke, haemorrhagic stroke, and cerebral venous sinus thrombosis (CVST).[163]

Let's provide a brief overview of selected research related to adverse events potentially associated with COVID-19 vaccine. For example, a study by MacMillan et al. outlined a case of a young female who ultimately suffered "fatal post COVID mRNA-vaccine associated cerebral ischemia" after developing a severe headache in the 24 hours after receiving the Moderna vaccination.[164] The authors concluded that while "correlational, her medical team surmised that the mRNA vaccine may have contributed to this presentation."[165]

Other potential complications include a temporary impairment of "semen concentration and total motile count among semen donors," as identified in a study by Gat et al.[166] Additional studies have outlined potential adverse events that may occur in the long-term post COVID-19 vaccination. For example, a study by Li et al. found that "individuals with first and second dose of BNT162b2 and mRNA-1273 had significantly increased risk of retinal vascular occlusion 2 years following vaccination."[167] Other studies corroborate these findings. Fraiman et al. have also found excess risks of serious adverse events, while Hui-Lee Wong et al. established potential associations between COVID-19 vaccinations and numerous adverse events (i.e., pulmonary embolism, heart attacks, intravascular coagulation).[168,169] Additionally, a new concern has been identified by Tindle that "COVID-19 vaccination per se might contribute to long COVID, giving rise to the colloquial term 'Long Vax(x)'."[170] Hulscher et al. has explained that "the spike protein of SARS-CoV-2 has been found to exhibit pathogenic characteristics and be a possible cause of post-acute sequalae after SARS-CoV-2 infection or COVID-19 vaccination. COVID-19 vaccines utilize a modified, stabilized prefusion protein that may share similar toxic effects with its viral counterpart."[171]

Furthermore, Uversky et al. has established that multiple vaccinations with mRNA vaccines can lead to abnormally high levels of immunoglobulin G4 (IgG4) antibodies. The authors noted that "the reported increase in IgG4 levels detected after repeated vaccination with the mRNA vaccines may not be a protective mechanism; rather, it constitutes an immune tolerance mechanism to the spike protein that could promote unopposed SARS-CoV-2 infection and replication by suppressing natural antiviral responses."[172] Uversky et al. further speculated that "increased IgG4 synthesis due to repeated mRNA vaccination with high antigen concentrations may also cause autoimmune diseases and promote cancer growth and autoimmune myocarditis in susceptible individuals."[173] In the last instance, the body's immune system will attack its own myocardium.

Lastly, based on COVID-19 vaccine batch labels that were conveyed to the Danish Medical Agency, Schmeling et al. found a temporal relationship between certain vaccine batches and adverse events.[174] The authors identified that "the observed variation in SAE rates and seriousness between BTN162b2 vaccine batches in this nationwide study was contrary to the expected homogenous rate and distribution of SAEs between batches."[175] Based on data from Schmeling et al., Hulscher et al. estimated that 4.2 percent of individuals potentially experienced more serious adverse events; this small group was responsible for over 70 percent of adverse events.[176] Hulscher and colleagues concluded that there may be different reasons for such possible adverse events, including over-concentration of mRNA, DNA, or LNP material in the actual vial, contamination with other materials, amount of degraded mRNA, and impurities. High levels of DNA contamination was also a concern raised by other researchers and was noted by both McKernan et al.[177] and Speicher et al.[178] A contamination of COVID-19 vaccinations was such a concern that it allegedly led to the suspension of 1.6 million doses of COVID-19 vaccines in Australia.[179]

Myocarditis and heart disease post COVID-19 vaccine

There is evidence of various heart problems potentially associated with COVID-19 injection. As reported in April 2024, "multiple studies have shown an increased risk of myocarditis after vaccination with mRNA encoding SARS-CoV-2 spike protein."[180] Cases of myocarditis potentially associated with COVID-19 injections were reported to the FDA and the CDC as early as February 2021 by the Israeli Ministry of Health. On June 25, 2021, the FDA even included an official warning about the risks of myocarditis and pericarditis in its own COVID-19 factsheet.[181] This information came out about two months before some universities in Canada implemented COVID-19 vaccination mandates to new and returning students. The FDA also issued other warnings, which were added to COVID-19 injection labels since their introduction. For example, in July 2021 the FDA issued a label warning for the Johnson & Johnson vaccine about the risk of Guillain-Barre Syndrome. By then, it had become evident that heart issues were on the rise, including an increased incidence of cardiac problems among young males aged 12-17 years, especially after the second dose of the COVID-19 vaccine.[182] Supporting evidence on this matter came from case studies, meta-analysis, large database analysis, and other sources. Needless to say, "myocarditis can be a potentially lethal complication following mRNA-based anti-SARS-CoV-2 vaccination."[183] In September 2021, the advisory committee of the FDA voted against administering the COVID-19 booster to adults, but the White House and the CDC overturned this recommendation. This decision resulted in the resignation of two FDA experts, namely Marion Gruber and Phillip Krause. Interestingly, while the White House and the CDC recommended vaccinations for children and young adults, other countries like Denmark did not make such recommendations. With regards to the booster campaign for young individuals, Bardosh et al. claimed that "booster mandates in young adults are expected to cause a net harm per COVID-19 hospitalization prevented."[184] They also argued that mandating boosters for young adults was unethical, citing numerous reasons for their conclusions.

There have been a multitude of studies focusing on the potential association between myocarditis and mRNA vaccines. For example, a study by Rose, Hulscher, and McCullough established that "the the number of myocarditis reports in VAERS after COVID-19 vaccination in 2021 was 223 times higher than the average of all vaccines combined for the past 30 years."[185] The authors also found that myocarditis commonly arose after the second dose of mRNA vaccines, as noted above. Baumeier et al. similarly noticed an increased risk of myocarditis after mRNA-based injections based on the cardiac biopsy of 15 young individuals, while importantly excluding infectious causes as a root of the myocardial inflammation and instead suggesting that "the inflammatory response triggered by the vaccine may be of autoimmunological origin" rather than viral.[186] One case study from Korea reported an instance of a healthy 22-year-old male who died a few hours after being admitted to the hospital where "the primary cause of death was determined to be myocarditis casually-associated with the BNT162b2 vaccine."[187] This case study confirmed that myocarditis can arise without any evidence of viral infection to the heart. In yet another study, Barmada et al., who sought to establish a pathogenicity of myocarditis after COVID-19 vaccines, confirmed that "our results demonstrate up-regulation in inflammatory cytokines and corresponding lymphocytes with tissue-damaging capabilities, suggesting a cytokine-dependent pathology."[188] Other researchers have also observed the pathogenic role of spike protein. For example, Tsilingiris et al. estimated that "the pathogenesis of mRNA-vaccine associated myocarditis has not yet been elucidated, although a number of mechanisms have been proposed, typically implicating the administered S-protein mRNA and likely mediated through an autoimmune mechanism."[189]

In another study, Krug and colleagues focused on adverse cardiac events in adolescents and established elevated risk levels associated with myocarditis and pericarditis post COVID-19 vaccination in the population of male patients ages 12 to 17 years.[190] In a more recent study from Saudi Arabia, Sherrif et al. estimated that 27.1 percent of respondents indicated potential various cardiac complications post COVID-19 vaccination.[191] The authors found that 15.8 percent were admitted to a cardiac critical care unit and 11.4 percent to general hospital wards, which represent a large proportion that required hospitalization so that they could be on a cardiac monitor and not necessarily because symptoms required it. The duration of hospitalization varied from less than one day (7.0 percent), to 1–3 days (11.1 percent), to 4–7 days (8.3 percent). These numbers appear extraordinarily high. In another study, "cardiovascular manifestations were found in 29.24 percent of patients."[192] In this case, one out of 301 Thai adolescents participating in the study (0.3 percent) developed clearcut myopericarditis while others had other cardiovascular symptoms such as tachycardia (7.6 percent), shortness of breath (6.6 percent), palpitations (4.3 percent), and other symptoms (such as hypertension).[193] In other words, 3 in 1,000 adolescents were identified as developing post-vaccination myocardial injury. The implication of this study is that in a school, college, or a small university of two or three thousand young individuals, one can potentially expect a handful of myopericarditis cases.

There is also evidence that heart muscle inflammation can potentially occur in asymptomatic individuals following vaccination. Nakahara et al. identified that vaccinated individuals had "overall higher myocardial

F-FDG [fluorodeoxyglucose] uptake compared to nonvaccinated patients" on PET scans.[194] This observation is important because damaged cells, a characteristic of myocarditis, normally take up more glucose than unaffected cells. Nakahara et al. have further shown that FDG uptake was visible in other organs such as the liver, spleen, and lymph nodes and could last for up to six months, consistent with earlier studies noted in this section. Lastly, it important to note that cardiac MRI changes frequently persisted beyond 6 months, indicating persisting risk of arrythmias and heart muscle loss rather than the rapid resolution that has sometimes been claimed.

A class action lawsuit against AstraZeneca

It is important to note that both the AstraZeneca vaccine (developed in cooperation with Oxford University) and the Johnson & Johnson COVID-19 vaccine are vector-based vaccines; that is, they are based on Chimpanzee adenovirus with the DNA for the spike protein in SARS-CoV-2. Here, the DNA is transcribed to mRNA which codes for spike protein. After years of legal proceedings, wranglings, and contestation on the part of the company, "AstraZeneca has admitted for the first time in court documents that its COVID vaccine can cause a rare side effect, in an apparent about-turn that could pave the way for a multi-million pound legal payout."[195] This admission follows a lawsuit initially filed by an individual who sustained "a permanent brain injury after having a haemorrhage the day after the COVID vaccine."[196] Subsequent to this initially filing, over 50 additional legal claims were filed against AstraZeneca. The approval of the COVID-19 vaccine that was once regarded by British Prime Minister Boris Johnson as a "triumph of British science" is now under intense scrutiny.[197] It is unclear what brought about this abrupt acknowledgment of side effects by AstraZeneca, although one can only speculate that the company may be trying to reduce potential payouts by early admission of its potential guilt and by settling the issue out of court. Note that adenovirus vector vaccines were known to cause blood clots before COVID-19.

One newspaper article summarizing the case has reported that "in the legal document submitted to the High Court in February, AstraZeneca said: 'It is admitted that the AZ vaccine can, in very rare cases, cause TTS. The causal mechanism is not known'."[198] The last part of AstraZeneca's acknowledgement is particularly surprising since

> [s]cientists from Cardiff University and Arizona State University worked with AstraZeneca to investigate vaccine-induced immune thrombotic thrombocytopenia (VITT), also known as thrombosis with thrombocytopenia syndrome (TTS), a life-threatening condition seen in a very small number of people after receiving the Oxford-AstraZeneca or Johnson & Johnson vaccines.[199]

Potential complications from the vaccine have also been found to "include stroke, failure, and leg amputations."[200] Early warnings about AstraZeneca also came from external sources in early 2021, such as from the chief medical officer of health in Ontario, who issued a statement confirming the first case of VITT in the province.[201] Other researchers have also investigated potential mechanisms of pathogenesis caused by COVID-19 vaccines that ultimately resulted in VITT.[202] While the legal case is ongoing, AstraZeneca decided to withdraw its vaccine from the market in May 2024.[203]

It is important to note that Norway was one of the first countries "to identify and react to rare blood clotting side effects associated with the AstraZeneca vaccine" and subsequently "responded very quickly to the side effects associated with some of the COVID-19 vaccines."[204] In their actions, Norway's authorities conceivably detected potential problems with AstraZeneca's vaccine about 3 years before its manufacturer formally admitted problems. More specifically, "on March 11, 2021, the NIPH [Norwegian Institute of Public Health] paused the use of the AstraZeneca (AZ) vaccine to review the evidence of significant side effects. This suspension was linked to similar actions in eight other countries due to reports of blood clots resulting in a death of a 60-year-old woman in Denmark."[205] About a month later, the AstraZeneca vaccine was removed from the national COVID-19 vaccine program, while another COVID-19 vaccine from Janssen Pharmaceuticals (a wholly owned subsidiary of Johnson & Johnson) was removed from the program in May. The Director of the Division of Infection Control and Disease in Norway put it succinctly: "since there are few people who die from COVID-19 in Norway, the risk of dying after vaccination with the AstraZeneca would be higher than the risk of dying from the disease."[206] Furthermore, the Norwegian Medical Association took an active role in warning about the AstraZeneca vaccine and "advised its members not to participate in making the Janssen vaccine available."[207]

Lastly, despite these potential complications, some may argue that millions of doses of AstraZeneca seemed to have been delivered without apparent complications. For example, Samir Gupta, a medical doctor, claimed that "ultimately we can't forget that the virus is worse than the vaccine, even with this complication."[208] Moreover, Gupta added that "the creation of the AstraZeneca vaccine, testing, roll out, discovery of complications and stopping of vaccine distribution played out as it should for a new pandemic virus."[209]

Healthcare scandal in the U.K.: Contamination of imported blood products

This chapter concludes with a brief description of the U.K. blood scandal. While the underlying events are different, the key question is whether the same or similar problems could arise in the context of the COVID-19 pandemic and mass vaccinations. Given the experience from the U.K., it could take a few decades to find out.

The story of the U.K. blood scandal begins in the early 1970s when the U.K. did not have a sufficient supply of blood donations to support its population. To address this problem, the U.K. government decided to import blood products from the U.S., which were prescribed to patients by the National Health Services (NHS). Imported blood products contained a critical blood clotting protein called Factor III, which, if defective or deficient, could lead to haemophilia. This disorder is characterized by a lack of blood coagulation or clotting, thereby leading to excessive bleeding or bruising. Haemophilia may be treated by increasing clotting proteins with lab-made clotting factors or human plasma concentrates. Unfortunately, these imported blood products were manufactured from blood collected "from prisoners, drug addicts and other high-risk groups who were paid to give blood" to manufacturers in the U.S.[210] In short, these products were disease-ridden and contaminated. When plasma from different donors was pooled, it only took a single person carrying a disease (i.e., hepatitis, HIV) to potentially infect the entire batch. Since these blood products were also not tested for viruses by the U.K. government or its agencies until the 1980s and 1990s, over 30,000 individuals were infected with various diseases under "NHS care between the 1970s and 1990s" and more than 3,000 died.[211]

More disturbingly, a 2,527-page report[212] prepared by Sir Brian Langstaff, chairman of the 5-year inquiry into contaminated blood products, revealed that "three crucial sets of documents were lost or destroyed in the 1980s and 1990s and this was 'a deliberate attempt to make the truth more difficult to reveal'."[213] Moreover, the report outlined that the state was "more concerned about reputational damage than openness and honesty" with the public.[214] Langstaff scathingly claimed that "this disaster was not an accident. The infections happened because those in authority–doctors, the blood services, and successive governments–did not put patient safety first."[215] Moreover, the U.K. government made decisions "against any form of compensation to people infected with HIV, with Lord Clarke, who was health minister at the time, saying there would be no state scheme to compensate those suffering 'the unavoidable adverse effects' of medical procedures."[216] It took decades for the truth to come out, on which point Langstaff has argued that:

> Hiding the truth includes not only deliberate concealment but also a lack of candour: the retelling of half-truths such as the "no conclusive proof" line; and failing to tell people about the risks inherent in treatment or the alternatives to that treatment, that they had been tested for infection, or been used in research, or were suffering from a potentially serious and fatal disease.[217]

Langstaff further claimed that "sometimes the truth was hidden by a treating clinician. Sometimes it was hidden by an organization. Sometimes it was hidden by the civil service. Sometimes it was hidden by (and sometimes from) politicians."[218] With respect to clinicians and public health, Langstaff's report outlines the many ways in which they failed patients.[219] A list of key problems outlined by the inquiry is included in table 1.1 below.

Table 1.1: A summary of problems identified in Sir Langstaff's report

- Failures in the licensing regime
- Deliberate destruction of some documents and the loss of others
- Failing to tell people of the risks of treatment and of available alternative treatments, thus treating them without their informed consent
- Adopting an attitude of denial towards the risks of treatment with factor concentrates
- Treating children unnecessarily with concentrates (especially commercial ones) rather than choosing safer treatments
- Failing to provide advice, guidance and information to clinicians to ensure that safer treatment practices were adopted
- Falsely reassuring the public and patients
- Taking a decision in July 1983 not to suspend the continued importation of commercially produced blood products
- Failing to warn patients of the risks of transfusion at least in situations where they reasonably had a choice
- Failing to offer people reasonable alternatives to treatment
- Failing, until 2017, to decide to establish a public inquiry
- A lack of openness, transparency and candour, shown by the NHS and government, such that the truth has been hidden for decades
- Difficulties and delays in accessing appropriate specialist treatment
- Refusal to provide compensation (on the ground there had been no fault)
- Long delays in agreeing to provide even ex gratia financial support
- Establishing ex gratia payment schemes which were underfunded and did not function in the best interests of those infected and affected
- Responding to calls for a public inquiry by producing flawed, incomplete and unfair internal reports

Source: These are direct quotes from "Infected Blood Inquiry: The Report." Note that the list of these was combined by Dr. John Campbell (U.K.)

PART II:
THE CHARACTERISTICS OF COVID-19 RESPONSE

2

Lockdowns, restrictions, and associated measures

When the coronavirus initially appeared, many political leaders, unelected public health officials, public administrators, medical doctors, experts, and advisors around the globe moved to implement a range of restrictive measures, mandates, and orders. Examples of such restrictions included closures of public spaces (i.e., universities, schools, government offices, courts, etc.), stay-at-home orders, travel restrictions (both domestic and international), border closures, and forced quarantines of healthy people. Other preventive actions included restrictions on social interactions and gatherings (such as visitations between family members, friends, co-workers, etc.), the implementation of curfews, and the enactment of social distancing measures. Most businesses were forced to operate on a restricted basis or were simply not allowed to open. Moreover, the decision by public health officials to restrict business operations was made on the basis of artificial and politically driven conceptions of what may be viewed as essential or non-essential services, with non-essential business mandated to shut down. This led to the determination that liquor stores were essential and allowed to remain open, while "optional" medical procedures or appointments, including surgeries or physiotherapy, were suspended. Practicing faith and service attendance was similarly deemed optional, so churches were either closed or severely limited in capacity.

Testing and the pandemic

One of the most frequently intonations repeated throughout the pandemic was to test, test, and test again. These calls not only came from medical doctors, unelected public health officials, and experts, but also from international organizations. For example, the head of the World Health Organization (WHO) Tedros Adhanom Ghebreyesus delivered a straightforward communication to the world early in the pandemic: "We have a simple message to all countries–test, test, test."[220] Such messages were repeated by the mainstream media all over the world. This testing was primarily done with polymerase chain reaction (PCR), which is a unique process of biochemical replication of the DNA developed by Kary Mullis in the 1980s (for which he subsequently received the Nobel Laureate Price in Chemistry in 1993). In essence, the process works by allowing "a small amount of DNA [to] be copied in large quantities over a short period of time. By applying heat, the DNA molecule's two strands are separated and the DNA building blocks that have been added are bonded to each strand."[221] With each thermal cycle of heating and cooling, the amount of DNA in a sample can be doubled. In practical terms, PCR functions as an "application for creating DNA mutations, DNA sequencing, for shuffling and merging nucleic acids of different origin (recombinant DNA technology), and for the creation of novel nucleic acids or even whole genome from scratch."[222] This process is useful for researchers because it allows a small sample of DNA to be amplified efficiently and inexpensively. Mullis himself was skeptical about using PCR as a diagnostic tool because, as he acknowledged, you can find anything in everything.

And yet, PCR testing became the primary method utilized during the pandemic. A six-inch nasopharyngeal swab was inserted into the nostril and rotated to accumulate nasal material. The sample was subsequently sent to a lab where the PCR test amplified the genetic material and matched with DNA or RNA of a specific segment of the coronavirus, which served as a reference DNA to determine positivity. If the genetic material obtained by the nasopharyngeal swab contained a significant amount of viral load, the diagnosis would be confirmed at limited number of C_t (cycle threshold) values. On the other hand, a sample with a small amount of viral load would require more C_t cycles to obtain a positive result. Of course, the higher the viral load in the person being tested, the higher the contagion potential.

The question of the number of C_t values needed to prove a positive coronavirus viral load is contentious. For example, Byram Bridle, a Canadian virologist, has observed in his testimony that "positive PCR tests for SARS-CoV-2 in asymptomatic people are often based on high cycle threshold (C_t) values, which in and of themselves, raise the question of whether these individuals harbor infectious viral particles."[223] He has further added that "several studies have been conducted to determine the highest C_t values at which SARS-CoV-2 could be successfully cultured in cells. The results were 25, 22-27, 30. This suggests that tests with C_t values above 22-30 are almost certainly not indicative of the presence of replication-competent SARS-CoV-2."[224] The studies Bridle references in his testimony are those conducted by Bullard et al.,[225] Corman et al.,[226] and Jansen et al.[227] The issue of the oversensitivity of testing when using PCR has been continually raised by scientists because positive PCR tests can arise from the identification of small fragments of viruses that are no longer contagious. Furthermore, although PCR can detect miniscule fragments of DNA or RNA, it cannot establish where these DNA or RNA fragments came from. Consequently, because of its testing oversensitivity and ability to produce positive results (either high or low) depending on the cycle threshold (C_t) values, the PCR test can become a powerful tool for political manipulation while providing "scientific" justification. In essence, governments can generate any number of positive COVID-19 cases they desire, which can provide further "scientific" rationalization in support of their preferred public narrative and policies. To avoid such problems, Florida Health, for example, required labs to report C_t values with each test.

An insightful discussion about PCR testing occurred during the legal dispute between Manitoba churches and the provincial government over restrictions on religious freedoms and freedom of assembly. The judge presiding over the case wrote in his final decision that epidemiologist Jay Bhattacharya from Stanford University "noted that the PCR test was never designed to measure infectiousness."[228] The Justice Center for Constitutional Freedom (JCCF) similarly highlighted in its article that PCR is not reliable "in determining whether a person is infectious with the actual COVID-19 disease."[229] Lawyers representing the applicants questioned Jared Bullard, a medical doctor, advisor to the Manitoba government, and associate medical director of the public health laboratory, who acknowledged the limitations of PCR and confirmed that "PCR test results do not verify infectiousness, and were never intended to be used to diagnose respiratory illness," as reported by the JCCF.[230] The judge also wrote in his decision that Bullard "acknowledged that PCR tests do not look for the whole virus, but rather parts or fragments of the nucleic acid particular to SARS-CoV-2."[231]

However, based on the end of paragraph 164, it is unclear whether the judge truly understood the nature of the PCR test and its critical role in potentially amplifying positive COVID-19 case numbers. For example, and as noted by the judge, Bullard "confirmed that Manitoba uses PCR test platforms that employ 40 and 45 cycles."[232] Interestingly, Bullard conducted his own research and knew that infectivity of patients with C_t values higher than 24 could be low. In his own research, Bullard stated that "ninety RT-PCR SARS-CoV-2-positive samples were incubated on Vero cells. Twenty-six samples (28.9%) demonstrated viral growth … There was no growth in samples with a Ct > 24 or STT [symptoms to test] > 8 days."[233] The judge in the case also confirmed that the chief provincial public health officer Brent Roussin was "aware that studies indicated only 28.9 per cent and 31 per cent of the positive PCR tests sampled were likely infectious."[234] As the JCCF concluded, "Dr. Bullard's findings call into question the practice used in Manitoba (and elsewhere in Canada) of the results of classifying positive PCR tests as 'cases', which implied infectivity,"[235] particularly because, in the eyes of public health, positive PCR meant infected, and even infectious individuals who needed to be quarantined.

The information exposed in the Manitoba lawsuit findings are consistent with other studies and on-the-ground observations. For example, Jafaar et al. noted, as early as 2020, that "it can be observed that at Ct=25, up to 70% of patients remain positive in culture and that at Ct=30 this value drops to 20%. At Ct=35, the value we used to report positive result for PCR, less than 3% of culture are negative."[236] In other words, a C_t value of 35 may have resulted in a 97 percent rate of falsely positive PCR tests. In another study, Sethuraman et al. concluded that "a 'positive' PCR result reflects only the detection of viral RNA and does not necessarily indicate presence of viable virus."[237] As reported by *The New York Times*, "in three sets of testing data that include cycle thresholds, compiled by officials in Massachusetts, New York and Nevada, up to 90 percent of people testing positive carried barely any virus."[238] A Harvard epidemiologist further found that "tests with thresholds so high may detect not just live virus but also genetic fragments, leftovers from infection that pose no particular risk–akin to finding a hair in a room long after a person has left."[239] These studies led officials from one of the New York labs to conclude that "with a cut-off of 35, about 43 percent of those tests would no longer qualify as positive. About 63 percent would no longer be judged positive if the cycle were limited to 30."[240] Surkova et al. added additional commentary which is consistent with our discussion above: "prolonged viral RNA shedding, which is known to last for weeks after recovery, can be a potential reason for positive swab tests in those previously exposed to SARS-CoV-2."[241]

Continuing with the example from Manitoba, which followed the guidelines set forth by the World Health Organization (WHO),[242] the province introduced new protocols during the pandemic related to PCR-testing of the deceased. This new protocol notes that "COVID-19 testing should be considered if the death was proceeded by influenza-like (ILI), upper or lower tract infection, or any symptoms compatible with COVID-19."[243] Manitoba defines "symptoms compatible with COVID-19" as "one or more of the following: fever/chills, new or worsening cough, shortness of breath, sore throat, loss of altered sense of taste/smell, runny nose/nasal congestion, fatigue (significant and unusual), muscle ache/join pain, headache, nausea/diarrhoea."[244] In effect, evidence that a single symptom from the above list occurred before death could trigger post mortem COVID-19 testing. Exhibiting any of the above symptoms was also sufficient to classify as "a probable case" of COVID-19.[245] Furthermore, Manitoba Shared Health defined COVID-19 related or associated fatality as "all laboratory confirmed COVID-19 cases who have died within 30 days after the earliest specimen collection date in the most recent investigation," and further stressed that "the reason for death does not have to be attributable to COVID-19."[246] These and other concerns are well described in the legal case of *Gateway Bible Baptist Church et al v Manitoba et al.*[247] The implications of these newly introduced protocols are worrisome, including the potential over-reporting of not only COVID-deaths, but also COVID-19 cases.

Thus, it is evident that PCR testing cannot tell the complete story of viral load and must be considered in view of other conditions. For example, Surkova et al. advocated that "any diagnostic test result should be interpreted in the context of the pretest probability of disease. For COVID-19, the pretest probability assessment includes symptoms, previous medical history of COVID-19 or presence of antibodies, any potential exposure to COVID-19, and likelihood of an alternative diagnosis."[248]

There is also a connection between asymptomatic transmission and PCR testing. One of the prevalent narratives throughout the pandemic was so-called asymptomatic transmission, which was described as situations where individuals were infected with COVID-19 but showed no signs of the disease so sole confirmation of the alleged disease was assumed by the presence of a positive PCR test. One compelling study of 10 million individuals in China concluded that "no new infections could be traced to persons that had tested positive for SARS-CoV-2 by PCR, but who did not exhibit any other signs of infections."[249] Furthermore, Cao et al. identified that "all close contacts of the asymptomatic positive cases tested negative, indicating that the asymptomatic positive cases detected in this study were unlikely to be infectious" and "there were no positive tests amongst 1,174 close contacts of asymptomatic cases."[250]

Lastly, it is important to include additional evidence that questions the reliability of PCR testing. In one instance from 2021, the Swedish Agency for Public Health stated that PCR tests were not able to differentiate between viruses ready to infect and those which have been neutralized by the immune system. The agency consequently concluded that PCR tests cannot be used to determine whether a person is infected or infectious.[251] Moreover, after reviewing expert evidence, the Lisbon Court of Appeal determined that a PCR test "is unable to determine, beyond reasonable doubt, that a positive result corresponds, in fact, to the infection of a person by the SARS-CoV-2 virus."[252] The judge in that case argued that,

> with so many scientific doubts, expressed by experts in the field, which are the ones that matter here, as to the reliability of such tests, ignoring the parameters of their performance and there being no diagnosis made by a doctor, in the sense of existence of infection and risk, it would never be possible for this court to determine that C ... had the SARS-CoV-2 virus, nor that A., B ... and D ... had high risk exposure.[253]

Thus, it is evident that PCR testing does not definitively prove a positive viral load, infection, or infectiousness. Especially at high Ct_t values, there is no assurance that the PCR test can properly detect the virus, which can replicate and infect.

Early criticisms of PCR testing in the context of the COVID-19 pandemic

Early in the pandemic a group of researchers commented on the study by Corman et al., known as the Corman–Drosten paper, which was critical in establishing a diagnostic approach to test for SARS-CoV-2. While this early procedure could have been perceived as beneficial, it had significant molecular and methodological problems that were subsequently multiplied in labs around the world. These errors could have been forgiven if not for the fact that it was based on these PCR protocols that public health officials, experts, and the state instituted massive lockdowns and restrictions, closed businesses, and violated human rights.

This section discusses at length a commentary written by Borger and colleagues in November 2020 regarding their extensive criticisms of PCR testing in the context of the COVID-19 pandemic. Firstly, the authors identified that the findings from the Corman-Drosten paper were "based on silico (theoretical) sequence, supplied by a laboratory in China because at the time neither control material of infectious ('live') or inactivated SARS-CoV-2 nor isolated genomic material of the virus was available to the authors."[254] Furthermore, it was found that "to date no validation has been performed by the authorship based on isolated SARS-CoV-2 viruses or full length RNA thereof."[255] Corman et al. confirmed this omission by claiming their goal was "to develop and deploy robust diagnostic methodology for use in public health laboratory settings without having virus material available."[256] In other words, Corman et al. developed a testing methodology for coronavirus without testing it on the actual virus. This raises multiple questions, such as if they knew with precision whether their testing protocol and approach worked. This concern was also raised by other researchers, including Pillonel et al., who asserted that "these observations based on in silico alignment should be confirmed by wet-laboratory experiment."[257] The U.S. Centers for Disease Control and Prevention (CDC) were also unable to test these results with the coronavirus "since no quantified virus isolates of the 2019-nCoV were available for the CDC use at the time the test was developed and this study conducted, [so] assays designed for the detection of the 2019-nCoV RNA were tested with characterized stock of in vitro transcribed full length RNA."[258] There are also questions as to what the gold standard for testing is, as Jessica Watson et al. found that "the lack of a clear-cut 'gold-standard' is a challenge for evaluating COVID-19 tests."[259]

Beyond a lack of actual virus testing, Borger et al. have found that "the Corman–Drosten test was not designed to detect the full-length virus, but only a fragment of the virus, which classified the test as unsuitable as a diagnostic test for SARS-virus infection."[260] Furthermore, it appears the Corman-Drosten findings are not even specific to coronavirus, as they admit that

> the assays can detect other bat-associated SARS-related viruses, we used the E gene assay to test six bat-derived fecal samples available from Drexler et al. and Muth et al. These virus-positive samples stemmed from European rhinophid bats. Detection of these phylogenetic outliers within the SARS-related CoV clade suggests that all Asian viruses are likely to be detected.[261]

The criticism from Borger et al. was that "this statement demonstrates that the E gene used in R_t-PCR test, as described in the Corman–Drosten paper, is not specific enough to SARS-CoV-2. The E gene primers also detect a broad spectrum of other SARS viruses."[262] Pillonel et al. have also found a significant problem, namely that "the proposed RdRp reverse prime contained an incorrect degenerate base (S), that does not match with the SARS-CoV-2 RNA sequence."[263]

In terms of the actual application of the PCR procedure, the Corman–Drosten study did not provide the specific C_t values at which the virus should be detected nor any standard operating procedures, including basic guidance and guidelines for labs.[264] Notably, the Corman–Drosten paper allegedly did not go through the peer review process, as noted by Borger et al., since it was submitted to *Eurosurveillance* on January 21, 2020 and accepted a day later. The paper had also previously appeared on the WHO's website on January 13, with updates provided on January 17. Most curiously, the Corman–Drosten paper, as observed by Borger et al., projected laboratory testing problems at a point when only a handful of deaths occurred due to SARS-CoV-2 worldwide. Specifically, Corman et al. wrote that "the ongoing outbreak of the recently emerged novel coronavirus (2019-nCoV) poses a challenge for public health laboratories as virus isolates are unavailable."[265]

In summary, while the PCR test was perceived to be the best analytical tool available at the time, the key problem was that based on the test people were isolated and quarantined, businesses were shut down, schools and universities were closed, families were prevented from visiting, travel was banned, and so on. Moreover, the test could be easily manipulated to fit the desired public narrative. It could also be used to exaggerate and amplify fear. Simply put, the PCR test could become a political tool masquerading as science since the public was unaware of the significance of specific C_t values and their influence on the number of declared COVID-19 cases and deaths.

Lockdowns: the global stay-at-home camp

Lockdowns were one of a "collection of severe and fairly long-lasting government restrictions on the normal activities of human beings."[266] These restrictions are regarded as non-pharmaceutical intervention (NPI) measures that were intended to reduce the spread of COVID-19 and included forms of confinements such as stay-in-place orders (SIPOs); the stoppage of economic activities including businesses; the closure of various social and public activities (i.e., education, arts, recreation, worship, etc.); mask mandates; social distancing; a restriction on assembly; and limitations on other forms of social gathering. While these restrictions were "originally presented as temporary measures in 2020 (e.g. two weeks to 'flatten the curve') [they] quickly transformed into many months of changing rules and regulations aimed at limiting human movement and interaction."[267] Importantly, these unprecedented but noticeably wartime-like measures were implemented without proper cost/benefit analysis.

Since the beginning of the pandemic there have been numerous studies discussing the advantages and disadvantages of lockdowns. One of the most affirmative studies was by Flaxman et al. from Imperial College of London, who claimed that "major non-pharmaceutical interventions-and lockdowns in particular-have had a large effect on reducing transmission" and may have even saved 3 million lives in Europe alone.[268] One economic study conducted by Thunstrom et al. further concluded that the "net benefits of social distancing are positive" and estimated its value equal to $5.16 trillion, although such praise was tempered with the caveat that "social distancing saves lives but imposes large costs on society due to reduced economic activity."[269] Chaudhry et al. concluded that "more restrictive public health measures (such as a full lockdown compared to partial or curfew-only measures) were associated with an increase in the number of recovered cases per million population. These findings suggest that more restrictive public health practices may indeed be associated with less transmission and better outcomes."[270] While Chaudhry et al. noted that these measures may prevent transmission (which may lead to runny noses, headaches, low-grade temperatures, and so on), they were quite clear that "full lockdowns and wide-spread COVID-19 testing were not associated with reductions in the number of critical cases or overall mortality."[271]

However, despite their claims, Canadian economist Douglas W. Allen has identified that these lockdown-affirming studies had significant problems and weaknesses. Firstly, these studies did not consider the long-term effects, implications, impacts, consequences, or costs of restrictive measures. Secondly, many studies were not evidence-based and were instead constructed from theoretical epidemiological models that were erroneous and favored ill-founded assumptions, which were then further fed into forecasting models. As Allen noted in his investigation, "an examination of over 80 COVID-19 studies reveals that many relied on assumptions that were false, and which tended to over-estimate the benefits and under-estimate the costs of lockdown."[272] Such incorrect assumptions pertained to overestimations of fatality rates, reproduction rates (i.e., the number of secondary infections reproduced from a single infection), and the economic value of singular lives saved. As an example, forecasting models assumed that infection fatality rates (IFR) were homogenous and did not differ with age, which was clearly not supported by data. Thus, "most of the early cost/benefit studies arrived at conclusions that were refuted later by data, and which rendered their cost/benefit findings incorrect."[273]

Furthermore, Allen has stated the importance of a cautious analysis when attempting to confirm that the benefits of public measures such as lockdowns outweigh the costs, since there is no evidence to suggest that governments simultaneously considered the costs and benefits when implementing their policy decisions. This evidence, or lack thereof, is apparent from legal cases adjudicated in Canada. While governments made general aspirational and declaratory proclamations of savings lives, limiting transmission, and reducing the number of cases and deaths through lockdown measures, they could not produce quantitative evidence as to how many lives they actually saved, how much they reduced transmission, or the true costs of the restrictions.

Another weakness of affirmative studies was that they implicitly assume that more action is better than no action. This rush-to-act perspective was also encouraged by Neil Fergusson, who modelled ICU predictions under different scenarios (i.e., do nothing, case isolation, case isolation and household quarantine, closing schools and universities, and so on). In comparison to "do nothing strategies", almost any strategy was assumed to be better, although in most cases their benefits were overstated, and any positive effects of lockdowns were amplified. One final issue was that researchers of affirmative studies utilize inappropriate economic comparisons of lockdowns benefits. For example, Mulligan et al. argued that it would be improper to trade lives for GDP, while stating that an appropriate trade-off is "between two things that people themselves value: health and other aspects of their lives."[274] The authors also concluded that a "suppression of the disease delays the development of 'herd immunity'."[275]

One of the earliest studies that cast doubt upon the positive effects of lockdown policy was a study by Atkenson et al., which warned that if basic facts and data (i.e., transmission rates, death rates, timing, declining trajectories in transmission, and so on) were not properly accounted for, predictions or models would overstate the benefits of lockdown.[276] In another study, Bjornskov concluded that when "comparing weekly mortality in 24 European countries, the findings in this paper suggest that more severe lockdown policies have not been associated with lower mortality. In other words, the lockdowns have not worked as intended."[277] Hunt et al. similarly found that lockdowns had a modest impact on the viral transmission of COVID-19 while highlighting the importance of taking population density into account when considering their validity.[278] In yet another study, Meunier prefaced his article by stating in its title that "full lockdown policies in Western Europe countries have no evident impacts on the COVID-19 pandemic."[279] This finding was echoed by Gibson, who, when reflecting on the lockdown measures in New Zealand, claimed that "there is no evidence that countries with a lockdown have fewer deaths."[280] Such findings prompted economists such as Allen to conclude that "it is possible that lockdown will go down as one of the greatest peacetime policy failures in Canada's history," particularly if the lockdown measures only prevented a minimal number of deaths.[281] In light of this regional evidence, Herby et al. conducted an exhaustive, detailed, and comprehensive meta-analysis and concluded that lockdowns were "a global policy failure of gigantic proportions."[282] Furthermore, Herby et al. have identified that "the draconian policy failed to significantly reduce deaths while imposing substantial social, cultural, and economic costs."[283] They further added that:

> Lockdowns prevented 1,700 deaths in England and Wales, 6,000 deaths across Europe, and 4,000 deaths in the United States ... Lockdowns prevented relatively few deaths compared to a typical flu season–in England and Wales, 18,500–24,800 flu deaths occur, in Europe 72,000 flu deaths occur, and in the United States 38,000 flu deaths occur in a typical flu season ... These results pale in comparison to the Imperial College of London's modelling exercises (March 2020), which predicted that lockdowns would save over 400,000 lives in the United Kingdom and over 2 million lives in the United States.[284]

Similar conclusions can be made when comparing cumulative deaths per 100,000 in Florida (which lifted restriction early) and California (which implemented full lockdowns with stay-at-home orders).[285] These and other findings have led Herby et al. to conclude that "meta-analysis support the conclusion that lockdowns in the spring of 2020 had little to no effect on COVID-19 mortality."[286] An earlier version of their study similarly stated that "lockdown policies are ill-founded and should be rejected as a pandemic policy instrument" and that lockdowns "imposed enormous economic and social costs where they have been adopted."[287]

A study from New Zealand, which predominantly pursued a geographic country-isolation strategy with initial lockdowns, confirmed that "lockdowns do not reduce COVID-19 deaths. This pattern is visible on each date that key lockdown decisions were made in New Zealand."[288] John Gibson, the author of this regional study, found that "the apparent ineffectiveness of lockdowns suggests that New Zealand suffered large economic costs for little benefit in terms of lives saved."[289] Another study by economist Martin Lally, which considered the costs and benefits of lockdowns in comparison to a basic mitigation strategy (i.e., selective isolation, quarantines, gathering limitations, social distancing, and masking on public transport, etc.), also concluded that "the lockdowns were not justified."[290]

Additional studies, such as that completed by Berry et al., "found no evidence that SIP [stay-in-place] policies led to reductions in new COVID-19 cases or deaths."[291] Others, like Mulligan and Arnott, focused on non-COVID excess deaths in the U.S. and outlined collateral damage from lockdowns and numerous abnormalities in death statistics (something which is explored in chapter 7). In the U.K., data from the Office for National Statistics (ONS) shows a significant increase in deaths from medical conditions other than COVID-19.[292] The official narrative from the Department of Health and Social Care (DHSC) attributes these excess deaths to circulatory diseases and diabetes. Thus, new evidence is emerging globally that lockdowns did not significantly limit COVID-19 transmission or death and may have instead caused drastic social and economic implications.

Additional areas that were impacted by lockdowns, as catalogued by Allen, include lost educational opportunities, the isolation of children, reduced labor force participation, inflated harms to children (including abuse and mental health issues), increased suicide rates due to loss of employment, loss of medical services and an associated increase in medical problems for patients, and even excess deaths unrelated to COVID-19. Allen also highlighted that many of these problems disproportionately affected lower income families, and particularly the children from such families. By April 2021, Allen had already anticipated that costs stemming from lockdowns "will not be known for years as they work out in reduced graduation rates, reduced future earnings, and reduced long run health status," which will be discussed in the following chapters.[293] Of the unanticipated impacts of lockdowns, the loss of educational opportunities is particularly worrisome because it can lead to a cumulative degradation of human capital. These losses are borne out in research as, for example, Engzell et al. found that "students made little or no progress while learning from home. Learning loss was most pronounced among students from disadvantaged homes."[294] A study by Rose et al. specifically indicated that students fell behind in reading and math.[295] As a result, Gajdorowicz et al. have estimated significant losses in these students' future earnings potential because of their educational shortcomings.[296]

There is another important point to make. It could be conjectured that some components of the lockdowns were politically motivated and intended to make life difficult for people in order to boost vaccination rates. It is difficult to argue that such actions do not represent coercion. For example, in a recording played during the House Select Subcommittee on the Coronavirus Pandemic in early June 2024 and in reference to the unvaccinated, Anthony Fauci admitted that "It's been proven that when you make it difficult for people in their lives, they lose their ideological bull****, and they get vaccinated."[297] In a similar vein, medical doctor and chief medical health officer for Vancouver Coastal Health and professor at the University of British Columbia Patty Daly stated in a recorded meeting that "the vaccine passport requires people be vaccinated to do certain discretionary activities such as go to restaurants, movies, gyms not because these places are high risk. We're not actually seeing COVID transmission in these settings … It's really to create incentive to improve our vaccine coverage."[298]

Interestingly, on July 26, 2024, British Columbia's Provincial Health Officer Bonnie Henry declared an end to "the public-health emergency for COVID-19 and rescind[ed] all related orders," which occurred about 2 years after the other Canadian provinces.[299] Unvaccinated healthcare workers who were prevented from working since 2021 could now return to work, although at the same time it was announced that "the Province is making it mandatory for health-care workers to disclose their immunization status" for COVID-19, influenza and other communicable diseases.[300] This disclosure requirement includes "doctors, nurses, allied health professionals, volunteers and contractors" and is allegedly aimed to "help keep people safe."[301]

The public and academics alike are left wondering: were lockdowns, restrictions, and vaccine passports put in place to keep people safe? Did public officials intend to punish the unvaccinated by restricting their movement, experiences, and opportunities? Was this all a ploy to boost vaccination uptake? Regina Watteel in her book *Fisman's Fraud* concluded that "testimonials from top government officials [in Canada] indicated that the true goal of the mandates and restrictions was not for public safety via reduced transmission but was to coerce all Canadians to take a vaccine that millions clearly did not want or need. Without scientific justification, these acts of coercion are akin to extortion."[302]

Lastly, it is important to touch upon the seminal paper by Donald Henderson (Johns Hopkins University) and others on the mitigation of disease through the implementation of different measures. The end of this paper refers to the "overriding principle" in mitigation, which prophetically concluded that:

> Experience has shown that communities faced with epidemics or other adverse events respond best and with the least anxiety when the normal social functioning of the community is least disrupted.

Strong political and public health leadership to provide reassurance and to ensure that needed medical care services are provided are critical elements. If either is seen to be less optimal, a manageable epidemic could move toward catastrophe.[303]

The obvious question, which will be analyzed in the last chapter of the book, is: how could such an important conclusion be disregarded? As noted by Allen, it was known by April of 2020 that epidemiological models for COVID-19 were based on erroneous assumptions. By the fall of 2020, "there was enough information available to show that any reasonable cost/benefit analysis would show that lockdown was creating more harm than good."[304]

The case of Sweden: A positive outlier

This section would not be complete without considering the case of Sweden, which broadly followed the suggestions outlined in the "Great Barrington Declaration" (which will be discussed in more detail in the following chapter). Sweden's controversial and "careless" approach to lockdowns, as it was considered by some, and their subsequent positive outcomes, may be somewhat awkward to international institutions, politicians, governments, unelected public health officials, epidemiologists, medical doctors, academics, and experts since the country did not fare any worse when compared to countries that implemented heavy-handed lockdown measures. In fact, Sweden scored better than other countries on many quantitative and non-quantitative measures. Of course, this is not to say that Sweden could not have done better in some areas of its public response, especially with respect to accommodating the elderly.

There are several specific features and characteristics related to the delicate and light-touch restrictions introduced in Sweden, the most striking being those measures including social distancing, remote work, and staying indoors if sick, were recommended by the government rather than ordered. Interestingly, Sweden was also constitutionally prevented from imposing society-wide lockdowns and closing down businesses.

Even though the Swedish "Parliament has the power to institute new laws very rapidly in case of emergencies", the state chose not to exercise this right.[305] Having said this, Sweden did introduce new policies and laws through amended legislation.[306] Also, "Sweden's agencies enjoy extraordinary autonomy from political interference."[307]

Furthermore, Sweden's approach was based on personal responsibility, meaning that individuals were perceived to be in the best position to judge their own circumstances and adjust their personal behavior in view of their own underlying risk factors. This approach to personal responsibility is well ingrained in Sweden. In fact, "Sweden's Communicable Diseases Act placed particularly high emphasis on the responsibility of each individual, reflecting a deep-rooted mindset in Swedish infection control that says the individual should be allowed to choose how to protect themselves on the basis of their own ethical considerations."[308]

The Swedish policies also did not aim to lockdown entire sectors of society but instead focused on protecting its most vulnerable groups (i.e., the elderly, individuals with significant comorbidities, etc.) while allowing the rest of the population to continue life as usual. Importantly, public health officials rejected the standard narrative illustrated by China and refused to implement policies that blindly followed those in other countries, including their neighbors. As Johan Norberg has identified, although it would likely have made "political sense" for Sweden to follow other countries, such decisions would have been based on "political science" rather than science.[309] To this point, Norberg has further stated that "if you followed the herd, and suffer on par with everybody else, then you can say that there was nothing much that could be done ... but if you act differently, from everybody else and face abysmal results ... then you put yourself in a terrible position as a politician."[310] This may be a possible explanation as to why so many politicians, health care officers, experts, medical doctors, and others took the standard route of enforced closures and lockdowns. But for Sweden, it appeared that "it was the rest of the world that was engaging in a risky, unprecedented experiment."[311]

Importantly, the Swedish population places a high level of trust and reliance in the idea that everyone will act in a responsible manner for the benefit of society. As noted by Norberg, "governments that police people's social life and enforce mask wearing might have problems retaining their residents' loyalty and trust."[312] Clearly, the Swedish state and public health officials had their sights set on longer-term outcomes rather than implementing lockdown mandates to solve a single problem with short-term results. The individuals responsible for public policy in Sweden clearly understood that "people don't just suffer from viruses, they also suffer from loneliness, mental illnesses, domestic abuse, unemployment, and other effects of stringent lockdowns."[313] Consequently, "gyms and training facilities were open and organized children's sports arrangements encouraged, based on a judgement that the benefit of socializing and being active outweighs the potential risks of COVID-19 for children."[314] This reflects the principles included in the Swedish Communicable Diseases Acts in Sweden, which specifies that "when infection preventive measures affect children, particular attention must be paid to what the child's best interests require."[315] In one sober but realistic assessment, it was understood that "countries that shut down will not avoid deaths, but just delay them, at a high social and economic cost."[316]

As a consequence of this unique approach, public health officials recommended, rather than mandated, that schools and universities switch to online modes of delivery between March and June 2020, and in December 2021. However, border closures were rejected as it was viewed that COVID-19 has already made entry into the country. Furthermore, it was determined that:

> There was no state of emergency, no curfews, no orders to stay at home or shelter in place. Young Swedes were encouraged to continue with their sports training and events. School remained open, and so did offices, factories, restaurants, shopping centers, gyms, and hairdressers ... There were no mask mandates and not even a recommendation for the public to use masks ... [Anders] Tegnell [medical doctor and Sweden's state epidemiologist] even warned against children wear them, saying that "school is no optimal place for face masks."[317]

Of course, there were times when the Swedish public policy strategy appeared to fail, especially in the short-term. The mainstream media was quick to criticize Sweden as a "disaster"[318], "catastrophe"[319], and "cautionary tale."[320] Early in the pandemic, Sweden had 517 COVID-19 deaths per million, which was lower than the rates in Italy and Spain but significantly higher than those in Norway and Denmark. COVID-19 deaths eventually reached above 2,000 deaths per million, which was a rate that was still greater than their neighboring countries but lower than those seen in the rest of Europe, the U.S., and the U.K. (about 3,300 deaths per million).

To fully appreciate the case of Sweden, it is important to observe other factors such as the rate of excess deaths, GDP, and individual well-being. In the first case, excess deaths refer to the percentage increase in mortality (or number of deaths) in comparison to a predetermined historical baseline point from all causes (i.e., all-cause mortality). Excess deaths represent an unusual or uncharacteristic increase in deaths during a specific time period and can be used to draw attention to unusual trends in mortality. In terms of the number of deaths per million, Sweden placed in the middle of comparable countries with 2,322 deaths between early 2020 and June 2023 (i.e., Norway: 1,204; U.S.: 3,332; U.K.: 3,378).[321] The excess death rate between 2020 and 2022 in Sweden was equal to 4.4 percent, which was the lowest in Europe and better than its neighbours (i.e., Norway: 5.0 percent; Denmark: 5.4 percent). In terms of economic activity, GDP in Sweden declined by only 2.2 percent in 2020 (Europe: -6.1 percent) but grew by 6.1 percent in 2021 (Europe: 5.9 percent), and 2.9 percent in 2022 (Europe: 3.4 percent). Finally, there are also softer considerations that have long-term impacts on individual heath, well-being, creativity, and life satisfaction. Importantly, Norberg has reported that "according to the World Happiness Report, self-reported well-being did not decline in Sweden during the pandemic."[322] These positive trends may also reflect the fact that in Sweden "the proportion of unemployed increased only slightly compared to previous years."[323]

COVID-19 response in other Scandinavian countries

While there are notable differences between Sweden and other Nordic countries, Sweden is by no means an exception in its approach to the pandemic. This section briefly describes the case of Norway because "the Norwegian policy response to COVID-19 is considered a success nationally and internationally."[324]

It is important to note that the Nordic countries (i.e., Finland, Norway, Denmark, and Sweden) have many similar characteristics, share "a special relationship", [325] and are regarded as "fraternal twin" nations.[326] Foremostly, these countries share similar cultures and languages. They operate on the basis of parliamentary democracies across different political spectrums, including left-green (Finland), social-democratic (Denmark), and center right (Sweden).[327] They also operate on a collaborative and "consensual form of decision making" approach rather than a more confrontational governing method.[328] As a result, people generally exhibit a high degree of trust in the governments and institutions and exhibit high levels of loyalty to public authority.[329] The Nordic countries similarly have high levels of social capital, which is defined as "the ability to cooperate without written rules and extensive contracts."[330] In terms of COVID-19 response, a comprehensive analysis of all the Nordic countries is provided by Saunes et al.[331] while Askim and Bergstrom deliver an insightful comparison of Sweden and Norway.[332]

Norway initially took "a wait-and-see approach to the epidemic"[333], but on March 12, 2020, the government introduced strict lockdown and quarantine measures. It "closed educational institutions and banned sports and cultural activities."[334] High schools, colleges, and universities were closed and restrictions on gatherings were introduced a few days later. Healthcare workers were prohibited from leaving the country, returnees were subject to quarantines, non-residents were not allowed to enter the country, and leisure travel was discouraged. Moreover, individuals were requested not to visit the elderly in long-term care facilities or other state institutions. Fines were even administered for violating quarantines restrictions. The strictness of these lockdown measures may have reflected the fact that people in Norway "believed that the [SARS-CoV-2] virus posed a large to a very large health threat to their family members."[335] Despite this, the Norwegian government did not invoke a state of emergency.[336] These strict measures lasted about 2 weeks and by early April the state announced that the initial pandemic outbreak had ended in view of a declining reinfection rate, which fell to 0.7. In fact, "Norway became the first European country to claim that the situation was under control."[337] Subsequently, the "COVID-19 Act" expired on May 27, 2020, and the country officially reopened in later September.[338]

Notably, "Norway has experienced very low levels of infection and death due to COVID-19."[339] As an example, as of March 24, 2022, from a population of about 5.4 million, Norway registered 1,393,058 cases, 11,098 hospitalized individuals, 1,835 cases that were treated in intensive care units, and 2,339 deaths. Interestingly, while the COVID-19 vaccination rates among the native Norwegian population (18–44-year-olds) was equal to about 93 percent for dose 1 and 89 percent for dose 2, the vaccination rates among immigrant populations were markedly lower.[340] The lowest vaccination rates (equal to about 45 percent for dose 1 and 40 percent for dose 2) were among Polish immigrants. Skjesol and Tritter noted that these lower rates among immigrant populations reflected hesitation about vaccine effectiveness and a fear of side effects. In addition, it important to note that the "government decided to force much stronger restrictions than recommended by the public health authorities … [which] did not recommend the closing of schools and kindergartens."[341] It is unclear why the government took more restrictive measures, and this very issue continues to generate controversy and considerable debate. One of the key concerns was whether the government over-reacted.

There are numerous key takeaways from a broad analysis of COVID-19 response related to the Nordic countries generated from a review of academic literature, mainstream media, and expert reports. Firstly, the Nordic countries placed significant levels of trust in their governments. In Sweden, for example, about 50 percent of people trusted their health authorities.[342] Individuals also believed that they "received good information from their health authorities."[343] It seems that unobstructed access to information fueled a general belief that "governments' decisions were based on scientific evidence."[344] Secondly, people in the Nordic countries were not only concerned about personal health and safety but also about the threat that the COVID-19 pandemic would pose to the broader economy, the family, and family economics. For example, "more than 60% of both Norwegians and Swedes agreed that the economic crisis would be a larger challenge than the pandemic itself."[345] Governments in these countries understood that there are trade-offs "between protecting citizens from the pandemic and protecting the economy"[346] while simultaneously maintaining concern for mental health. Thirdly, the countries relied on a decentralized response to the pandemic since local health authorities were broadly responsible for the development and implementation of regional emergency and preparedness plans.

While the Nordic countries differed somewhat in their approach to the pandemic (and certainly in comparison to Sweden), their policy measures were relatively short-lived. Olagnier and Mogensen have characterized this strategy as "act fast and act with force."[347] As noted in table 2 by Saunes et al., many measures were temporary.[348] Importantly, "successive re-opening phases started in late April, as concerns for businesses and the broader economy started to dominate policy discussions."[349] In practice, this meant that "schools started to open on 15th April in Denmark and on 27th April in Norway. Finland reopened educational facilities on 13th May."[350] In Norway, reopening efforts prioritized children since kindergarten re-opened April 20, young students (6-10-year-olds) returned to class April 27, and other schools opened on May 11. On June 15, "Nordic countries opened for travel" and "public events for 200 [were] permitted."[351] Interestingly, "schools and daycare centers were open for children of essential health care personnel throughout the period."[352] In comparison, while many Western countries (including Canada, the U.S., the U.K., and many others) were focused on continuing (or even increasing) restrictive measures and lockdowns, the Nordic countries prioritized re-opening initiatives and returning lives to normal. Notably, while there were calls for collective solidarity and "special considerations were given to protect older people and other vulnerable groups in all [Nordic] countries", there was a strong emphasis on "voluntary efforts."[353]

The Nordic countries also relied on independent and various ad-hoc commissions, expert groups and hearings, internal meetings, and independent advisors (from outside of the government system) to offer a wide range of perspectives and advice (i.e., socioeconomics, mental health, and so on). While governments of the Nordic countries depended upon epidemiological models and projections, they also strived to institute evidence-based decisions rather than be swayed by a particular dogma, political calculus, or other political consideration.[354] Importantly, as demonstrated in the case of Norway, "the political leadership did not sideline professional experts, as in the United States."[355] In addition to evidence-based considerations, the Nordic countries also focused on the cost side of lockdowns and restrictions. In Norway, for example, economists' concerns led a group of experts under the leadership of economics professor Steinar Holden from the University of Oslo, who were employed by the Directorate of Health, to calculate the costs associated with three contemplated strategies.[356] These findings led to a report which was completed by early April 2020. Other studies were undertaken to estimate the costs related to school closures, among other restrictions. As noted throughout this book, most governments around the world outright ignored the economic costs of lockdowns and restrictions.

Finally, in terms of vaccination, the Nordic countries pursued voluntary vaccinations even though there was more pressure to vaccinate individuals in healthcare and social services, which did not occur without significant opposition. In Finland, for example, "these regulations on forced vaccinations have sparked debate on social media and raised objections among some health and social care workers."[357] Importantly, however, the Nordic governments took seriously their decisions to invoke special powers, acts, policies, or laws. Consequently, governments in these countries "have all appointed national commissions to reevaluate the entire course of the COVID-19 crisis."[358]

Masks and masking

Masking was one of the most polarizing issues during the COVID-19 pandemic, as some individuals swore by mask-wearing while others outright rejected it. The proponents of masks relied on a few affirmative arguments, such as that masks could prevent sick people from infecting others or that healthy people could be protected by wearing masks, especially in view of so-called asymptomatic spread. Another popular defense was that even if protections from masks were imperfect, they may be better than nothing. Some of these convictions will be explored below.

The different forms of masking behavior and belief in their efficacy reflected confusing messaging around the topic. For example, Anthony Fauci, director of the National Institute of Allergy and Infectious Diseases (NIAID) advised on the March 7, 2020, episode of *60 Minutes* that "right now in the United States, people should not be walking around with masks."[359] Fauci further claimed that "when you're in the middle of an outbreak, wearing a mask might make people feel a little bit better and it might even block a droplet, but it's not providing the perfect protection that people think that it is."[360]

Fauci's advice in early March was consistent with that of the CDC, which made a Twitter (currently X) post on February 27, 2020, stating that the "CDC does not currently recommend the use of facemasks to help prevent novel coronavirus. Take everyday preventive actions, like staying home when you are sick and washing hands with soap and water, to help slow the spread of respiratory illness."[361] In an article published in *The Journal of the American Medical Association* in March 2020, Angel Desai was also clear that "face masks should not be worn by healthy individuals to protect themselves from acquiring respiratory infection because there is no evidence to suggest that face masks worn by healthy individuals are effective in preventing people from becoming ill."[362] A study posted on the CDC's website in May 2020 further concluded that "although mechanistic studies support the potential effect of hand hygiene or face masks, evidence from 14 randomized controlled trials of these measures did not support a substantial effect on transmission of laboratory-confirmed influenza."[363]

However, once the pandemic got going, the CDC, Fauci, and others changed the narrative. In June 2020, on the basis of evidence from two hair stylists who serviced about 140 clients and subsequently tested positive for COVID-19, the CDC began to argue that mask wearing may be a contributing factor to transmission prevention.[364] At this point, Fauci estimated that "if you have a physical covering with one layer, you put another layer on, it just makes common sense that it likely would be more effective."[365] By early December 2020, the WHO advised that the public should wear a mask,[366] and shortly after in January 2021, President Joe Biden signed an order which mandated "masking and physical distancing in federal buildings, on federal lands, and by government contractors."[367] Just two months later, in March 2021, CDC director Rochelle Walensky announced to Americans that "You can visit your grandparents if you have been vaccinated and they have been too."[368]

And yet, not all countries changed their approach so quickly. Contrary to advice from other governments and public health officials, chief epidemiologist of Sweden Anders Tegnell advised that:

> The findings that have been produced through (the use of) face masks are astonishingly weak. I'm surprised that we don't have more or better studies showing what effect masks actually have. Countries such as Spain and Belgium have made their populations wear masks but their infection numbers have still risen. The belief that masks can solve our problem is in any case very dangerous.[369]

Additional problems with masks, which particularly pertain to children, have also been raised in Canada.[370] The most significant issue, as identified by Canadian scientist Byram Bridle, is that constant mask wearing prevents children from being exposed to the microbial environment, and thus hinders the development of children's immune system because it typically self-adjusts based on interaction with pathogens. In the long run, a lack of interaction with the microbial surroundings and the complete isolation of children for the better part of two years can compromise immunological development and consequently increase the prevalence of chronic diseases such as allergies, asthma, and autoimmune diseases in the future.[371] Byram also argued that masking children can also hinder their development in different spheres of life, including speech, emotions, and psychology, in addition to becoming addictive as a result of long-term use.

After this brief introduction to masking, the next section will review the historical evidence on using masks and present evidence on masking during the COVID-19 pandemic, and close with a discussion of the negative consequences of mask wearing.

Studies on masks prior to the pandemic

There have been numerous studies in the past regarding masks and virus transmission that provided a range of conclusions, although none of them argued decisively that masks worked. It is important to cite a few examples. A meta-analysis study by bin-Reza et al. published in 2012 found that "none of the studies established a conclusive relationship between mask/respirator use and protection against influenza infection."[372] Another meta-analysis by Smith et al., published in 2016, similarly confirmed that there were "no significant differences between N95 respirators and surgical masks when used by health care workers to prevent transmission of acute respiratory infections from patients."[373] One study by Zhou et al., which specifically assessed issues of masking for surgeons, identified that "there is a lack of substantial evidence to support claims that facemasks protect either patient or surgeon from infectious contamination."[374] In yet another study, Beder et al. noticed "a decrease in the oxygen saturation of arterial pulsation (SpO_2) and a slight increase in pulse rates" among surgeons, which could be a result of wearing a facemask, the stress of surgery, or a combination of the two.[375] Furthermore, Xiao et al. identified that "although mechanistic studies support the potential effect of hand hygiene and face masks, evidence from 14 randomized controlled trials of these measures did not support a substantial effect on transmission of laboratory-confirmed influenza."[376] Jacobs et al., who studied the use of masks among health care workers (HCWs) in Japan, noted that "face masks used in HCWs was not demonstrated to provide benefit in terms of cold symptoms or getting cold."[377] In another systematic review, Cowling et al. concluded that "there is little evidence to support the effectiveness of face masks to reduce the risk of infection."[378]

In terms of masking outside of the health care system, Dugre et al. reasoned that "the use of masks in the community did not reduce the risk of influenza, confirmed viral respiratory infection, influenza like illness, or any clinical respiratory infection" and "found limited evidence that the use of masks might reduce the risk of viral respiratory infections."[379] With regard to the types of masks used, a study by MacIntyre et al. cautioned against using cloth masks, a style more readily available to the public, because "moisture retention, reuse of cloth masks and poor filtration may result in increased risk of infection."[380] The authors further added that penetration of cloth masks by particles was equal to 97 percent. On the other hand, a study by Oberg and Brousseau confirmed that "none of these surgical masks exhibited adequate filter performance and facial fit characteristics to be considered respiratory protection devices."[381] Additional studies by Long et al. and Radonovich et al. have reached similar conclusions.[382,383]

Thus, there is limited historical evidence to suggest any benefit from either cloth or surgical masks at preventing the spread of infection. Research evidence on masks is at best inconclusive with respect to the prevention of transmission, meaning that there may be a net-negative impact when taking into consideration the potential harms to their wearers (as noted below). While some studies point to mechanistic prevention of transmission from droplets which can arise when sneezing, coughing, and even talking, these studies are heavily qualified.

This section closes this review of the historical evidence on mask efficacy by illuminating some disputes over mask policies in the workplace, and particularly in the health care setting (note that these disputes arose prior to the COVID-19 pandemic). In these cases, the arbitrators argued that mask requirements must be scientifically justified rather than capriciously decided upon by hospital administrators. In the case of *St. Michael's Hospital and the Ontario Hospital Association v Ontario Nurses' Association*, arbitrator William Kaplan noted the following:

> The fact that there is some evidence, for example, that masking can prevent transmission of large droplets–unlikely in asymptomatic transmission–is not enough to confer reasonableness of the policy. Little evidence–negligible evidence–cannot serve as the justification for this policy. The "ask" is significant, but the benefit is so limited that the former cannot balance the latter. Independent of any other finding in this award, the VOM policy fails on a reasonableness basis for these reasons alone ... The argument was advanced by St. Michael's that masking was especially important to reduce the risk of nosocomial influenza by asymptomatic or pre-symptomatic HCWs [health care workers]. At best, the evidence indicates that asymptomatic transmission is not a significant factor in nosocomial influenza.[384]

In another case, that of *Sault Area Hospital v Ontario Nurses' Association*, Arbitrator James Hayes judged that forcing employees who were not vaccinated with a flu shot to wear a mask in the flu season was not a proper exercise of management rights. Specifically, Hayes "found the 'vaccinate or mask' policy was unreasonable, and 'a coercive tool' to force health-care workers to get the flu shot."[385] Hayes also claimed that "*Irving* balancing demands nuance and it is not sufficient to claim that scant, weak, "some", or imperfect data is better than nothing. While the precautionary principle ("reasonable efforts to reduce risk need not wait for scientific certainty") surely applies in truly exceptional circumstances, one could not live in a society where only 'zero risk' was tolerated."[386] It is noteworthy that medical doctor Bonnie Henry, who is a current provincial chief health officer in British Columbia, testified in the latter case in support of the hospital's vaccinate-or-mask policies.

Masking during the pandemic

In terms of masking during the COVID-19 pandemic, there have been numerous studies conducted on the effectiveness on masking since 2020 that considered the efficacy of N95 respirators, surgical masks, and cloth masks in different settings (i.e., healthcare, public space, home environment, and so on). One of the most deliberate and carefully designed randomized control trial studies on masks during the COVID-19 pandemic was executed by Bundgaard et al. in Denmark. The authors identified two key points in their findings, the first of which, as noted by researchers in the past, was that observational studies that make considerable claims about the benefits of masks in mitigating SARS-CoV-2 should be viewed with substantial skepticism. Instead, a reliance on randomized control trials should be the gold standard, especially in cases that inform important policy matters and considerations. Secondly, the authors concluded that "a recommendation to wear a surgical mask when outside of the home among others did not reduce, at conventional levels of statistical significance, incident SARS-CoV-2 infection compared with no mask recommendation."[387] Another important study, the so-called Cochrane review led by Jefferson and others, represents a systematic review of all available scientific research on masks and masking and is highly regarded in the medical research community. Importantly, this notable review concluded that "wearing masks in the community probably makes little or no difference to the outcome of influenza-like illness (ILI)/COVID-19 like illness compared to not wearing masks."[388]

In conclusion, mask wearing was one of the most polarizing issues during the pandemic. Often succumbing to fear and anxiety, people wore them when indoors and outdoors, while being in groups, or in cars alone. The most dedicated masks wearers even forcefully insisted that others wear them. Masks were seemingly regarded as a pandemic panacea, which they were not.

Hesitations about masks

The Cochrane review outlined the need to investigate potential problems related to masks, while Jefferson et al. specifically noted that "more attention should be paid to describing and quantifying the harms of the interventions assessed in this review, and their relationship with adherence."[389] One of the key concerns about wearing masks pertains to the risk of elevated carbon dioxide (CO_2) levels when wearing a mask, which has been confirmed in numerous studies (see for example Pifarre et al.).[390] In simple terms, wearing a mask for prolonged periods of time can reduce blood oxygenation (i.e., hypoxia) while increasing blood carbon dioxide (CO_2) levels (i.e., hypercapnia). Proper oxygenation in the blood is known to be critical for maintaining energy levels, mental functions, and emotional wellbeing.

The typical air composition in a room consists of about 20 percent oxygen (O_2), about 80 percent nitrogen, and about 0.1 percent carbon dioxide.[391] In contrast, fresh outside air has about 0.04 percent CO_2. Various public organizations set the appropriate safety limits for exposure to CO_2. For example, the Occupational Safety and Health Administration (OSHA) in the U.S. set the permissible exposure limits (PELs) and threshold values for carbon dioxide at the level of 5,000 particles per million (ppm), which equates to about 0.5 percent of air in a room. OSHA also defines oxygen deficiency at the level of 19.5 percent or less. The CDC has similar recommendations for CO_2 thresholds and exposure limits. These limits are important because humans respond differently to variable levels of CO_2. For example, studies confirm that slightly elevated levels of CO_2 concentrations can result in headache, agitation, color distortions, vertigo, and numbness, while higher levels can lead to tachycardia, arrythmia, acidosis, metabolic stress, convulsions, unconsciousness, and even death.[392] On the other hand, lower levels of O_2 can cause increased heart rate, labored breathing, weakened physical coordination, attention and concentration deficits, and diminished mental functions.

Notably, the studies regarding increased CO_2 exposure due to mask use indicate that the percent of CO_2 found within inhaled air may be as high as 3.5 percent, which is equal to 35 times the normal levels of CO_2 indoors (3.5%/0.1% = 35) and even much higher outdoors. The level of CO_2 generated by humans also depends on the time spent wearing a mask. For example, "wearing masks more than 5 minutes bears a possible chronic exposure to carbon dioxide of 1.41% to 3.2% of the inhaled air," which are between 14 to 32 times normal levels (1.4%/0.1% = 14; 3.2%/0.1% = 32).[393] Kisielinski et al. have provided a detailed summary of the possible toxic effects of chronic exposure to CO_2. The possibility of negative effects is no surprise since wearing a mask necessitates re-breathing CO_2 which the lungs are desperately trying to expel. According to Kisielinski et al.'s review, elevated levels of CO_2 caused by chronic mask wearing can lead to various pathologies and oxidative stresses, which have multiple negative health impacts that disproportionately affect vulnerable groups such as pregnant women, adolescents, and children.[394]

In the case of pregnant women, Kisielinski et al. report that "US Navy toxicity experts set the exposure limits for submarines carrying a female crew to 0.8% CO_2 based on animal studies which indicated an increased risk for stillbirths" above this level.[395] Furthermore, "there is circumstantial evidence that popular mask use may be related to current observations of a significant rise of 28% to 33% in stillbirths worldwide."[396] To support this assertion, Kisielinski et al. compared stillbirth data from Australia and Sweden, since no mask mandates were implemented in the latter country, and noted that "no increased risk of stillbirths was observed in Sweden."[397] The authors also identified potential negative impacts of masking-related increased CO_2 levels on male fertility through examinations of testicular tissue. In terms of masking children, Kisielinski et al. observed issues related to the amplification of anxiety levels, diminished learning capacity, and weakened memory.[398] Another study by Walach et al. that focused on children who wore nose and mouth coverings (NMC) noted that "wearing of NMC (surgical masks or FFP2 masks) raises CO_2 content in inhaled air quickly to a very high level in healthy children in a seated resting position that might be hazardous to children's health."[399]

There are also other potential concerns. For example, a study by Cosalino–Matsuda et al. noted that in response to poor oxygenation, the body can produce an immune response which negatively affects cell functions in the lungs and blood vessels. Specifically, the authors "found that hypercapnia downregulated the expression of 183 genes and upregulated 126 ... The overwhelming majority of these genes were not previously known to be regulated by CO_2."[400] Other studies confirm that hypoxia can lead to the impairment of immunity, due to an increase of hypoxia inducible factor-1, which subsequently hinders T cells, stimulates immune powerful suppressor cells called Tregs, and suppresses natural killer cell functions.[401,402,403] This in turn can lead to an increase in contracting infections as well as an inability to fight infections and other diseases. A study by Ji-Won et al. also found that "hypoxia-inducible factor (HIF-1) is an oxygen-dependent transcriptional activator, which plays crucial roles in the angiogenesis of tumors and mammalian development."[404] In another paper, Pezzuto and Carico concluded that "there is increasing evidence that hypoxia plays an important role in cancer dormancy and cancer metabolism, increasing stemness activity and bringing about cancer initiation and progression."[405]

Beyond these instances of potentially serious health concerns, there is also evidence that mask wearing is associated with less severe health problems including oral hygiene issues, gum disease, cavities, facial rashes, fungal infections, and bacterial infections, among others. The possibility of "unknown and harmful volatile chemicals and dyes in medical masks" also means there is a potential to inhale microfibers and carcinogens.[406,407]

Social distancing: Enforcement of unjustified science

It is evident that public health officials relied on the assumption that coronavirus is transmitted by air when implementing masking and social distancing restrictions, but this hypothesis was not able to be proven in the pandemic. The WHO even stated that "the evidence is not compelling" on this issue.[408] Two years after the onset of the pandemic, there was still no clarity as to the real transmission methods, while in the meantime masking continued to be severely enforced. In Ontario, for example, just before restrictions and mandates were lifted, some uncertainty remained as a publication from Public Health Ontario reported that "air sampling data supports that aerosol transmission is plausible at both short and longer distances; however, virus-laden aerosols may not reach infectious dose during transient or long distance exposures".[409] Among the studies that argued SARS-CoV-2 was airborne, there was still some debate about its actual viral infectivity and its duration of contagion. In one study, for example, authors investigated "the infectivity of the airborne virus over timescales from 5 s [seconds] to 20 min [minutes]" and demonstrated "the role of two microphysical processes in this infectivity loss, namely, particle crystallization and aerosol droplet pH change."[410] There were studies which "proved" aerosol transmission of coronavirus, but these studies predominantly focused on hospitals, nursing homes, and long-term care facilities. Thus, these studies "confirmed" aerosol transmission only through airflow modelling studies which coincided with a strong possibility of spread through physical contact with contaminated areas.

Lastly, it is worthwhile to note some testimonies regarding the six-foot social distancing rule, which was insisted up on by politicians, unelected public health officials, medical doctors, medical boards, experts, and ordinary people who often believed this rule to be instituted based on science, and its true "scientific" underpinnings. Firstly, former commissioner of the FDA Scott Gottlieb spoke about this issue in the program *Face the Nation* on CBS. An article in *Forbes* described the interview in the following manner:

> The six-foot rule, Gottlieb said, was a compromise between the Centers for Disease Control and Prevention, which had recommended 10 feet, and an unnamed political appointee in the Trump administration who called 10 feet "inoperable." Both the 10-foot and six-foot recommendations were unfounded, said Gottlieb, and show "the lack of rigor" in how the CDC made public health recommendations.[411]

Secondly, in a closed-door session of the House Select Subcommittee on the Coronavirus Pandemic, Anthony Fauci allegedly admitted that "the six-feet rule for social distancing 'sort of just appeared' without a solid scientific basis."[412] It may be difficult to accept that these questionable and unscientific rules contributed to the closure of businesses, schools, places of worship, churches, and other venues.

Interestingly, in Norway, for example, the authorities recommended "distance of 1m [meter or about 3 feet] between persons who are not living in the same household."[413] It is also unclear whether these recommendations were based on any science.

3

COVID-19 response and centralization of political power

It is important to note that the cause of many social and economic afflictions experienced by individuals during the COVID-19 pandemic was either a direct or indirect consequence of public policy implemented by the state and its associate stakeholders. To clarify, what individuals and economies experienced was directly or indirectly reflective of political decisions that were made at the federal, provincial, state, or municipal levels. Viruses, including coronaviruses, have been a part of human existence for many years and are known to cause sickness and even death despite high vaccination rates and modern medicine. What was atypical during the outbreak of novel coronavirus was the response of public authorities to what was perceived as a health crisis; this is what is termed in this book as "COVID-19 response."

Public policy restrictions and centralization of political power

Public authorities had numerous policy alternatives at their disposal, with countries like Sweden, Norway, Japan, South Korea, and even some states in the United States (U.S.) implementing different policy approaches and stances toward SARS-CoV-2 that resulted in the continued operation of small businesses, schools, and universities, avoidance of personal restrictions, sidestepping of lockdowns, and prevention of vaccine mandates. Other countries, especially those located in Central and Eastern Europe, did not fully engage in COVID-19 vaccinations due to a general mistrust of the state stemming from years of experience under communist rule. For example, according to data from Johns Hopkins Coronavirus Resource Center, only 36.1 percent of the population in Ukraine, 30.3 percent in Bulgaria, and 42.6 percent in Romania received at least one dose of the vaccine.[414] By comparison, vaccination rates for at least one dose among Western countries was equal to 90.9 percent in Canada, 87.3 percent in Australia, and 81.8 percent in the U.S. China's vaccination enforcements led to 92.8 percent vaccination rates.

Public officials who avoided restrictions often recommended basic hygiene measures, individually implemented precautions depending on personal circumstances, and generally responsible behaviour. An example of one of such policy alternatives was the "Great Barrington Declaration", signed by professors Martin Kulldorff (ex-Harvard University), Sunetra Gupta (Oxford University), and Jay Bhattacharya (Stanford University), which focused on the notion of protecting and assisting the most vulnerable parts of the society (i.e., people with underlying medical conditions as well as older people in homecare, their own residences, or multi-generational homes) while allowing the rest of society to function as normal.[415] In furtherance of their goal, the declaration states that "adopting measures to protect the vulnerable should be the central aim of public health responses to COVID-19 ... Those who are not vulnerable should immediately be allowed to resume life as normal."[416] The key framework behind the Barrington Declaration is deeply rooted in economics.

Despite these available alternative responses, most leaders across the political spectrum supported restrictive public health measures, mandates, and orders in a similar manner. These restrictions were implemented without any cost-benefit analysis, examination of net harms, proportionality analysis (i.e., proving that actual benefits outweigh actual harms), or analytical approaches. Even now, years after the onset of the pandemic, there is still no evidence that any cost-benefit analysis was performed by the state ahead of the implementation of restrictions. Although politicians from different countries were happy to express generalities such as "if we could only save one life, it would be worth it," "no life is worth losing," or "if everything we do saves just one life, I'll be happy,"[417] one is left to ponder why these same politicians did not previously express such dedication to other health issues (i.e., cancer, cardiovascular problems, suicides, diabetes, obesity, etc.), poverty, homelessness, addiction prevention, or similar social problems.

In any case, political leaders in most countries implemented society-wide restrictions and lockdowns that primarily resulted in the closure of recreational facilities, retail outlets, places of worship, schools and universities, and other public places of gathering. Some politicians ordered stay-at-home orders and cancelling cultural, arts, music, sports, and educational events that would have been held outside the home. [418] Gatherings for funerals, weddings, and holidays, especially Christmas and Easter, were also limited and subsequently prevented a free flow and exchange of information between friends and family. It is estimated that at the height of the pandemic, about 3 billion people were effectively under house arrest.[419] Although people voluntarily agreed to be confined to their homes, this would not have occurred if not for state restrictions. [420,421]

As further consequences of the imposed restrictions, firms were closed, family members were separated (especially from the elderly), people were not permitted to read books in parks or walk on beaches, and children were prevented from going to playgrounds or building snowmen. In effect, politicians had the power to determine whether families could visit each other, and when. Politicians and the state also pre-determined which sectors of the economy were "essential" and "non-essential," thereby deciding which businesses were to continue operations, close, become bankrupt, and be liquidated. For example, large grocers and big-box stores were open, but smaller stores were closed. There was limited economic justification for the division of businesses into essential versus non-essential categories.

Such restrictions led to the cancellation of elective medical procedures, appointments, surgeries, and other forms of treatment. The fear of contagion also led to an increased reluctance for sick individuals to seek medical assistance, even in emergency situations. Furthermore, government offices (i.e., the judicial system, healthcare, social support, and so on) moved online and became less accessible to the public.

It is difficult to believe that the public would agree to such restrictions without asking questions, seeking alternative solutions, and working through a cost/benefit analysis.[422] While not necessarily irrational (especially in view of overwhelming fear and anxiety), how is it possible that people simply accepted the reduction or outright elimination of their freedoms, rights, entitlements, and privileges without asking any basic questions? How is it that people agreed to give almost unlimited rights to unelected officials? What prevented them from seeking additional information? From an economics point of view, how "costly" was it for individuals to obtain additional information to make an informed and independent decision?

Such behavioural patterns may be explained in part by the reliance of some politicians on the ideas of behavioural scientists from academic institutes to force people into compliance. This approach of relying on a massive state campaign of fear has been well documented, for example, in the United Kingdom by Laura Dodsworth's book *A State of Fear: How the UK Government Weaponized Fear During the COVID-19 Pandemic.* Douglas Farrow, a professor of theology and ethics, also noted that "it is remarkable what a coordinated effort to generate, nurture, amplify, and sustain fear can achieve."[423] On the top of this, there were many "doctors who won't doctor and hospitals that won't treat."[424] In Canada, for example, there were "alarming claims that the Canadian military used information warfare tactics to monitor (and perhaps influence?) public opinion during the pandemic."[425] More specifically, "the military deployed propaganda techniques in Canada without approval during the pandemic and gathered information about Canadians' online activities without permission from authorities."[426] Another explanation may be the concept of "mass formation psychosis" developed by Mattias Desmet in his book *The Psychology of Totalitarianism*. The World Economic Forum (WEF) also promoted the use of psychology and marketing techniques to overcome their alleged hesitancy to the restrictions and mass vaccinations by employing "more assertive approaches," providing incentives (i.e., giveaways, lotteries, money, etc.), and using "medical providers, political and faith-based leaders" as promoters.[427]

Significantly, as it is discussed in more detail in the last chapter of the book, politicians did not act alone in their implementation of restrictions and lockdown. They relied on unelected officials working in lockstep who, in many cases, operated with "insufficient political oversight" and were not subjected to the "democratic accountability" that was expected of "democratically elected representatives."[428] While some of these unelected participants, who were employed in the sectors of media, healthcare, banks, transportation, military, police, educational systems, and labour unions resisted such power, others did not.[429]

One of the most influential international organizations during the pandemic was the World Health Organization (WHO), which, in addition to sounding the pandemic alarm, also propagated the idea that viruses can spread through handling cash and subsequently advocated for the diminished usage of physical money.[430] Medical doctors, various experts, advisors, scientists, and academics, who rarely calmed people down with balanced perspectives, comprised another group of powerful yet unelected officials. While some medical doctors proved to be timid, or were ultimately silenced, only a few questioned the mainstream public narrative.[431] The final group who executed these restrictions were unelected public health officials who were directly or indirectly responsible for the closure and cancellation of non-essential businesses and activities, imposition of gathering restrictions, testing requirements, capacity limitations (i.e., 10, 25, or 50 percent of actual capacity), mask mandates, vaccination thresholds, vaccination-status verification cards, and so. They were also responsible for invoking emergency measures and public orders, which were sanctioned by the state.

These lockdowns, restrictions, and mask mandates that were created by public health officials and endorsed by politicians were subsequently enforced by public agencies (i.e., health services, border services, etc.) and law enforcement. Police and by-law officers pursued people for not wearing masks, handcuffed others not willing to cooperate, and arrested priests for holding religious services. Otherwise, law-abiding individuals were criminalized for protesting their freedom against the various restraints and mandates. The judicial system remained largely silent on the issue of restrictions and their participation was marginal at best, especially at the beginning of the pandemic.[432] With rare exception, judges were unwilling to engage in independent evaluations of public health measures and orders with respect to COVID-19 and thus did not wish to challenge emergency declarations, lockdowns, public health orders, travel restrictions, quarantine requirements, vaccination mandates, or the suspension of government operations. In Canada specifically, where the judges are obligated to consider such instances under the *Canadian Charter of Rights and Freedoms* by the application of the so-called Oakes test (*R v Oakes*), many still did not want to consider arguments regarding the harms caused by lockdowns.[433]

During this period, academics who are normally keen to get involved in open debates on issues related to science, human rights, poverty, the underprivileged, the oppressed, or other social considerations were largely quiet, withdrawn, and absent. Many academics agreed with the policies that were developed by the state and implemented by unelected officials. Academics who did choose to become involved in open debates about COVID-19 policies became marginalized, demoralized, oppressed, and in some cases, were terminated from their positions. In Canada, for example, professor of medicine and practicing medical doctor Francis Christian was suspended and terminated from the University of Saskatchewan due to his public statement related to the COVID-19 vaccine, and particularly to the vaccination of children.[434] The local health authority similarly terminated its contract with Christian and the legal case remains ongoing.[435] As outlined in the statement of claim, among other points raised, Christian "presented his professional opinion regarding the relative risk of vaccinating children" and "expressed concern about the censorship of scientific facts and opinions during the pandemic and the deplatforming, intimidation, and persecution of eminent scientists and physicians around the world."[436] Ethics professor Julie Ponesse from Huron University College, a part of Western University, was similarly suspended from teaching and has since reflected on her experience at her academic institution during COVID-19, her treatment from colleagues, and the ethical considerations surrounding vaccine mandates in her book *My Choice: The Ethical Case Against COVID-19 Vaccine Mandates*.[437] Numerous other academics were placed on unpaid leaves as a result of their public statements or disobeying with vaccination mandates. Because of this public pressure, and in combination with personal and financial circumstances, many felt coerced into taking the vaccine.

Also, one of the most disturbing facts was the cooperation between public health officials and the social media.[438] The so-called "Facebook files" reveal that the Centers for Disease Control and Prevention (CDC) in the U.S. played a significant role in censoring and moderating content related to COVID-19 vaccines. In other words, CDC "played a direct role in policing permissible speech on social media throughout the COVID-19 pandemic. Confidential emails obtained by *Reason* show that Facebook moderators were in constant contact with the CDC, and routinely asked government health officials to vet claims relating to the virus, mitigation efforts such as masks, and vaccines."[439]

Rather than make public statements, some public officials instead chose to raise concerns about their observations to immediate supervisors and department heads. If their findings were not in line with the general public narrative, they were often intimated, dismissed, or even subtly threatened. One example is the case of Ronald F. Owens, information officer at the California Department of Public Health's Office of Public Affairs. His account is captured in the book *The Muzzled Truth: How the California Department of Public Health Rejected COVID-19 Treatment and Vaccine Health Risks Warnings*. Despite the multitude of instances to the contrary, there are some examples of successful academic advocacy. For example, a group of German academics and medical practitioners have been active in symposiums, informal exchanges of ideas, and formal collaborations regarding vaccine and mandate efficacy. Furthermore, there has been an inquiry in the United Kingdom (U.K.) Parliament about excess deaths.[440,441]

Interestingly, vaccination mandates at some Canadian and U.S. universities came at a time when it was clear that COVID-19 vaccines could not prevent transmission and that both the vaccinated and the unvaccinated could transmit COVID-19. For example, in August 2021, director of the CDC Rochelle Walensky admitted during a CNN interview with Wolf Blitzer that "[o]ur vaccines are working exceptionally well … They continue to work well for Delta, with regard to severe illness and death–they prevent it. But what they can't do anymore is prevent transmission."[442] Janine Small, a senior executive at Pfizer, when asked by a Dutch member of the European Parliament Robert Roos in October 2022 whether Pfizer's COVID-19 vaccine was tested for its ability to stop transmission before being rolled out in the marketplace, she simply said "No."[443] Small further added that "we had to really move at the speed of science to really understand what is taking place in the market. And from that point of view we had to do everything at risk."[444] "Fact-checker" posts at Reuters, AP News, and other news agencies were quick to point out that Pfizer was not required to test for viral transmission (which it could easily have done) and that Small's response was somehow taken out of context.[445,446] But the main issue here is different, namely whether the public knew early in the pandemic that Pfizer had not tested its COVID-19 vaccines for stopping SARS-CoV-2 transmission.

With respect of Pfizer-BioNTech's application for licensure for COMIRMATY, an FDA briefing document dated September 17, 2021 from the Vaccine and Related Biological Products Advisory Committee Meeting, confirmed that "an additional analysis appears to indicate that incidence of COVID-19 generally increased in each group of study participants with increasing time post-Dose 2 at the start of the analysis period."[447] In other words, vaccination did not reduce chances of obtaining coronavirus and those vaccinated can also become sick. Research confirmed that the vaccinated and the unvaccinated have comparable viral loads when testing positive for SARS-CoV-2. For example, Singanayagam et al. noted "fully vaccinated individuals with breakthrough infections have peak viral load similar to unvaccinated cases and can efficiently transmit infection in household settings, including to fully vaccinated contacts."[448]

In some cases, universities allowed unrestricted student registration and only triggered vaccine mandates in the middle of the semester (while offering tuition reimbursements) or immediately prior to the start of the semester, thereby placing students in difficult financial situations as many were already committed to a particular educational institution and had pre-paid for tuition and housing.

The geography of political restrictions

China focused on "zero COVID" policies with its draconian restrictions. As exemplified by events in Shanghai, a city of about 25 million people, the state's enactment of a full-scale lockdown included roadblocks and physical barriers, the ability for police officers to forcefully enter private residences to enforce quarantines, the requirement of permits to leave residences, and the implementation of travel bans.[449] Furthermore, the state also moved people into makeshift quarantine centres, tested people in housing blocks, and sealed (or even welded) doors to housing compounds. While local officials promised the lockdown would only last for a few days to "flatten the curve," this allegedly quick "circuit breaker" lasted for more than 70 days. These restrictions tested (and confirmed) the state's ability to control people.[450] To that end, Farrow has identified that "plagues call for vaccines; that is, for delivery systems. Vaccines call for passport; that is, for control systems. Control systems require Controllers."[451]

In comparison to other countries, severe restrictions were implemented in Australia, Canada, and other countries. At the height of its restrictions on January 5, 2022, Canada scored 78.2 points on the Oxford Pandemic Stringency Index, which was comparable to China's 79.2 points.[452] At the same time, other G7 countries scored the following: France–66.7, Germany–56.5, Italy–73.2, Japan–47.2, the U.K.–46.8, and the U.S.–58.8.[453] In Australia, as evidenced in the case of New South Wales (NSW), individuals were only allowed to shop for essentials and exercise outside for 1 hour in a radius of no more than 5 kilometres from their home, although the state graciously granted an additional hour of outside recreation time for those who were vaccinated. Individuals were also subjected to curfews. In the province of Victoria in the country, the police resorted to firing rubber bullets at construction workers protesting the vaccination mandates.[454]

However, one of the most politically awkward experiences with respect to the behaviour of the state occurred in Canada during the so-called Trucker Convoy. In the words of Prime Minister Justin Trudeau, the convoy was comprised of a "small fringe minority of people who are on their way to Ottawa, who are holding unacceptable views."[455] Under the *Emergencies Act*, which aimed to shut down the convoy, the liberal left government in Canada jailed convoy organizers and froze or seized the bank accounts of about 280 individuals, who contributed to the convoy through crowdfunding efforts or by purchasing convoy-protest merchandise, without due authorization or judicial process.[456] Specifically, the *Emergencies Act* allows for the seizure of bank accounts, crypto holdings, financial securities, and private property.[457] While Canadian banks and the Canadian police agreed with such actions and participated with relevant enforcement, this form of intervention on the part of the state, the police, and the banking system are unprecedented in modern Western memory. In this case, individuals were punished for supporting a particular social movement which opposed the state and its public narrative. It is worthwhile to note that at least one Canadian bank (i.e., Scotiabank) apologized to its customers for being involved in this practice.[458] However, on January 24, 2024, the federal court rendered that the invocation of the *Emergencies Act* did "not satisfy the requirements of the *Emergencies Act* and that certain of the temporary measures adopted to deal with the protests infringed provisions of the *Canadian Charter of Rights and Freedoms*" (Para. 7).[459] In short, the actions of the Canadian liberal government were proven to be illegal, unconstitutional, and unreasonable (i.e., breaching principles of minimal impairment).

This section on concludes by pointing to comments made by Associate Justice of the Supreme Court of the United States Samuel Alito during his speech at a Federalist Society in late 2020. At this talk, Alito asserted that:

> The pandemic has resulted in previously unimaginable restrictions on individual liberty ... And whatever one may think about the COVID restrictions, we surely don't want them to become a recurring feature after the pandemic has passed. All sorts of things can be called an emergency or disaster of major proportions. Simply slapping on that label cannot provide the ground for abrogating our most fundamental rights. And whenever fundamental rights are restricted, the Supreme Court and other courts cannot close their eyes.[460]

With reference to the extent of executive authority exercised during the pandemic, Alito noted that the restrictions happened by "executive fiat, rather than legislation."[461] In terms of religious freedoms, Alito also specifically highlighted that "in certain quarters, religious liberty is fast becoming a disfavored right. And that marks a surprising turn of events."[462] The Justice's further argumentation regarding these disfavored religious rights is concise and compelling:

> So, if you go to Nevada, you can gamble, drink, and attend all sorts of shows to your heart's content. But here is what you cannot do: If you want to worship at a church, synagogue, or mosque and you are the fifty-first person in line, sorry, you are out of luck. Houses of worship are limited to fifty attendees. The size of the building does not matter. Nor does it matter if you wear a mask and keep more than six feet away from everybody else. And it does not matter if the building is carefully sanitized before and after a service. The

State's message is this: Forget about worship and head for the slot machines or maybe a Cirque du Soleil show.[463]

The economic impact of COVID-19 response worldwide

Due to COVID-19 response restrictions, lockdowns, and limitations imposed by public authorities, member economies belonging to the OECD (Organization for Economic Co-operation and Development) shrunk by more than 4 percent on average in 2020. Countries which experienced the highest declines in GDP (gross domestic product) were Spain (-11.6%), the United Kingdom (-11.2%), Greece (-10.2%), and Mexico (-9.2%). The least affected countries were those that did not implement such heavy-handed state restrictions, including South Korea (-1.1%), Norway (-1.2%), Turkey (-1.3%), Sweden (-3.2%), and Ireland (-3.2%). Poorer and richer countries were affected in different ways, as wealthier countries experienced increased economic slowdown and contractions and "suffer[ed] greater losses of life years per capita than poorer countries."[464] There was also significant growth in the inequality gap within some countries, with higher-skilled and more educated employees able to easily transition to online jobs while others could not. However, the clear victor was China, which grew its economy by 1.8 percent, the only nation among the OECD countries which demonstrated positive economic growth while returning to its normal historical growth trajectory by the end of 2020.

Furthermore, the global economic slowdown decreased demand for raw materials, weakened consumer spending, reduced investments, and lowered cross-border trade. There was also an unprecedented disruption of local, national, and international supply chain structures. The most significant effect on local economies was an unparalleled level of state spending, printing of money by central banks, and a decrease of interest rates to near-zero levels. For example, in the U.S., the Federal Reserve (FED) dropped its fund rate to 0.05 percent in April 2020 and retained near-zero rates until January 2022. Simultaneously, U.S. government spending increased from $7.6 trillion in the first quarter of 2020 to $10.8 trillion in the second quarter of that year. The federal debt increased sharply from $23.2 trillion to $26.5 trillion over the same period, ultimately culminating in debt exceeding $35 trillion in 2024 with an annual interest payment of over $1 trillion. Moreover, the level of debt-to-GDP in the U.S. increased from 107.0 percent in the first quarter of 2020 to 133.0 percent in the second quarter of 2024.

A rapid increase in money supply and massive spending led to predictable consequences, namely an increase in inflation. For example, in the U.S., the consumer price index (CPI) increased from 2.5 percent in January 2020 (declined to near zero in May 2020) and reached about 9.0 percent by June 2022. Alternative calculations of inflation (for example, based on 1980 methodology) indicated that the CPI increased to above 12 percent.[465] Other measures illustrate that the loss of purchasing power from January 2020 to May 4, 2024, was more substantial and equal to 25.3 percent.[466]

Another visible manifestation of COVID-19 response at the macro level was a rise in unemployment on a massive scale. Job losses materialized quickly and reached levels not seen for decades as at its peak, it was estimated that about 500 million people lost their jobs worldwide. About "120 million people [were] pushed into extreme poverty" at the height of the restrictions.[467] The global unemployment rate in OECD countries increased from 5.2 percent in December 2019 to 7.1 percent in November 2020. The unemployment rate exceeded 10 percent in the European Union, with some countries (i.e., Estonia and Latvia) exceeding 15 percent. In the U.S., it was estimated that 24 million jobs were lost, resulting in an unemployment rate equal to 14.7 percent in April 2020.

As noted above, COVID-19 response resulted in pressures on small businesses, families, and individuals. In the former case, this resulted in loss of revenue, financial challenges related to increase in cost, and supply chain issues. As it is discussed in other parts of the book, financial and operational challenges impacted businesses differently, as COVID-19 response restrictions disproportionately affected small firms vis-à-vis large corporations because they did not have the appropriate defence structures in place, such as financial resources, access to capital, and ability to adjust their business models. Economic pressures on individuals and families arose because of high unemployment rates, loss of income, and decline in savings. Moreover, owners of small firms, individuals, and families alike experienced significant mental health challenges.

Furthermore, the available assets, cash, and appetite for risk taking made a significant difference in wealth creation and redistribution during the COVD-19 pandemic. Massive liquidity injection (or printing of money) fuelled growth in capital and other markets (i.e., real estate, for example), which offered significant financial opportunities for those who had freely available financial resources, stable employment, or were independently wealthy. These individuals could deploy capital by purchasing financial and hard assets at depressed prices. Others, who worried about potential job losses, mortgage payments, and other adverse effects focused on limiting their expenses, avoiding larger purchases, increasing savings, reducing debt, and cashing investments. Based on research from Oxfam International, evidence from Canada and the U.S. suggests that "billionaires have had a terrific pandemic. Central banks pumped trillions of dollars into financial markets to save the economy, yet much of that has ended up lining the pockets of billionaires riding a stock market."[468] In terms of fiscal success, big pharma (i.e., Pfizer, Moderna, Johnson & Johnson), online platforms (i.e., Amazon), and social media firms (i.e., Alphabet, Facebook) led the way in financial windfalls. Since the end of March 2020, for example, the share price of Pfizer has increased by about 129 percent, Moderna by 4,182 percent, Johnson & Johnson by 70 percent, and BioNTech by 1,452 percent. Alphabet increased its share price by 199 percent, Facebook by 179 percent, Microsoft by 155 percent, Netflix by 140 percent, and Amazon by 130 percent. In addition to increases in stock prices, state budgets were also redirected toward special initiatives, including indirect funding of large corporations.[469,470]

Public surveillance and censorship

Public restriction measures also included COVID-19 passportization in the form of vaccination cards or QR codes to enter planes, public transportation, community spaces, and restaurants. The system was widespread and represented one of the most oppressive sets of worldwide restrictions ever imposed on people in modern times. In many cases, these restrictions were equal to or exceeded those implemented under the most totalitarian regimes ever known to man and represented a suspension of human rights and freedoms, including freedom of worship, assembly, movement, speech, and so on. These measures broke individual freedom of conscience and belief, especially if non-compliance for vaccination meant a loss of employment, which may subsequently lead to loss of home. These restrictions also corresponded with an increase in digital surveillance, which it was claimed would assist public health officials and the state to spot, monitor, and track outbreaks to allegedly reduce viral transmission and keep populations healthy. Technology was also used to track vaccination progress among different races and ethnic backgrounds.[471]

The state often argued that the SARS-CoV-2 outbreak justified the use of surveillance methods including contact tracing, exposure notification application systems, and other applications and devices.[472] To facilitate the implementation of surveillance systems, the federal government, provinces, and states introduced new legislation, bylaws, and regulations for data collection, sharing, and privacy.[473] While individuals, non-government bodies, and institutes expressed concern about the accountability and oversight of such widespread data collection efforts, they were often ignored, and invasive data surveillance measures were implemented without public consent. For example, the Public Health Agency of Canada (PHAC) tracked the location data from 33 million mobile devices to monitor compliance with COVID-19 restrictions.[474] China similarly relied on facial recognition, thermal scanners, and artificial intelligence linked to personal information to ensure proper observance of their COVID-19 restrictions.[475,476] Other countries implemented their own invasive surveillance measures. Interestingly, these technologies were also used to identify people who participated in demonstrations against state restrictions and vaccination mandates.

Another form of restrictions involved reduced access to information and censorship. For instance, people had difficulty accessing information from alternative (i.e., non-mainstream) media related to SARS-CoV-2, COVID-19 vaccines, mRNA technologies, or alternate treatments. In fact, many social platforms (i.e., Twitter, YouTube, Facebook, etc.) banned individuals, academics, specialists, experts, and medical doctors from sharing their observations, conclusions, and recommendations that countered the state's narrative. YouTube in particular regularly suspended user accounts for allegedly spreading misinformation and disinformation. As a result, alternative information was only available on independent online media platforms.

Lastly, there is the small matter of the FDA's release of documents, information, and data related to their decision to approve the use of the Pfizer and BioNTech COVID-19 vaccines. This amounted to about +329,000 pages of relevant documentation, which the FDA promised to release at a rate of 500 pages per week.[477] With such a proposal the FDA assured that it "values transparency" and was fully committed to truthfulness and protecting public interest.[478] And yet, the FDA's originally planned release schedule would roughly translate to a period of over 70 years needed to disclose the relevant information.[479]

In August 2021, a group of scientists, researchers, and medical professionals collaborating with a group called Public Health and Medical Professionals for Transparency (PHMPT) submitted a request for documents under the Freedom of Information Act (FOIA), pertaining to the approval of the Pfizer COVID-19 vaccine. When the FDA was slow to respond, PHMPT sued the FDA in September 2021 in the state of Texas. Although the FDA began to release some smaller batches of information while the legal case was ongoing, the federal judge ordered in a February 2022 ruling that the FDA had to release redacted documents according to a specific schedule of disclosure. While mainstream media mostly ignored the FDA's disclosures, some articles reported the information contained within them as standard, run-of-the-mill, or even mundane,[480] others defended Pfizer.[481] Some media outlets expressed concerns that recipients would "cherry-pick" the data, and still others reported that the FDA was willing to release documents but contested the expedited release schedule due to staffing issues.

So, what could be found in the released information? Let's have a quick look at the "Cumulative analysis of post-authorization adverse event reports of PF-072048 (BNT162B2) made public through 28-Feb-2021" (section 5.3.6) released by the FDA under court order following the EUA (Emergency Use Authorisation).[482] Firstly, Pfizer-BioNTech reported 42,086 cases of adverse events of interest associated with their vaccine, over 1,000 of which are listed on page 8 in Appendix I. Since the vaccine was officially approved under an EUA on December 11, 2020, these adverse events occurred in only about 3 months. Secondly, Pfizer-BioNTech noted that the reporting of adverse events was "regardless of causality assessment."[483] Thirdly, the information regarding the number of vaccines shipped around the world is redacted (paragraph 3.1.1, page 6), meaning it is not possible to calculate the percentage of individuals experiencing adverse events associated with the vaccine or the percentage of people who died after receiving it on the global scale. Fourthly, in terms of case outcomes, there were 1,223 fatalities and 9,400 cases with "unknown" conclusions, which, in other words, suggests that Pfizer-BioNTech does know what happened in these cases but did not report it, or they failed to follow up (p. 7). It is worth to reiterate that the 1976 swine vaccination program in the U.S. was suspended when only 10 deaths occurred as a direct result of the vaccine. Lastly, in terms of missing information, Pfizer-BioNTech disclosed that regarding pregnancy outcomes, there were 23 cases of spontaneous miscarriages and 2 cases of premature birth resulting in neonatal death, and 2 cases of spontaneous miscarriage with intrauterine death. Unfortunately, Pfizer-BioNTech was not able to account for 238 pregnancies, which represent 86.6 of pregnancy cases (p. 12). The FDA finally approved the

Pfizer-BioNTech vaccine on August 23, 2021, although the FDA notably pleaded in court that the information and data surrounding its approval effectively be withheld from the public.[484]

Oppression of medical professionals

This use of censorship also impacted medical doctors. For example, some of the most censored medical doctors in Canada were Charles Hoffe, William Makis, Mark Trozzi, Patrick Phillips, Rochagne Kilian, Daniel Nagase, and Crystal Luchkiw, just to name a few. In the U.S., medical boards similarly pursued doctors, who, in many cases, were disciplined for prescribing alternative treatments for COVID-19, signing vaccine exemption forms, sharing information publicly about COVID-19 vaccines, criticizing COVID-19 response state restrictions, and not wearing a mask or not requiring patients to wear one.[485]

The use of experimental COVID-19 vaccines was deemed acceptable by the state but using alternative treatments and off-label medications to treat COVID-19 was rejected. Such prohibited alternative protocols for treating COVID-19, which could be used on an outpatient basis and offered as a solution when the conventional and procedural medicine proved ineffective early in the pandemic, included the Zelenko protocol,[486] McCullough protocol,[487] and others.

There was also the mockery of ivermectin as a horse de-wormer, when it is a multifaceted, well-tolerated, safe, and broad-spectrum drug used for the treatment of infectious diseases, the discovery of which was awarded a Nobel Prize for Medicine in 2015 (see, for example, a study by Kerr et al. describing its use as prophylaxis for COVID-19).[488,489] Another drug, hydroxychloroquine, an anti-malaria and anti-inflammatory agent approved by the U.S. Food and Drug Administration (FDA) in 1955, offered opportunities for a wider acceptance of usage against COVID-19 but was also directly attacked by an academic article that claimed it caused harm to COVID-19 patients.[490] Even though the paper was retracted from one of the most prestigious scientific journals, *The Lancet,* due to "a shocking example of research misconduct,"[491] the "science-based" attack on hydroxychloroquine proved irreversible, halting any further trials.

Regarding ivermectin, the FDA decided to settle a lawsuit filed by three medical doctors over the agency's post in August 2021 on the social platform X (formerly Twitter) which read: "You are not a horse. You are not a cow. Serious y'all. Stop It."[492] There were additional social media posts from the FDA in a similar vein, such as "You are not a horse. Stop it with the #ivermectin. It's not authorized for treating #COVID" and "Hold your horses, y'all. Ivermectin may be trending, but is still isn't authorized or approved to treat COVID-19."[493] The three medical doctors involved in the lawsuit claimed that the FDA "acted beyond its legal authority with its campaign to prevent the use of ivermectin to treat COVID"[494] and that the "FDA was interfering with their ability to practice medicine."[495] The lawyers representing the medical doctors stated that the resolution "vindicates our position that the FDA overstepped its regulatory authority by trying to dictate appropriate medical care."[496] The Fifth Circuit Court further confirmed that the "FDA is not a physician. It has authority to inform, announce, and apprise–but not to endorse, denounce, or advise."[497] While it is difficult to truly understand the FDA's motivations behind its post on X, its effect was the suppression, discreditation, and obstruction of ivermectin as an early treatment of COVID-19, and the discouragement of doctors from prescribing it. This impact was noted by the court, which stated that:

> in an internal email, a member of FDA's communications team referred to the Posts as a part of a new engagement strategy. This strategy played well, and media outlets nationwide ran headlines and stories emphasizing FDA's 'horse' message. Medical organizations also took note of the Posts, as did pharmacy boards and hospitals. Federal and state courts, too began citing the Posts in cases involving ivermectin.[498]

As a result of the FDA's X campaign, the medical regulatory apparatus subsequently began to persecute and threaten physicians who prescribed ivermectin with the loss of their medical license. Most astonishingly, it is difficult to find another period in history when physicians were not allowed to attempt early treatment of their patients, as this has been the key premise of medicine for years.

In terms of specific oppression experienced by individual medical doctors, in the province of Ontario in Canada, the College of Physicians and Surgeons of Ontario (CPSO) conducted over 40 investigations of medical doctors who challenged the mono-thematic vaccine approach as the only solution to COVID-19 and prescribed alternative treatments for coronavirus.[499] As a result, the CPSO revoked the medical license for Trozzi, only one of many under investigation, in January 2024. Doctors in Alberta were similarly accused of spreading misinformation and prescribing alternative treatments. They were also pursued by the local College of Physicians and Surgeons of Alberta (CPSA).[500] However, on a more positive note, the CPSA recently dropped the case against medical doctor Michal Princ for providing his patients with COVID-19 exemptions following the *Ingram v Alberta* court decision. Regarding this decision, John Carpay, president of the Justice Center for Constitutional Freedoms (JCCF), noted that the CPSA "violated the ethical principle of informed and voluntary consent for medical treatment, by threatening medical doctors with the loss of their license if they exercised their independent clinical judgment about the safety and efficacy of new vaccines for which no long-term safety data existed."[501]

Despite this recent success, many of these dissenting doctors were also targeted by mainstream media for allegedly "undermining the fight against COVID-19."[502,503] To provide just a couple of examples from the U.S., medical doctor Mary Talley Bowden, an independent doctor (i.e., not under contract with insurance firms), has been targeted by the Texas medical board for using monoclonal antibodies to treat COVID-19, prescribing a combination of drugs (i.e., ivermectin and hydroxychloroquine), raising concerns about prescribed medical protocols against COVID-19, criticizing vaccine mandates, and allegedly spreading "dangerous misinformation."[504] As a result of her rejection of the mainstream narrative, Bowden was suspended from hospital duties at the Houston Methodist Hospital, the hospital that also terminated about 150 healthcare workers who opposed the COVID-19 vaccine after they successfully worked through the initial onset of COVID-19.[505] The hospital reversed its decision only after the Texas House passed Senate Bill 7 which "would ban private businesses from requiring employees and contractors to get the COVID vaccine."[506] On another occasion, the same medical board indefinitely suspended doctor Eric Hensen for violating a Texas mask mandate by not requiring his patients to wear one, only to lift his suspension after he retained legal counsel.[507] There are innumerable stories like this across the U.S.

In sum, it may appear that local medical licensing colleges, associations, boards, and other regulatory bodies pursued multi-pronged approaches to punish doctors for not complying with the mainstream narrative. Firstly, medical bodies often claimed that these doctors were guilty of "professional misconduct by making misleading, incorrect or inflammatory statements about vaccinations, treatments, and public health measures concerning COVID-19."[508,509] Medical bodies would frequently move to expand their list of accusations, and if these efforts failed or proved insufficient, they shifted to raise the argument that dissenting medical doctors did not cooperate in the investigations. Following the accusations, disciplinary hearings or tribunals were conducted, although these initiatives could not be viewed as having been conducted by independent and impartial adjudicators.[510] Dissenting doctors defended themselves using various approaches but often argued that alternative medicines may not have been recommended by state medical bodies, but they were not expressly prohibited or contra-indicated either. These doctors also presented scientific data and evidence related to their actual concerns with COVID-19 vaccinations, which were frequently ignored, denied, or downplayed.

The level of vigour, drive, and determination exhibited by these medical licensing bodies in persecuting dissenting doctors was unprecedented and raised questions about the bodies' level of objectivity, independence, and impartiality. In effect, these licensing bodies investigated, reprimanded, or de-licensed medical doctors for prescribing alternative treatments or providing vaccine exemptions.[511]

Covid-19 science and scientism

Human rights, individual freedoms, and other constitutional protections took a back seat to COVID-19 scientism (which is defined here as an unjustified application or even manipulation of science to achieve desired political objectives) because the only acceptable narrative promoted by the mainstream media, social media, politicians, public health officials, and various sorts of experts claimed that the way to deal with COVID-19 were lockdowns, social distancing, mask wearing, and of course, mass vaccination. Anthony Fauci, director of the National Institute of Allergy and Infectious Disease (NIAID), became a reflection and embodiment of this scientism through the claim that criticisms directed at him represented a direct attack on science itself.[512] Debate over alternative courses of actions and policies were thwarted and shut down. Thus, it was clear that these pandemic measures were not to be questioned or publicly challenged. As noted above, alternative methods of treatment were disallowed, reprimanded, and even ridiculed.

During the pandemic, the general public was certainly persuaded that scientists, medical doctors, and academics were unbiased and were not driven by financial motivators or incentive structures that would effectively constitute a conflict of interest.[513] In this way, science became an unquestionable guide and source to control the public narrative.[514] The term "follow the science," like an everyday mantra, was repeated again and again during the COVID-19 pandemic by politicians, public health authorities, the media, experts, academics, and average people. Individuals assumed that the mainstream media would offer objective, well-considered, balanced, and truthful information.[515]

Another approach was the use of "science" to support government policy. For example, authors of a theoretical model published in a prestigious medical journal in Canada "found that the choices made by people who forgo vaccination contribute disproportionately to risk among those who do get vaccinated." [516] However, the study was quickly debunked by statistician Regina Watteel (and other researchers) in her book *Fisman's Fraud: The Rise of Canadian Hate Science*, in which she observed that "the Trudeau government was in desperate need of 'scientific' justification for extending their federal vaccine mandates and travel restrictions." [517] Watteel further argued that:

> The research trio concocted a faux scientific model to fabricate data indicating that those people who opt out of COVID-19 vaccination (the 'unvaccinated') constitute a disproportionate risk to the vaccinated population, a trend contrary to reality ... David Fisman, Afia Amoaka and Ashleigh R. Tuite, conducted fraudulent research, funded by the Canadian Institutes of Health Research, then proceeded to present the fabricated results as scientific fact in order to inform government policy to defraud millions of Canadians of basic rights and freedoms ... Can't get an operation? Blame the unvaccinated! The 'science' says so. [518]

Watteel also articulated the illogical contradiction that "the vaccine was touted as powerful at stifling COVID-19, yet, it was incapable of protecting the population so long as the unvaccinated were present." [519] Most interestingly, the Deputy Prime Minister of Canada, expressed gratitude and appreciation of Fisman's science by writing in one tweet, "As we fight the COVID-19 pandemic, scientific guidance and analysis has been an essential weapon." [520] When politicians directly acknowledge their weaponization of science, it must be asked, who is it being used against, and for what purpose?

This section is closed with a quote an article by Kamran Abbasi, editor-in-chief of well-respected *British Medical Journal*, which appeared in the fall 2020:

> Politicization of science was enthusiastically deployed by some of history's worst autocrats and dictators, and it is now regrettably commonplace in democracies. The medical-political complex tends towards suppression of science to aggrandize and enrich those in

power. And, as the powerful become more successful, richer, and further intoxicated with power, the inconvenient truths of science are suppressed. When good science is suppressed, people die.[521]

Abbasi further added: "Politicians often claim to follow the science, but that is a misleading oversimplification. Science is rarely absolute. It rarely applies to every setting or every population."[522]

Public communication during COVID-19 response

In the 21st century, the most effective tool to influence public opinion is social media. The most popular social media platforms are Facebook, YouTube, WhatsApp, Instagram, TikTok, WeChat, X (formerly Twitter), and so on. There is also the mainstream media, which still has significant influence over parts of the population and played a key role during the COVID-19 pandemic. Specifically, social and mainstream media can be used to manipulate public opinions through the divergence of attention, creation of a problem and proffered solution, introduction of incremental changes, focus on pathos-evoking rhetoric, and the elevation of the feeling of guilt in people.[523] This practice of manipulation has been well captured in the book *Propaganda* by Edward Bernays, who was related to Sigmund Freud. Other experts in the field, like psychologist Richard Grannon, have noted other techniques of social manipulation, including gaslighting (i.e., disruption of the perception of reality), forcing the preferred narrative, preaching the future, finding the guilty, isolation of people, direct attacks on people who oppose the main narrative, and other tactics.[524]

On March 11, 2020, WHO announced to the world the existence of SARS-CoV-2, which was given the abbreviation COVID-19. The initial predictions regarding its impact on humanity were grave. On March 26, Neil Ferguson, together with his colleagues from Imperial College London, released an epidemiological model noting that "in the absence of interventions, COVID-19 would have resulted in 7.0 billion infections and 40 million deaths globally this year."[525] These estimates were for 2020 alone. In this report, Ferguson and his team also compared the potential impact of this novel coronavirus to the devastation caused by the H1N1 influenza, or Spanish flu, of 1918. For example, they specifically claimed that "whilst our understanding of infectious diseases and their prevention is now very different compared to in 1918, most of the countries across the world face the same challenge today with COVID-19, a virus with comparable lethality to H1N1 influenza in 1918."[526] The scare tactics and fear continued because once these claims were officially verbalized and placed in the public domain, they were not corrected. Many people believed these claims.

It is important to note that the report from Imperial College London, its claims, and its modelling codes were not independently verified, peer reviewed, or academically scrutinized.[527] It was later discovered that these codes were in fact incorrect, leading the projections made from Imperial College London's epidemiological model to be deemed problematic or even outright flawed. The initial analysis was not retracted. There were also major problems in the key assumptions related to the "reproduction number" (too high), the infection fatality rate (too high), a "do nothing" scenario (i.e. it was assumed that people would not undertake even basic safety precautions), and so on. Fergusson and colleagues also assumed that hospital bed capacity remains unchanged (temporary beds can be added, as shown in practice around the world) and that people's behaviour is unadjusted in the face of risk (people rationally adjust behaviour on their perception of risk). Small adjustments to Ferguson's model would have made significant changes to his predictions. At the time, this did not seem to matter since worries, concerns, and fears were already amplified. The prestige of Imperial College London, regarded as one of the most respectable academic institutions in the world, served as further scientific underpinning for the political action taken, which manifested as COVID-19 response. Many countries spiralled into complete fear and implemented strict restrictions to an extent that prompted Farrow to claim that "the modelers themselves are the new Wise Man. They follow the Star and discern the path to the greater good. [C.S.] Lewis called them the Controllers."[528]

The cornerstone of the suppression strategy recommended by Ferguson and his colleagues included protection for the elderly, the institution of wide-scale social distancing measures, isolation of the sick, household quarantine, and the closure of schools. These measures were intended to be implemented swiftly and for a period of at least 18 months, the probable length of time required to develop a vaccine. However, Ferguson and his team did not recommend complete lockdowns, stay-at-home restrictions, or work-from-home measures.

The recommendation from Imperial College London was an attempt to slow down the spread of COVID-19, but not to suppress it entirely (as currently insisted upon by many public health officials and political leaders), to allegedly avoid overwhelming the healthcare system during the initial stages of viral spread. This suppression strategy was based on the initial evidence from China that 80 percent of coronavirus transmissions occurred within households. Importantly, Ferguson and his colleagues stated that the recommended strategy did not estimate "wider social and economic costs of suppressions," or in other words, the strategy that at its core advised the disruption of millions of lives had no related background analysis of socio-economic consequences.[529] With some notable exceptions, it does not appear that the majority of public authorities around the world conducted any such analysis on their own despite widely implementing these restrictive mandates.

The preliminary epidemiological model projections from Imperial College London estimated 2.2 million deaths in U.S., 1.4 million in Japan, 510,000 in the U.K., 326,000 in Canada, and 85,000 in Sweden (table 3.1 below presents details for selected countries related to these projections and relevant calculations). Although Ferguson subsequently revised his initial estimates, public authorities around the world had already unleashed their enhanced versions of what experts from Imperial College London hypothesized, the magnitude of which led to and subsequently exacerbated widespread panic, fear, and outright hysteria. Interestingly, as noted above, countries that ignored this advice and did not instigate lockdowns, had limited or no restrictions, and relied upon general hygiene standards and other recommendations to be followed at one's discretion completely discredited Imperial College London's unmitigated worse case scenarios.

In this vein, it is also relevant to document Ferguson's track record of sensational and apocalyptic projections. For example, in the case of mad cow disease, Ferguson estimated up to 150,000 deaths (actual 2,704); for the swine flu, he predicted 65,000 deaths in the U.K. alone (actual 457 total); and for the bird flu, he estimated up to 200 million deaths (actual 455).[530] If only the deaths related to mad cow disease and the swine flu are considered, Ferguson overestimated the actual deaths in his worst-case scenarios by a factor of 98.9 times. Commenting on the apparent imprecision of Ferguson's predictions, Andrew Bridgen, former member of the U.K. Parliament and organizer of parliamentary debate on excess deaths in the U.K., noted the following:

> It is this sort of thing that allowed us to slaughter millions of cattle during the apparent foot and mouth outbreak, when we were persuaded not by science but by plausible potter of provable idiots such as Professor Neil Ferguson–yes, the same. His advice led to the bankruptcy, immiseration and utter despair of countless farmers who were forced to destroy their livelihoods in a futile attempt to prevent the spread of an airborne virus, which has already managed to pass in the air all the way from France to the Isle of Wight.[531]

Table 3.1 presents several COVID-related statistics for selected countries, including the U.S., the U.K., and Canada. The table includes Ferguson's initial projections of death vis-à-vis actual deaths and the overestimation factor (i.e., initial death projections divided by actual deaths). However, Ferguson was no exception since epidemiological models by the Burnet Institute in Australia, the World Health Organization (WHO), and others did not do better. These models failed because of

poor data input, wrong modelling assumptions, high sensitivity of estimates, lack of incorporation of epidemiological features, poor past evidence on effects of available interventions, lack of transparency, errors, lack of determinacy, consideration of only one or a few dimensions of the problem at hand, lack of expertise in crucial disciplines, groupthink and bandwagon effects, and selective reporting.[532]

Table 3.1: Selected countries and key COVID-19 related statistics

Selected countries	Projected deaths	Population	Actual deaths[1]	Overestimation factor
U.S.	2,200,000	328,200,000	419,000	5.3
Japan	1,400,000	126,300,000	5,063	276.5
U.K.	600,000	66,650,000	97,329	6.2
Korea	381,000	51,710,000	1,349	282.4
Canada	326,000	37,590,000	19,094	17.1
Taiwan	212,000	23,780,000	7	30,285.7
Sweden	85,000	10,230,000	11,005	7.7
Averages				**85.0[2]**

Source: Based on information from St. Onge (2020) and other sources. Own calculations.
[1] Numbers of actual deaths as of January 24, 2021, which were associated with COVID. [2] This calculation excludes Taiwan, which would unduly increase the average.

Consequently, the state, public officials, and local experts embraced these worst-case scenarios and justified restrictions on their basis while further amplifying existing fear and doom-mongering. The initial response to "flatten the curve," an exercise undertaken to allegedly prevent overwhelming the healthcare system, ultimately lasted for about 2 years. Using this alarmist data, the media unleashed its campaign on the people through frightful headlines, the propagation of anxiety regarding coronavirus, and general fearmongering, which became more pronounced than the disease.

Was there evidence to confirm that COVID-19 overwhelm the healthcare system? There is limited available evidence about the capacity utilization of hospitals either early in the pandemic or later in 2021 and 2022. One example of evidence about the allegedly overwhelmed hospital system came from Alberta. Evidence obtained by the Justice Center for Constructional Freedom (JCCF), based on its freedom of information requests, confirms that the healthcare system in Alberta was not overwhelmed in 2020 and early 2021. Table 3.2 presents capacity utilization in acute and intensive care units (ICU) beds in Alberta. Based on this data, it is difficult to conclude that hospitals were overwhelmed by COVID-19 patients. Evidence from Ontario also confirms the difference between the official narrative and the actual experience on the ground. As noted in one article, "over the weekend, spokespeople for the biggest hospitals in Toronto said they were at a tipping point" while "across the entire system, there are 16 COVID-19 patients and fewer than 10 of them in an ICU."[533]

Table 3.2: Acute care and ICU beds utilization in Alberta between 2016 and early 2021

	2016	2017	2018	2019	2020	2021
January	95.81%	96.43%	96.84%	94.36%	95.21%	90.12%
February	96.66%	95.39%	96.94%	95.25%	94.81%	90.63%
March	96.46%	95.70%	96.15%	95.87%	86.29%	93.19%
April	95.12%	94.63%	94.79%	94.59%	74.51%	
May	93.93%	94.65%	93.76%	94.20%	83.07%	
June	94.81%	95.63%	93.07%	94.09%	85.43%	
July	92.55%	94.35%	91.60%	91.82%	88.26%	
August	92.74%	93.99%	92.22%	93.12%	89.42%	
September	95.14%	94.65%	93.83%	95.00%	90.33%	
October	94.55%	95.90%	95.10%	94.15%	93.18%	
November	95.70%	96.39%	95.31%	92.51%	91.82%	
December	94.51%	94.53%	92.21%	91.44%	88.39%	
Acute care beds average	**94.83%**	**95.19%**	**94.32%**	**93.87%**	**88.39%**	**91.31%**
ICU beds average	**79.8%**	**80.7%**	**79.5%**	**79.8%**	**75.6%**	**N/A**

Source: Data from Alberta Health Services obtained by JCCF. Own calculations.

Division among people

Mask wearing, hand washing, and social distancing became everyday rituals, an expression of sorts of Covidian tribalism. A mask became a talisman, a reflection of almost religious belief after individuals established their own view of how they are to understand their belief in the pandemic and the necessary behavior needed to enact this belief. This, in turn, led to tribe formations which often operated along political divides (i.e., Republicans and Democrats in the U.S.), a concept described by medical doctor Clare E. Craig in her book *Expired: Covid the Untold Story* in the context of the 12 most common beliefs about COVID and their well-balanced counterarguments. In any case, these behaviors were often grounded in emotional reactions and fear. Individuals not only succumbed to their emotions, but also surrendered their own ability to think by deferring to experts and fact-checkers.[534] This illogical behavior is exemplified by the phenomena of mask-wearing by solo motorists or single pedestrians, who walked, engaged in cross-country skiing, or ran without another person within 50 or 100 meters, when the threat of spreading or contracting COVID-19 was not present.

Such behavior was promoted through collectivist slogans such as "we are all in this together." Of course, it was unclear how individuals promoting or adhering to these new social norms were unified with those who lost businesses and life savings due to COVID-19 restrictions, were fired from jobs due to vaccination non-compliance and were unable to pay the bills since an unvaccinated person was unable to collect unemployment benefits, plummeted into depression because of isolation, segregation, or exclusion, or were unable to visit loved ones in the hospital. The rhetoric itself of being "all in this together" did not resolve anything and certainly did not create any substantial level of camaraderie among people. Instead, restrictions created major problems: "[d]espite the talk of 'essential workers' and everyone being 'in this together,' the stark reality is that job and income losses are likely to have hit lower skilled and uneducated workers the hardest."[535]

Since mask wearing, vaccination status, and proper six-feet social distancing became social symbols of belonging to a collective, Covidian tribalism set the stage for the widespread division of people. Those who did not belong to the COVID-19 collective were easily identified because they did not wear a mask, did not adhere to social distancing rules, visited family members, or refused vaccination; hence, two clusters of people (i.e., the vaccinated and the unvaccinated) were created. As a result of this strict division, it became easy to unleash attacks against the unvaccinated. Just to cite one example of media involvement in exacerbating division among people, the Canadian newspaper the *Toronto Star* ran a front-page article on August 26, 2021, with the following text: "If an unvaccinated person catches it from someone who is vaccinated, boohoo, too bad. I have no empathy left for the wilfully unvaccinated. Let them die. I honestly don't care if they die from COVID. Not even a little bit. Unvaccinated patients do not deserve ICU beds."[536] Two days later, the *Toronto Star* ran another article, this time with the title "Toronto Star front-page design exacerbated division between readers."[537] The newspaper aptly identified the consequences of publishing such a story, namely the amplification of division and magnification of antipathy toward the unvaccinated. In its "apology," the newspaper noted that it simply "cited an Angus Reid poll that most vaccinated Canadians are indifferent to the unvaccinated getting sick with the virus, with 83 percent saying they have no sympathy for those who choose not to get the COVID-19 vaccine and then fall ill."[538]

The *Toronto Star*'s publications were not benign and caused the increased polarization of the vaccinated and unvaccinated against each other.[539] However, news headlines continued to argue that the pandemic was exacerbated due to the actions of the unvaccinated, which created both feelings of guilt on the part of those who did not want to get vaccinated, and resentment from the vaccinated toward the former group.[540] Thus, the media actively garnered dislike, disrespect, and disgust against the unvaccinated. Individuals who did not succumb to this collective Covidian tribalism were excluded from participation in society at many levels, including family life. It is interesting to note that this division was not only focused on urban centers, but also on farmers, who are traditionally religious, conservative, faithful to traditions, and loyal to their farmland; as such, farmers also became targets due to lower vaccination rates.[541,542]

Furthermore, politicians further entrenched this division through various forms of discrimination and intimidation. For example, Quebec Premier announced that "the province would be imposing a health tax on Quebecers who refuse to get their first dose of a COVID-19 vaccine in the coming weeks."[543] One exceptional admission of these discriminatory practices toward the unvaccinated came from Alberta's newly elected Premier, who noted that the unvaccinated were "the most discriminated against group that I've ever witnessed in my lifetime."[544] This acknowledgment may only be a single example from among many senior public servants in Canada.

Furthermore, the unvaccinated endured rampant name calling and were labelled as conspiracy theorists, irresponsible, egotistic, "granny killers," antivaxxers, "Covidiots," and many other terms indicating their alleged threat to the moral fabric of society. In other words, they were stigmatized.[545] Most significantly, the unvaccinated were branded as immoral in comparison to the vaccinated, who may have viewed their actions as virtuous, moral, and righteous.[546] The use of name calling led many people to turn on the unvaccinated, as in Canada, for example, in a survey conducted by Maru Public Opinion, 37 percent of people believed that the unvaccinated people should be denied access to public healthcare while 27 percent were in favour of a short jail sentence.[547] In the U.S., a similar survey confirmed that "a majority of Democrats embrace restrictive policies, including punitive measures against those who haven't gotten the COVID-19 vaccine."[548] More specifically, 59 percent of Democratic voters would restrict unvaccinated to their homes, 48 percent would recommend that the state fine or imprison those who questioned the efficacy of COVID-19 vaccines, and 45 percent would require the unvaccinated to live away from home and in designated facilities.[549]

Lastly, it is important to highlight one of the most egregious examples of prejudice against unvaccinated people, namely that some medical doctors and local health authorities refused to place them on transplant lists. In Alberta, for example, this decision of the Alberta Health Services (AHS), sanctioned by the provincial court system which ruled that "charter [is] not violated in denying transplant to patient who refused COVID-19 vaccine," actually resulted in a death.[550,551] The article summarizing this case specifically noted that the judge "found that if Lewis's [patient] application were successful, it would have significant negative public policy implications, be unfair to other patients and disrupt the transplant program."[552] The Supreme Court subsequently refused to hear the case.[553] There are also similar decisions in the U.S.[554,555] Most interestingly, while some hospitals in Canada and the U.S. required vaccination for transplant, others did not.[556] In terms of the debates on the issue, most arguments advanced by doctors, health authorities, and hospitals related to notions that organs would be "wasted" on the unvaccinated, unvaccinated patients posed risks to other patients in hospitals, and that refusal to vaccinate somehow provides evidence of nonadherence to medical protocols. And yet, these arguments appear illogical, erroneous, and unethical, especially since the medical system appeared to by hypersensitive to even singular deaths during the COVID-19 era.[557]

PART III:
THE MAIN AREAS OF IMPACT OF COVID-19 RESPONSE

4

COVID-19 response and its impact on the family and the middle class

COVID-19 response and its impact on family life

There were two main components that drove the pandemic and COVID-19 response, namely fear and division. In the first case, fear was often weaponized by governments, politicians, political party narratives, public health officials, experts, medical professionals, academics, and the media. Throughout 2020, and again at the height of 2021, fear of disease appeared to be more pronounced than the disease itself. Worse yet, the levels of fear were not static. Like the frequently changing levels of blood pressure in the human body, oscillating levels of fear promoted in lockstep campaigns led to mental and physical effects on human health and emotional exhaustion.[558] Fear was also comprised of many distinct parts, including fear of contagion, the sudden emergence of a new strain of coronavirus and its advancement through society, and general uncertainty about life and economics going forward. The latter case proved to be one of the most stress-generating characteristics of COVID-19 response.[559] Fear also amplified the erroneous perception of the inevitability of death if one caught coronavirus. Fear was further used to disrupt and redefine human relations through social distancing and disengagement.

Most significantly, however, is that fear fed division. COVID-19 response resulted in divisions among people, family members, friends, workers, students, sports teams, and other normally cohesive groups. Division was readily promoted, and the media played a key role.

Justin Trudeau, Canada's Prime Minister who routinely expressed conviction about inclusivity, contrarily described the unvaccinated as people who "don't believe in science or progress and are very often misogynistic and racist ... This leads us, as a leader and as a country, to make a choice: Do we tolerate these people?"[560] With respect to the Freedom Convoy (i.e., truckers' convoy), Trudeau labelled the unvaccinated truckers and others who wanted to protest the vaccine mandates and restrictions as "the small fringe minority of people who are on their way to Ottawa, who are holding unacceptable views."[561]

There was also new language invented to name the behaviour of scepticism of COVID-19 vaccines. The unvaccinated were called "covidiots," a form of language meant to shame the unvaccinated into compliance and obedience by stigmatizing them.[562] The headline from Global News that appeared on March 20, 2020, emphasizes this intention: "Spot a COVIDIOT? Here's how to report coronavirus rule-breakers."[563] For faster reporting or snitching, some provincial governments and municipalities set up online forms, including the provinces of Alberta (through the website of the Alberta Health Services) and Newfoundland and Labrador. Other countries, like the United Kingdom (U.K.), for example, also set up online forms to report people breaking COVID-19 response restrictions.[564] At the height of the vaccine campaign in the fall of 2021, the unvaccinated were further stigmatized with the so-called "pandemic of the unvaccinated," which implied that they were allegedly more of a health risk than coronavirus or the vaccinated.

When data from COVID-19 testing did not support the narrative marketed by the Canadian government that the unvaccinated were entering hospitals, filling intensive care units (ICUs), and dying, politicians and public health officers resorted to other strategies. In Ontario, as an example, methods of reporting COVID-19 cases and hospitalizations changed, which effectively reduced the number of cases found in the fully vaccinated from the dataset by about 50 percent.[565] In the province of Manitoba, data reporting was halted altogether, and reporting formats were changed so historical data was not comparable. Furthermore, Manitoba officials refused to provide data upon a freedom of information request.

To further help with the division of people, the website of the Canadian Broadcasting Corporation (CBC) provided expert advice on how to deal with COVID-19 rule breakers.[566] As a consequence of such entrenched fears and divisions, about 57 percent of people polled across Canada said that they would not invite unvaccinated people into their home (with this aversion as high as 70 percent in British Columbia).[567] The Leger poll also suggested that 78 percent of Canadians supported COVID-19 passportization (i.e., proof of vaccination) for individuals to access public spaces (with the highest percentage again found in British Columbia).[568]

The aggregate and long-term effects of constant fear mongering and division is difficult to imagine, especially when considering the consequences of prolonged chronic stress, isolation, separation from loved ones, and social estrangement. At the very least, it is evident that the culmination of general uncertainties about one's health, economic wellbeing, ability to pay off one's mortgage, and employment has led to elevated levels of loneliness, poor community relations, family separations, increased mental illness, and emotional stress, further leading to the manifestation of anxiety, depressive behaviour, and post-traumatic stress disorder (PTSD). It has also been reported that the level of stress reached such a point of mental paralysis that about a third of people were unable to make basic life decisions.[569] Of course, there were expert predictions that COVID-19 response would result in increased cases of PTSD, mental burnout, chronic stress, emotional exhaustion, and other forms of mental illness. However, while projections of deaths from COVID-19 were quickly and deeply internalized by the state, politicians, and unelected public health officials, predictions of impending mental health crises and catastrophes were ignored.

Changes to normal patterns of family life

The state's implementation of lockdowns, quarantines, stay-at-home orders, and other sorts of restrictions during the onset of COVID-19 caused significant changes to normal patterns of life. This, in turn, led to a broad array of developments which varied from country-to-country. However, one key area of similarity was that home became the centre of gravity for the entire family. Due to a fear of contagion, the heightened perception of risk, COVID-19 restrictions, and social distancing measures, individuals spent increasingly more time away from other natural settings. Thus, home became everything: a gym, personalized coffee shop, classroom, office, bar, restaurant, theatre, practice hall, and so on. However, this rapid transformation of the home into an everything-space created numerous problems. Firstly, being at home blurred the line between work, rest, and play for the entire household; it became easy to confuse family life and work life.[570] Secondly, the loss of healthy levels of daily separation between children and parents often led to excessive argumentation, disrespectful interactions, and improper communications. While there may normally be a manageable level of tension within the home, these levels were often exceeded due to constant space sharing, and even led to abuse in some cases. Scars from these negative engagements among family members may require years to heal, if ever. Thirdly, it was relatively easy during extended stays at home to pick up some negative habits, including watching too much TV, spending too much time on the Internet, engaging excessively with social media, exercising less, or avoiding person-to-person socialization outside of home.

A further adjustment to normal patterns of family life came from the mass adoption of online and digital solutions. These disruptive innovations, inventions, and new applications of existing technologies led to the development of new business products and services. The acceleration of these trends has been astonishing as they would normally take decades rather than months to implement and embrace. Individuals turned to television, social media, live-streams, gaming, and other Internet-based activities to occupy their time. Evidence from different countries confirms a 15–25 percent increase in time dedicated to these media during COVID-19 response. However, the prominence of social media and Internet-based entertainment is likely to stay post-COVID-19 because these media are often sticky and can easily become part of one's daily routine.

Parenting became more difficult since parents were expected to perform their usual employment duties in a work-from-home setting while simultaneously taking care of children. This structure inevitably led to mental exhaustion and burnout for parents. Parents' anxiety, chronic extreme stress, and uncertainty related to COVID-19, and state-led restrictions contributed to exacerbated familial conflicts, which in turn led to child neglect, physical mistreatment, and even abuse.[571] In fact, parents reported significantly worse mental health issues while under COVID-19 restrictions. These mandates further inhibited families from gathering for both normal interactions and special events, such as holidays, religious celebrations, weddings, and funerals. Moreover, familial separations occurred at various levels: children from grandparents, parents from adult children, children from places of education, and so on. The unvaccinated were additionally restricted from visiting family members in hospitals and long-term care homes. All these pressures served to increase the chance of domestic violence and aggression, substance abuse, and addictions, as new, previously unknown tensions appeared at home.

There were numerous consequences of this excessive home nesting, which varied from country-to-country and will be discussed further in the following pages. For example, stay-at-home orders proved to be a considerable strain on marriage in the U.K., resulting in a 9.6 percent increase in divorces in 2021 (up to 113,505 from 103,592 in 2020), which exceeded the 10-year average equal to 104,642.[572] Fortunately, the number of divorces decreased to 80,057 in 2022, which is one of the lowest statistics to be seen since the early 1970s. The divorce rate in the United States (U.S.) per thousand of population similarly increased between 2020 and 2021 to 2.5 percent from 2.3 percent.

Mental health issues as a consequence of COVID-19 response

The sudden arrival of social distancing, self-quarantine, forced stay-at-home orders, self-isolation, a lack of socialization, community disengagement, economic and financial uncertainty, limited travel and vacations, inadequate downtime, and other disruptions to regular life had a significant impact on the mental health of many individuals. The list of mental health issues experienced during the pandemic is long and may include depression, emotional problems, insomnia, fatigue, and the deterioration of cognitive functions, all of which disproportionately affected women, particularly younger women. The increase in these conditions is reflected in a synonymous uptick in calls to emergency departments during the height of COVID-19 restrictions. The Centers for Disease Control and Prevention (CDC) in the U.S. reported that 40.9 percent of respondents had "at least one adverse mental or behaviour health condition, including symptoms of anxiety disorder or depressive disorder."[573]

Children, adolescents, and young adults seemed disproportionately affected with the high rates of depression and anxiety among the latter group. The extent of depression rates among children was even estimated to be equivalent to those seen during wartime.[574] There is also the issue of youth suicides, which increased immediately during the pandemic but tapered off thereafter. Many youths went into their adulthood in a state of isolation due to disruptions to their social networks, disconnection from peers, separation from physical and extracurricular activities, and a dislocation from extended family members. [575] These negative effects on mental health occurred despite the alleged benefits of social media; it is therefore evident that an over-reliance on the virtual world did not help.[576]

Specifically, children were affected in terms of their educational outcomes, physical and emotional development, and growth of language and communication skills. In terms of educational outcomes, school closures in addition to a shift to online and hybrid learning proved harmful to children. For example, Halloran et al. established early in the pandemic that, on the basis of an analysis of 12 states, "pass rates declined compared to prior years and that these declines were larger in districts with less in-person instructions."[577] Researchers further noted that "passing rates in math declined by 14.2 percentage points on average", although scores in other subjects were affected less.[578] Thus, Halloran et al.'s analyses "demonstrate that virtual or distanced schooling modes cannot support student learning in the same way as in-person schooling."[579] Kuhfeld, Soland, and Lewis argued that "the COVID-19 pandemic has been a seismic and on-going disruption to K-12 schooling" and confirmed that "achievement gaps between students in low-poverty and high-poverty elementary schools grew" substantially.[580] These weaker educational outcomes are more significant when understood in a broader context. For example, the senior economist from the Federal Reserve Bank of Richmond confirmed that "switches to hybrid/virtual learning due to the pandemic adversely affected student achievement through several channels, including a decline in skill accumulation and a disruption of peer effects and peer-group formation."[581] He also noted that educational "losses took place early in the pandemic and that there has not been an apparent recovery."[582]

In terms of increased mental health challenges, children reported anxiety, feeling unsafe, emotional over-reactions, mood and personality swings, irritability, compulsive behaviours, obsessions, and depression. One cause of these increased issues was the inability for children to attend school in a consistent manner, which was detrimental to their development. The overall negative impact of state-led restrictions on children is well documented in research.[583] Additionally, 13.3 percent of young adults started or increased substance use, 40.9 percent showed symptoms of anxiety disorder (including 30.9 percent who displayed symptoms of depressive disorder), and 26.3 percent presented symptoms of trauma- and stressor-related disorder (TSRD).[584] Many studies across different countries corroborate these findings. It is worrisome that actual consequences of these psychiatric conditions that arose because of COVID-19 response are likely to continue to emerge well into the future.[585]

Politicians in the U.K. were warned about these potential outcomes but chose to ignore them.[586] The former U.K. parliamentarian Andrew Bridgen noted the following:

> We inflicted social distancing, masking and school closures on healthy children who were at no risk from the virus. We did that to protect the adults, at the expense of our children's social and mental health. People raised the alarm, but nobody listened. A society that consciously and knowingly sacrifices perfectly healthy children for adults is sick.[587]

There were also negative trends among older adults, especially older men, due to their long-term isolation from family, disruption of normal social support networks, and deterioration of mental and physical health.[588,589] In fact, entire households were impacted by a long laundry list of physical and mental health issues including depression, emotional problems, insomnia, fatigue, and a deterioration of cognitive functions. COVID-19 response particularly impacted people with pre-existing economic and social vulnerabilities.[590] Some of these individuals included minorities, the unemployed, the underprivileged, the disabled, children with special needs, and immigrant communities.

Another distinct group of people profoundly affected by the pandemic were healthcare workers. In their case alone, research confirms that about 70 percent reported worse mental health than prior to COVID-19 response and nearly 50 percent had symptoms of depression.[591,592] These consequences should not have been a surprise, as academics warned early in the pandemic about its delayed impact on mental health and suicide rates. For example, it was speculated in 2020 that the "mental health consequences of COVID-19 crisis including suicide behaviour are likely to be present for a long time and peak later than the actual pandemic."[593] Many professionals realized that as it became "normalized to be shut in and isolated at least for the better part of 1 or 2 years."[594]

COVID-19 response and the elderly

One of the most affected groups by COVID-19 response were seniors. The impact of isolation, separation, social distancing, and visitation restrictions upon seniors included loneliness, depression, chronic stress and anxiety, PTSD, mental burnout, emotional exhaustion, and relational disassociation. Bridgen also observed that "with unbearable cruelty, we isolated even those who would gladly have made the individual choice to see their grandchildren."[595] However, the elderly were not only isolated from their families, but also from networks of old friends and support.

Research also confirms the extent of mental health disasters in long-term care facilities where the elderly were often mistreated while being utterly alone. This isolation was absolute and kept children from their parents, siblings from each other, and even forced married couples apart.[596] Thus, "although this isolation was initially imposed to protect residents and staff from COVID-19 infection, the collateral consequences were devastating … COVID-19 took its greatest toll on older persons."[597] Research also indicated that:

> Virtually all nursing homes [were] in lockdown mode with residents unable to see their families or participate in communal meals or activities … in effect, residents were placed in solitary confinement for six months … it is almost impossible to underestimate the harm and mental anguish that barring entry to nursing, care and residential homes has caused to thousands of residents, their families and significant others. Such actions also support the dangerous narrative that elderly and vulnerable people matter less.[598]

This behaviour was exhibited in view of the fact that, for example, under the regulations of the Centre for Medicare and Medical Services (CMS) in the U.S., a nursing home resident "has a right to a dignified existence, self-determination, and communication with and access to persons and services inside and outside of the facility."[599] However, it is evident that these long-term care facilities and nursing homes did not become places of dignity, respect, and autonomy for the elderly, but instead functioned as "golden prisons."[600]

COVID-19 response and suicide ideation

Understanding suicide data and rates is a complex matter that should be approached from sociological, psychological, and economic points of view because these statistics reflect a combination of factors, including unemployment rates, financial worries, deteriorating wages, substances abuse, family dynamics, drug use and overdose, and so on.[601] When scrutinizing suicide statistics, some researchers focus on the five Ds (i.e., depression, disease, disability, disconnection, and deadly means) of suicide; it is easy to see how some of these five D-components were present during the pandemic.[602] The complexity also stems from the significant variability of the impact of COVID-19 response across the globe. For example, females were the most affected group in some countries early in the onset of the pandemic, while in others it was children, young adults, or the elderly.[603] In the U.S., for example, the CDC reported that 25.5 percent of respondents aged 18-24 "having seriously considered suicide in the in 30 days before completing the survey."[604] Furthermore, the dynamics of suicide statistics often changed as COVID-19 response progressed.

The impact of COVID-19 response on suicide came in two phases. The first phase of the pandemic (i.e., throughout 2020) saw a meaningful decline in the number of suicides, which was a phenomenon observed across the globe.[605,606] This decline may be explained by heightened unity in view of a common threat, an external focus (rather than internal one), or a greater tolerability to the nature of suffering in view of others' pain.[607] More time was also spent with families and loved ones at home, which fostered a sense of unity, belonging, understanding, appreciation, cohesiveness, and empathy–all enemies of depression, anxiety, and suicidal ideation. Interestingly, this decline during the pandemic was not uncommon or unexpected as "suicidologists have long observed that suicide rates tend to decline after a catastrophe."[608] The second phase of the pandemic, however, was marked by the loosening of the initially strong bonds, the aggressiveness and intensification of lockdowns and restrictions, and the desire to return to regular patterns of life, which became more difficult. This phase resulted in a rapid increase in suicides as the effects of global trauma set in. These two distinct phases in suicide statistics have been observed within the U.S., whose number of suicides has been increasing by about 1.9 percent since 2012 (see figure 4.1). The suicide rate fell by 3.3 percent in 2020 to 45,979 from 47,571 in 2019. This decline was followed by an accelerated rate of 4.8 percent and 2.6 percent in 2021 and 2022, respectively, and exceeded 50,000 in 2023.

Figure 4.1: Suicides in the United States

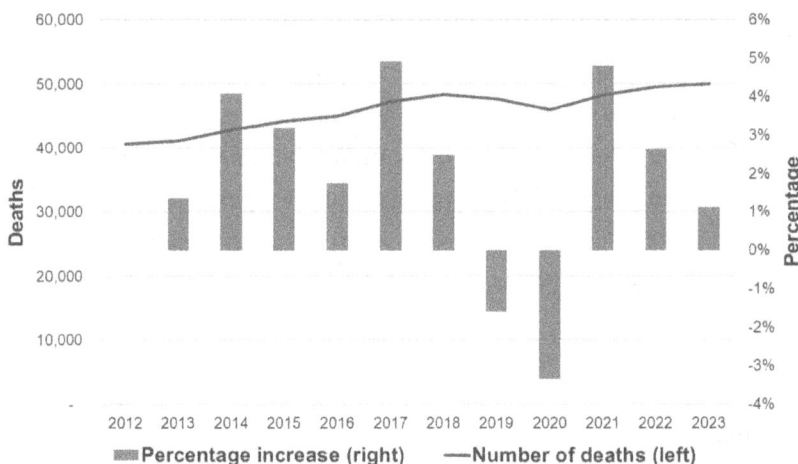

Source: Various sources.

Turning now to mental health issues in Canada specifically, Kevin Bardosh, applied medical anthropologist, provided a reference to more than 100 studies describing the effects of COVID-19 response on mental health of Canadians in his written affidavit.[609] The most important points of Bardosh's report are summarized below.

To begin with, the level of suicide ideation among adults in Canada was equal to 4.2 percent in 2021, which is higher than the baseline average of about 2.7 percent in 2019.[610] Secondly, increased levels of chronic stress, panic, depression, emotional disturbances, and anxiety were reflected in simultaneous increases in the dispensation of mental health medications such as antidepressants.[611] This was primarily seen in adolescents who, in addition to feelings of depression, anxiety, and self-harm,[612] also experienced less satisfaction, greater sadness, and lower optimism about life.[613] The deteriorating mental wellbeing of adolescents led to an over 50 percent increase in emergency department visits and hospitalizations related to mental health, especially for younger females.[614,615] It also led to the increased consumption of alcohol, cannabis, and other substances, as well as elevated levels of social conflict, especially with parents and siblings.[616] Moreover, 45 percent of parents were also significantly affected themselves by higher alcohol consumption, suicidal ideation, extreme stress, and emotional issues, which placed even more stress on the family and disrupted normal patterns of communication and behaviour.[617]

Economics of the family post COVID-19 response

Assessing the economic wellbeing of the family is a complex issue because it can involve multiple measures such as hourly wages, unemployment levels, family incomes, and so on. Beyond these issues, however, the family has been subjected to several other concerns, including housing affordability and levels of debt. This section will assess the economics of the family in the U.S. and Canada prior to and following COVID-19 response.

Americans have generally struggled in terms of wages and family income over the last fifty years (see figure 4.2a). Specifically, when expressed in 1982-1984 constant dollars, real wages declined from $9.0 in 1978 to $7.6 in 1998, which represented a 17-year period of decline. This interval was followed by a 23-year period of slow increase back to the $9.1 level in 2018. The fact that labour wages have remained flat is particularly disappointing considering the U.S. labour force has generated significant productivity gains over the years, which has not been reflected in increases to actual purchasing power. Since the onset of COVID-19 response, individuals lost about a quarter of their purchasing power. Although nominal average wages in the U.S. rose post-pandemic, when adjusted for inflation, real wages in the U.S. remained flat.

The median nominal family income in the U.S. has increased from $6,569 in 1964 to $86,100 in 2019, which represents an annual increase of 4.7 percent over the period (see figure 4.2b). However, expressed on an inflation-adjusted basis (i.e., in real terms), median family incomes increased at less than one percent per annum. In more recent years, American family budgets were increasingly affected by food costs. In 2022, Americans spent 11.3 percent of their disposable income on food, which was comparable to the level seen in 1991 (equal to 11.4 percent).[618]

Figure 4.2: Hourly wage and annual family income statistics in the United States

a)   Nominal and real hourly wages in the U.S. between 2000 and 2023.

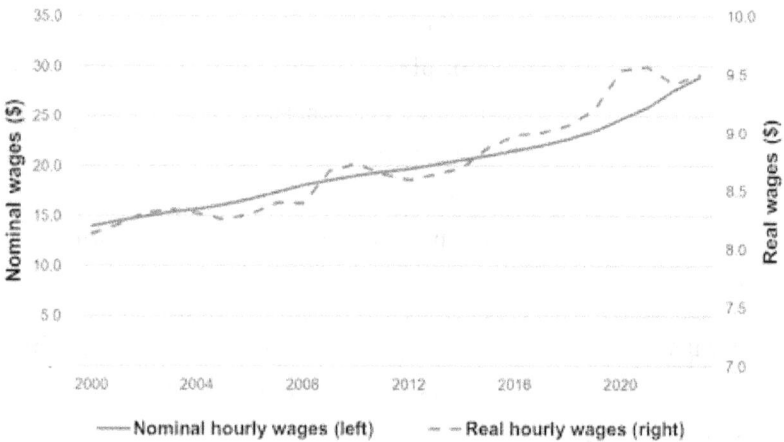

b)   Nominal and real median income in the U.S. between 2001 and 2023.

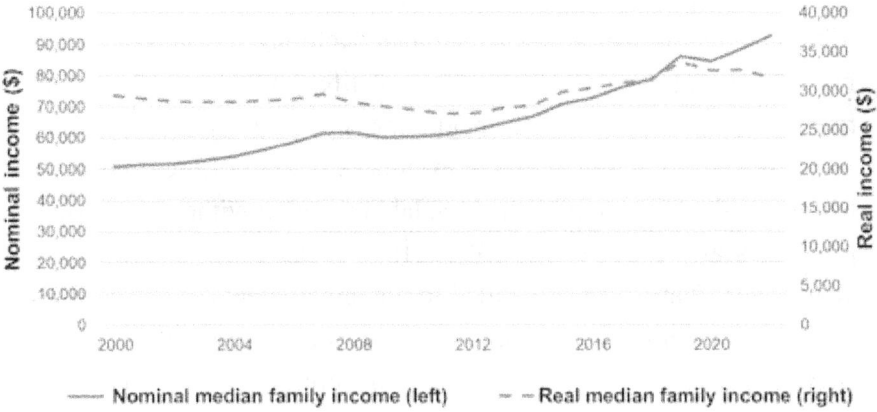

Source: Various sources, including Federal Reserve Bank of St. Louis and the U.S. Bureau of Labor.

Another key statistic affecting families is the unemployment rate. Over the last 50 years the unemployment rate was equal to about 6.0 percent in the U.S., with the highest rates occurring during the tenures of Barack Obama (7.4 percent) and Ronald Reagan (7.5 percent). Labor market dynamics are also influenced by the labour force participation rate, which reflects workers' ability to secure employment. In the long-term, this rate was equal to an average of 64.0 percent. The U.S. labour market has, over the years, also been affected by a significant shift in the quality of employment opportunities. For instance, there has been a visible increase in precarious employment, which has been associated with the substitution of higher-paid employees in favour of lower paid, dispensable workers. Furthermore, the growth rate of this form of precarious employment has often exceeded the job creation of better-quality jobs. In other words, the creation of low paying jobs has outpaced higher paying jobs. Moreover, terminated workers who are unable to find local employment at similar wage

145

levels to their previous positions have been forced to accept low-pay service positions. Workers have also tried to pursue self-employment opportunities, which are often unstable and pay less. The implications of these labour dynamics contribute to a declining standard of living, inability to pay for basic necessities of life, and increased poverty rates. Importantly, although beginning pre-pandemic, COVID-19 response saw a continuation and even acceleration of these negative labour trends. For example, the U.S. labour market witnessed massive job losses at the outset of COVID-19 response, and in May 2020 alone, over 30 million people filed for unemployment assistance. This caused the unemployment rate to increase from 3.5 percent in 2019 to 14.8 percent in 2020, although it subsequently declined to about 6.9 percent by yearend. In Canada, on the other hand, the unemployment rate increased to 13.5 percent in 2020, with over 3 million Canadians applying for unemployment benefits. The unemployment rate similarly declined to 9.8 percent by year end, which was still about 1.4 percent higher than the 50-year average.

Another issue affecting the economics of the family has been the extraordinary increase in housing costs. For example, Canadian households have spent exceedingly higher amounts of income to cover home ownership costs, which normally include mortgage payments, property taxes, and utility costs, among other expenses. In fact, evidence confirms that the average share of household income in Canada required to cover house ownership expenses was equal to 51.9 percent at the end of 2018. In other words, about half of the family's income was dedicated to fulfilling the Canadian dream of house ownership. Thus, house ownership has become extremely difficult to attain for Canadian families in major Canadian cities. Furthermore, while the average house cost four years of labour time in Canada in the 1970s, this figure was equal to eight years by 2016, which coincided with the average level of debt to disposable income reaching high levels (see figure 4.3a). This situation has only worsened post-COVID-19 response. For instance, while the level of household debt as a percentage of disposable income increased, the real impact on Canadian households came from increased interest rates. In fact, in 2022, Canada had one of the highest levels of household debt among G-7 countries at 1.87, with the U.K. being at 1.47 and Japan at 1.26.[619,620] The lowest levels are found in Italy at 0.88. Moreover, "Canadian households [are] now the third most indebted in the world", only behind Switzerland and Australia, in terms of household debt as a percent of GDP.[621] Canadians were warned of this likelihood in 2023 when the International Monetary Fund (IMF) stated that "Canada runs the highest risk of mortgage defaults among advanced economies."[622]

Figure 4.3: Debt and insolvencies in Canada

a)   Canadian credit card and household debt between 2000 and 2023

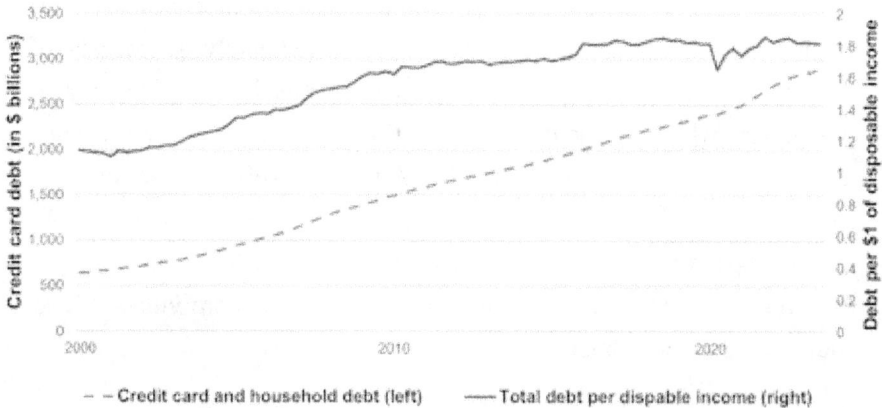

- - Credit card and household debt (left)   ——Total debt per dispable income (right)

b)   Consumer insolvencies in Canada between 2011 and 2023

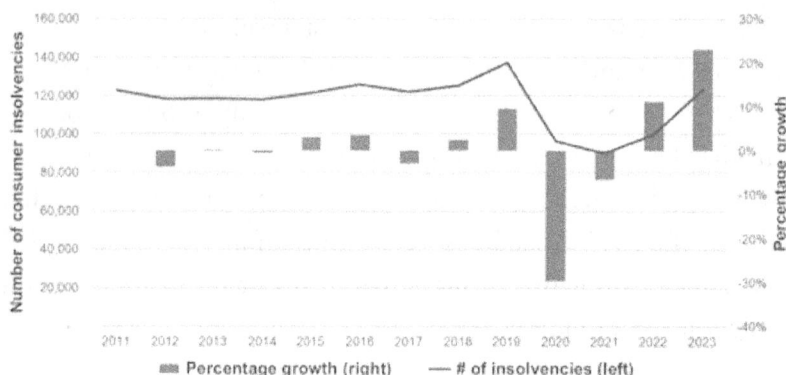

Source: Government of Canada.

Additionally, many Canadians have already incurred a mortgage "payment shock" after renewing their home loans. Moreover, "between 2024 and 2026, an estimated $900-billion worth of Canadian mortgages at chartered banks are set to renew."[623] Approximately 40 percent of Canadians will renew their mortgages with higher interest rates during this period, which means that over 2 million Canadians will experience the financial jolt related to renewal.[624] And it is likely that the financial strain on Canadian household will increase as they renew mortgages.[625] As mortgage payments increase, Canadian households will not only struggle to cover the basic necessities, but they will also be more vulnerable to additional financial shocks.

Specifically, about 20 percent of mortgages in Canada are variable and have seen a significant increase in their payments since the onset of the pandemic.[626] There are many others who had to renew their mortgages during this period that were unduly impacted by the vast increase in mortgage interest rates in Canada from about 2.15 percent in 2020 to 6.65 percent in just three years.[627] In practical terms, this means that on a $500,000, 30-year mortgage, a monthly mortgage payment for individuals with a variable rate increased from $1,885.8 to $3,209.8, or a whopping

70.2 percent. One Bank of Canada publication estimated broadly that "median payments are expected to increase by 54%."[628]

In light of these challenges, it is estimated that "63 percent of Canadians say they are concerned about their ability to repay their debts."[629] This, in turn, negatively influences mental health and "causes them anxiety (60%), stress (59%), isolation (48%) or embarrassment (40%)."[630] Moreover, such high interest rate levels and mortgage payments are likely to prevent new homeowners from entering the housing market, especially in view of grossly inflated home prices. Since the onset of the pandemic, Canadians' pocketbooks were hit twice, initially with high inflation and then with high interest rates. It appears that this detrimental combination of high inflation and increased interest rates may prevail for some time in the future.

How have Canadians dealt with such difficult, and ongoing, financial circumstances? Many Canadians have resorted to reverse mortgages (i.e., loan-like financial instruments backed by home ownership, where cash can be released from home equity), which charge interest rates equal to between 7 or 10 percent that are payable upon relocation, sale, or death. The value of these reverse mortgage transactions increased from about $0.8 billion in 2019 to over $1.0 billion in 2021 and 2022.[631] However, there has also been a significant depletion of Canadians' savings "for repayments and daily expenses."[632] Additionally, in 2022 and 2023, Canadians pulled "billions from Canadian mutual funds in the high interest rates era."[633] Also, many Canadians may be forced to sell their homes.[634] Interestingly, due to house affordability problems, one third of Canadians are now considering different ways to own a house. These scenarios include renting-to-own or house ownership with non-family.[635] Another now considered method is renting out a part of one's owned home, which is a practice already used in some of the most expensive cities in Canada.

The financial pressures on the Canadian family are further reflected in consumer insolvency statistics. Figure 4.3b presents a steady increase in consumer insolvencies in Canada between 2011 and 2023. Although consumer insolvencies declined by 29.7 and 6.6 percent in 2020 and 2021, respectively, the years 2022 and 2023 saw rapid increases. Consumer insolvencies continued in 2024 hitting "4-year high in Canada as interest rates weigh on households."[636]

Credit card debt and delinquencies

Total consumer debt in the U.S. is equal to about $17.5 trillion and is comprised of mortgages (about $12.3 trillion), auto loans ($1.6 trillion), and student loans ($1.6 trillion).[637] By the end of 2023, credit card debt in the U.S. was equal to $993.3 billion and reached $1.1 trillion in early 2024, while revolving credit exceeded $1.2 trillion. As illustrated in figure 4.4, credit card debt (including other revolving plans) increased from $233.5 billion by 7.3 percent per annum on average since 2001. Similarly to other statistics discussed above, the level of credit card debt fell by 5.0 percent and 2.6 percent in 2020 and 2021 respectively, reaching the level of $763.6 billion. The years 2022 and 2023, however, saw a rapid increase in the level of credit card debt (15.3 percent in 2022 and 12.8 percent in 2023), reflecting the financial stress and deterioration of the financial standing, especially among younger people and lower-income families.[638] In addition to increased debt, the personal savings rate decreased to 3.8 percent in early 2024, which dropped from 5.3 percent in May 2023 and from above 7 percent immediately prior to the pandemic.[639] It is estimated that excess savings have been declining in the U.S. at a rate in excess of $1 billion per month since early 2022. In short, credit card debt and savings rates are moving in opposite directions and creating an ever-widening gap, which does not bode well for the future.

Figure 4.4: Credit card debt and delinquency rates in the United States

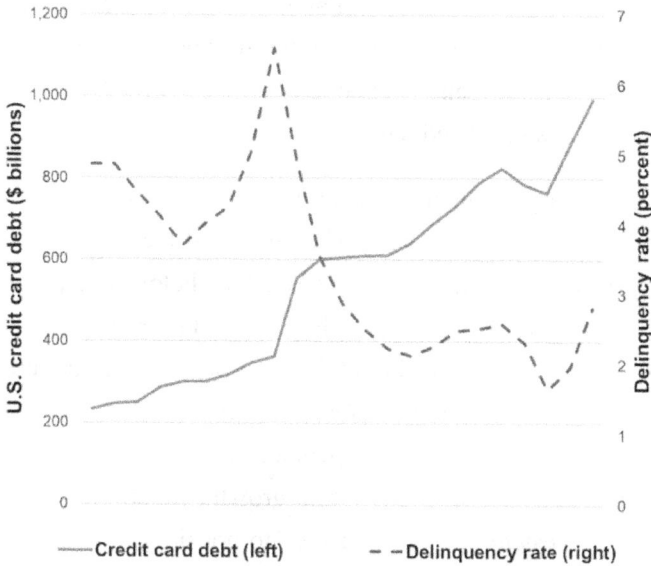

Source: Federal Reserve Bank of St. Louis

Another critical debt statistic is the delinquency rate, which represents the percentage of debt that is overdue. The delinquency rate in the U.S. has declined steadily since it reached its peak at 6.3 percent in 2009. The delinquency rate fell to its lowest point in 2021 (1.6 percent) and began to rise from thereon, reaching 2.8 percent in 2023 due to a rapid increase in the interest rates and higher prices.[640] Millennials were the mostly affected age group, especially with respect to car loans and credit card debt.[641] Research also confirms that younger Millennials (up to the age of 30) fell into delinquency, especially serious delinquency (exceeding 90 days).[642]

Poverty rates: Evidence from Canada and the United States

It was noted in the preface that early in the pandemic about 300 million people fell below the poverty line, which is in addition to those already living in poverty around the world.[643] The total number of people living in poverty is currently equal to about 1.1 billion (with about 700 million living in extreme poverty), including about 500 million children.[644] This section on the economics of the family would not be complete without some reference to issues related to poverty post-COVID-19 response. An example from Canada is used here.

The topic of poverty is inherently complex. Poverty rates are defined on the basis of economic determinants (i.e., personal income) and reflect a percentage of the population whose income falls below a certain income threshold called a poverty line, which is often determined "as half the median household income of the total population."[645] But poverty goes beyond simple personal economics and reflects a wide combination of socioeconomic factors. In addition to personal income, poverty may reflect general economic conditions, economic growth, inflation, employment opportunities, access to education, access to housing, food security and nutrition, sanitation, and so on.[646] In addition to official statistics of poverty rates, there is also "hidden poverty" wherein an individual earns income above the predetermined poverty line but struggles to make ends meet in terms of securing adequate food and housing, paying basic bills (i.e., hydro, water, gas, etc.), and affording other basic necessities of life.

Evidence from Canada, for example, confirms that poverty rates are rapidly growing. While poverty rates declined steadily from 14.5 percent in 2015 to 10.3 percent in 2019 and reached even lower levels in 2020, this positive trend was reversed post-COVID-19 response. Since 2020, poverty rates in Canada have increased from 6.4 percent to 9.8 percent in 2022 (provisional data).[647] The official poverty rates for the U.S. in 2022, as reported by the U.S. Census Bureau, was equal to 11.5 percent, which also increased from the pre-pandemic levels of 10.5 percent (2019). This equates to about 38.0 million individuals in the U.S.[648]

Moreover, "a new report by Food Banks Canada suggests that more Canadians may be living in poverty than previously estimated, with 25 per cent potentially falling into this category."[649] These conclusions were reached by Food Banks Canada through an application of the standards of the Material Deprivation Index (MDI), a measure commonly used in the European Union (EU) to ascertain poverty, to official Canadian statistics.[650] In its report, Food Banks Canada reported that "in March 2023, there were almost 2 million visits to food banks across Canada, representing a 32 per cent increase compared to March 2022, and a 78.3 per cent increase compared to March 2019, which is the highest year-over-year increase in usage ever recorded."[651]

The attack on the middle class

The social, economic, and political trends which emerged post COVID-19 response were negative for many individuals. For example, over 60 percent of Americans lived paycheque-to-paycheque. About 40 percent of Canadians felt that they were in a worse financial position than they were prior to 2020. However, the discussion of the economics of the family would not be complete without referring to the middle class.

Although a definition of the middle class may be somewhat elusive and abstract, it can be defined by its economic, social, educational, and occupational parameters. Other things that can impact the definition may include the geographic region of residence, family size, levels of investment, and potential for earnings improvement. The middle class can also be defined on an individual, household, or familial basis and can be further divided into lower middle class, middle class, and upper middle class.

In terms of economic-driven descriptions, the most prevalent understanding of the middle class is related to income. One characterization of the middle class is the broad demarcation between the poor and the rich. In this case, a middle-class income simply resides in the middle of income distribution. Another way in which the middle class can be defined is as the middle third quintile of economic distribution, or sometimes the middle fifth. Alternative conceptualizations of the middle class may pertain to people who do not belong to the bottom or top 20 percent, or those who earn between certain percentages of the median household income after tax. However, in the latter case, the percentage range is often defined so broadly that it becomes impractical. Furthermore, the percentage spread can vary from country-to-country.

Despite the variety in definition, the most used income band is between 50 and 150 percent of the median income. In Canada, for example, the middle class is defined in terms of the income band between 75 and 200 percent of the median income, while in the U.S. it is defined as between two-thirds and double the median family income. Since the median family income in the U.S. was equal to $92,750 in 2022, a family income between $61,864 and $185,500 would be classified as the middle class. However, the lower end of the middle class may be considered around $50,000 while the upper end may exceed $300,000. Of course, the extent of the spread of income in the band means that families placing in the upper middle class can comfortably withstand increases in inflation and maintain normal patterns of consumption, retirement preparation, and vacations, while families at the lower end of the spectrum will experience a financial squeeze because of acceleration in the cost of living. In other words, families struggle to make ends meet at the lower end of the middle-class spectrum. This phenomenon has only accelerated since the onset of the pandemic, as it is estimated that about 70 percent of middle-income families have not been able to cover cost-of-living increases.[652] The most progress in terms of income improvements were made by older adults (65-years of age), Black adults, married men, and married women.[653]

In broad terms and beyond basic economics, the middle class may be defined as those who can comfortably afford to implement their unique lifestyles, have job security, have a reasonable amount of discretionary income, have suitable health insurance, sustain savings, own a home, have time and money to afford holidays, and have decent prospects for retirement. In terms of occupational distribution, the middle class may be comprised of professional managers, owners of small and medium-sized businesses, and salaried workers (i.e., teachers, social workers, engineers, nurses, administrators, skilled craftsmen or people in technical positions), among other employment possibilities. Since the middle class often represents a desirable economic and social outcome, many people define themselves as belonging to this class. For example, about 70 percent of Canadians view themselves as middle class while 50 percent of U.S. families define themselves as such (this percentage declined from over 60 percent in the last 50 years).[654] But, when more comprehensive economic and social measures are used, only between 30 and 40 percent of Americans can qualify as middle class.[655]

The middle class has been badly affected by COVID-19 response, experiencing impacts that are both wide and multidirectional. These consequences include the stagnation of the inflation-adjusted hourly wage, downward pressure on salaries, the rise of unemployment, a decline in labour force participation, poor housing affordability, limited savings, and enormous personal debt (i.e., student debt, consumer debt, and mortgages). There are also consumer insolvencies and bankruptcies that were described earlier in the chapter. In addition to the statistics already provided in this chapter, there is more bad news for the middle class: because of the financial squeeze, Americans are increasingly relying on savings and credit cards to supplement their monthly incomes, in addition to dipping into retirement savings. For example, the 401k balances (a retirement savings plan in the U.S. with contributions from employees and employers) fell by about 4 percent in 2023.[656] Moreover, it is estimated that only around 20 percent of Americans still have excess savings and liquid assets.[657] The key reasons for these withdrawals are attempts to avoid home foreclosure and evictions, paying for medical expenses, and covering normal life expenditures.

Evidence further indicates that young adults are likely to be economically worse off than their parents, which is historically unprecedented. Post-COVID-19 response, young adults are likely to continue experiencing problems starting professional careers and earning reasonable wages, even with a strong educational background and preparation. Young but less educated adults are similarly projected to see a downward pressure on wages throughout most of their adult lives. Although education is normally correlated with higher wages, a four-year bachelor's degree may no longer be a guarantor of higher and steadily increasing wages, stable employment, and a secure career. Thus, Americans intuitively know that they do not experience the same quality of living as their parents and grandparents.

5

COVID-19 response and its impact on religious practice

COVID-19 and COVID-19 response impacted the world at a very peculiar time since many people, especially in the West, have predominantly held materialistic views.[658] They have aimed to maintain comfort and peace, pursue pleasures, secure great careers, chase money, watch sports, and focus on food-related experiences.[659] Furthermore, the key "values" for many have been the pursuit of different pleasures, fun and entertainment, and experimenting with different substances.[660] There has also been an acute sensitivity and over-fixation toward healthy lifestyles, looking young, and living longer. Many have become addicted to digital media and social platforms, and other Internet-driven activities, while a primary worry has been whether they are able to attend gyms and maintain Internet connectivity. In simple terms, the historical social order based on *logos* (Word of God), *ethos* (ethics, ethical behaviour), and *pathos* (quality of life, pleasures) has given way for many to the sole concentration on *pathos* while avoiding *logos* and *ethos*. One corollary to the cultural attitudes described above is that if these activities and priorities are threatened, a quicker and more vigorous emotional response to a particular situation or event would likely result.[661] Of course, there have also been many people who hold oppositional views to those described above.

Materialism has many drawbacks, but one of the most significant is the fact that people consumed by it often have difficulty dealing with death, and more specifically, their own death.[662] The widespread fear of death and poor health in our current culture has created the conditions wherein human activities are centred on physical activity and wellbeing. Another consequence of this passion has been the profound medicalization of human life and an overreliance on the pharmaceutical industry for solutions to physical, as well as mental, health. Put simply, the more people become concerned about their physical wellbeing, the more they believe they can distance themselves from death, and the easier it will become for all sorts of medical authorities, experts, and advisors to manipulate them along the spectrum of physical wellbeing. However, as noted by Ivan Illich in his book *Limits to Medicine*, "after a century of pursuit of medical utopia, and contrary to current conventional wisdom, medical services have not been important in producing the changes of life expectancy that occurred. A vast amount of clinical care is incidental to the curing of disease, but the damage done by medicine to the health of individuals and populations is very significant. These facts are obvious, well documented, and well repressed."[663] Illich has further identified that "awe-inspiring medical technology has combined with egalitarian rhetoric to create the impression that contemporary medicine is highly effective."[664]

As materialism-oriented priorities have become central to modern human life, many individuals have moved away from the search for and pursuit of God. Consequently, the last few decades saw a negative impact on religiosity and religious practice due to an increase in secularization, atheism, and "religious privatization" (i.e., individual spiritualization without any involvement of the church).[665] There are numerous global examples of this trend. In Poland, for instance, attending Sunday Mass declined from 45.2 precent in 2002 to 36.9 percent in 2019. This decrease may reflect a combination of factors, including Poland's integration with the European Union (characterized by growing secularization and atheism) and a transition from traditional to allegedly more progressive and modern values. In the United States (U.S.), a growing part of the population attends church infrequently, rarely, or even never. The most severe erosion of faith has occurred among Evangelical Protestants, who exhibit the most substantial corrosion of religious beliefs and a diminishing influence of biblical worldviews on their lives and decisions.[666] Meanwhile, religious affiliation in Canada were reported by about 70 percent of people in 2022, with the biggest decline found in various Protestant denominations. Australia has seen a similarly stark change, as attendance at Sunday Mass declined from over 70 percent in the 1950s to about 11 percent in 2016.[667]

Religious beliefs have been under attack because they are fundamental to the formation of human values, norms, traditions, and beliefs across the globe.[668] Attacks on the family and religiosity may be interconnected since religion strengthens the family, and strong families in turn nurture religiosity from one generation to another.[669] Moreover, the attack against religion may arise because "the power of all religions, such as Christianity, Islam, Hinduism, or Buddhism, and their ability to create large civilizations, arises from the fact that they are able to emancipate people from materialistic and animalistic approach to life."[670]

COVID-19 response restrictions and religion

There has been a significant curtailment of religious freedom, freedom of conscience, faith, and expression because of COVID-19 response. Restrictions not only negatively affected traditional religious practices, but they also impacted other aspects of religious life and religiosity such as faith-based teaching and education (i.e., preparatory classes, courses, and seminars); methods of civil engagement (i.e., serving the poor and the underprivileged, evangelizing, organizing children's activities, participating in community services, etc.); preparing couples for marriage; organizing religious events (i.e., festivals, retreats, and pilgrimages); holding religious work meetings; executing spiritual care for the elderly; and so on. One pastor from Nigeria described COVID-19 response and its impact in the following manner:

> The lockdown felt like being under attack. The fact that we no longer would be able to gather together and pray, hold hands, sing songs of praise, and act like brothers and sisters that we are, and

hold church services that help strengthen the bond we share, was baffling. It was like being hit by a meteor from space.[671]

In terms of the Catholic faith, as an example, public celebrations of Mass were suspended in Vatican City in March 2020, which prompted many local Catholic churches to follow suit. Other Catholic churches suspended Mass but kept churches open for prayer ahead of Easter, which is the most important celebration for Christians around the world. Importantly, these closures occurred at a time when experts were not entirely clear about the nature of the disease or how deadly it was.

For a specific period, Catholic churches were required to keep attendance lists, maintain mask requirements, disallow singing, remove the Holy water, disinfect the pews, and discourage parishioners from receiving the Holy Eucharist on the tongue, among other alterations. In Poland, for example, the state cancelled "All Saints" celebrations and posted police and by-law officers near cemeteries. The state also cancelled religious pilgrimages as part of COVID-19 response, thereby ending a tradition that has spanned hundreds of years. In comparison, churches in Poland were not even closed during the Second World War. From a historical perspective, as reminded by Reverand Derek Remus from the Diocese of Calgary, the closure of Catholic churches has been unprecedented in modern times. The closest comparison is Archbishop Charles Borromeo's decision to introduce health restrictions during the plague that affected Millan in 1576, although even these restrictive measures did not involve full closures of churches or denial of Sacraments.

There were many arguments put forward by country leaders, politicians, political parties, medical doctors, unelected public health officers, and all manner of experts and advisors (i.e., epidemiologists, virologists, etc.) in favour of significant restrictions to religious rights. Firstly, it was argued that religious services and freedoms could not be granted at the expense of people's physical health and wellbeing. In-person religious services needed to be shut down, it was purported, because such actions could allegedly save lives, although no specific data was provided to support these arguments. However, public officials "permitted" religious believers to worship in different ways, such as online or through personal prayers at home, although as discussed below this private option became religious adulteration for many religions, including Catholicism and Islam, because it deprived the faithful of some essential services for their spiritual and mental wellbeing. A second argument put forward by many political and unelected officials, including non-religious people, was that staying away from communal prayers at churches could be viewed as community service, an expression of neighbourly love, and an act of self-sacrifice. Thirdly, it was stated that spending half an hour or an hour inside of a church or place of worship (with proper safety measures) was different than buying groceries over the same period (where shoppers frequently pass each other). Arguments were made that physical proximity (even though appropriate spacing was possible), religious singing, and loud praying could lead to viral transmission and cause so-called "super spreader events." Of course, there was limited or no medical evidence for such claims. Lastly, it was expected that everyone "trust the science" and that religious leaders should not be second-guessing appropriate medical experts, health officers, and politicians who allegedly understood what was best for the human being and the human soul. The notion of trusting in God in the face of substantial adversity was rarely mentioned.

In a publication on the constitutionality of lockdowns in Canada, it was argued that in-person church attendance was viewed as a super-spreader event. And yet, in one locational analysis "[i]n British Columbia, [merely] 48 places of worship were affected by COVID-19 between 15 March 2020 and 15 January 2021, with 180 associated COVID-19 cases."[672] This means that each church on average had less than 4 cases of COVID-19 over a period of 9 months; hence, it is unclear how attending religious service could be classified as a super-spreader event. While the information provided does not state if there were any deaths related to these churches, a runny nose, which could also result in a positive COVID-19 test, does not provide confirmation of a super-spreader event. It is evident, however, that the closure of churches was based on theoretical "predicted infections" without sufficient, or any, empirical justification and evidence-based analysis.[673]

However, none of these seemingly plausible reasons noted above can be supported by the evidence. Firstly, SARS-CoV-2 did not discriminate against religious and non-religious gatherings that exhibited the same physical circumstances, conditions, and characteristics. There was no scientific evidence to confirm that religious gatherings somehow resulted in excess levels of viral transmission that could be classified as super-spreader events, and it proved difficult to come across any reporting that a religious gathering resulted in COVID-related deaths. Secondly, and as discussed further below, research confirms that regular participation in religious practices and the maintenance of active communal prayer can serve as an effective protection against various human challenges, mental health issues, and other life difficulties. Active faith proved particularly important during the time of the pandemic and subsequent COVID-19 response, as research clearly verified that religious people experienced higher levels of happiness and lower levels of stress during the pandemic and COVID-19 response in comparison to secular people.[674] Hence, religiosity cushioned the difficulties related to COVID-19 response.[675] Thirdly, regarding the restrictions, Portland Archbishop Alexander Sample observed that "it seems strange to us ... no one has a constitutional right to go to a restaurant, a bar or a gym. But there is a right to the free exercise of religion."[676] The director of communications for the Portland Diocese further noted the inconsistency with which restrictions were applied, stating that "it's really frustrating since all 141 Catholic churches in Maine have followed the protocols set forth by the state and have had zero outbreaks or cases stemming from the Mass."[677] Lastly, religious liberties, the freedom to seek God in the way that He calls people to do, and religious practices, are constitutionally protected in the vast majority of countries around the globe.

There were also issues related to basic human dignity, personal autonomy, and respect, especially related to the treatment of the elderly and those living in long-term care facilities. In many cases, under severe hospital restrictions "heartbreaking stories emerged of many who died alone, without either family or sacred religious rituals in their final hours."[678] Did anyone ask the elderly what they wanted? Were the elderly consulted as to whether they approved of not seeing, holding, and hugging their children for a brief period? Did anyone check if they would prefer to risk their lives in return for living fulsomely, regularly meeting with family members, and receiving emotional support? Did they agree to the cancellation of religious services, sacramental practices, and communal prayer at their long-term facility?

It is evident that human dignity is lost "when people are treated as nothing more than possible conduits of viral infection from a contagious disease."[679] When violations of basic human rights are profound and freedoms are taken away, individuals may be placed on an accelerated path to disenfranchisement or even enslavement.

Lastly, there may be questions to political leaders, politicians, and unelected health officers in relation to their views on religious practices. What were some of the other reasons that they may have insisted on closing places of worship? Why did they not regard religion and religious practices as essential services? It is difficult to guess, although one can think of several reasons. One possible answer may be that many politicians did not appreciate the importance of religiosity to people of faith. It is possible that, even if the decision makers claimed to be from specific religious backgrounds, there was a lack of appreciation of the nature of religious life and practices.[680] If they did not believe in God themselves, it is conceivable that they did not consider public worship of God to be important. Many potentially overlooked the benefits of religion on mental health during a time of crisis.

Moreover, some perhaps did not appreciate the nature of religious practices across different religions. For example, religious practices such as the Holy Eucharist, Baptism, and the Anointing of the Sick, and penitentiary services could not be done online or by telephone and were thus effectively suspended. One's physical presence at religious services is a key aspect for many religious denominations. Archbishop Sample expressed this sentiment in 2020 by stating that "we are a sacramental church … We need to have physical presence to the mysteries, to hold communion, the centrepiece of the life of a Catholic, the mass, to physically be present."[681]

Another reason for this political decision could have been that politicians responded to demands from their local constituents out of fear of attacks and pressures by the media. It is also conceivable that decision makers also had limited tolerance and appreciation of religious freedoms, constitutional protections, and human rights; it may be that they simply did not care. Politicians and public health officers perhaps wanted to signal to the public that liquor and cannabis stores, restaurants, casinos, and other such venues were more important than faith and religious services. Another possibility is that the unjustified and unprecedented lockdowns were preparation for the acceptance of mass vaccination to regain one's freedom.

The consequences of COVID-19 response on religiosity

Different religions were affected in alternate ways by COVID-19 response due to the nature of religious practices and the variable extent of required in-person attendance. Research confirms that Catholics and Muslims experienced the greatest disruption by COVID-19 response because they rely on "weekly communal attendance" and engagement in regular religious practices.[682] In Catholicism, as mentioned previously, Catholics engage in several essential in-person celebration of the Sacraments, such as Baptism, Confirmation, the Holy Eucharist, the Anointing of the Sick, Penance, and Holy Matrimony. It is also pertinent that the Catholic clergy participate in in-person Holy Orders. Importantly, these constitute the seven sacraments in the Catholic Church, and each play a vital, in-person role within Catholic spiritual life. These sacraments are also practiced in the Orthodox Church.

In particular, the Sacraments of Penance and Holy Eucharist are critical for faithful Catholics. This is because "Catholics believe that the Holy Eucharist is the Body, Blood, Soul and Divinity of Jesus Christ, really, truly, and substantially present, united in His one Divine Person (*Catechism of the Catholic Church*, 1993)." [683] According to the *Catechism of the Catholic Church* (#1324), "in the blessed Eucharist is contained the whole spiritual good of the Church, namely Christ himself, our Pasch."[684] The *Catechism* also notes that "the Eucharist is the memorial of Christ's Passover, the making present and the sacramental offering of his unique sacrifice, in the liturgy of the Church which is his Body" (#1362).[685] Importantly, Budeav has observed that "from approximately IX century [onward], reverently receiving the Holy Eucharist while kneeling and on the tongue has been the only allowed practice."[686]

However, the practice of receiving the Holy Eucharist has changed over the years, and especially in modern times. For example, in May 1969 the Congregation for Divine Worship issued the "Memoriale Domini, the Instruction on the Manner of Administering Holy Communion"[687] wherein the "Holy See gave bishops permission to distribute Holy Communion in the hand but said that the conventional way of receiving on the tongue must be retained."[688] In other words, Communion on the hand was allowed in certain parts of the world because permission was granted by the Holy See, although it was subject to several conditions. The document does issue warnings about certain vulnerabilities, which may include "a lessening of reverence toward the noble Sacrament of the altar, its profanation, or the adulteration of correct doctrine."[689] Thus, receiving Holy Eucharist on the tongue has been, and continues to be, practiced "not only because it rests upon a tradition of many centuries but especially because it is a sign of the reverence of the faithful toward the Eucharist."[690]

In more recent times, according to the General Instruction of the Roman Missal (GIRM) published in 2008, the communicant "receives the Sacrament either on the tongue or, where this is allowed, in the hand, the choice lying with the communicant" (paragraph #161).[691] In spite of these changes, receiving Communion on the tongue is still the universal norm in the Catholic Church while Communion on hand, even though it has become widespread in some parts of the world, is not. Catholics continue to practice receiving the Blessed Eucharist on the tongue in accordance with the Church's long-lasting practices and traditions. A recent survey of Catholics in the United States conducted by Real Presence Coalition has even concluded that receiving the Holy Eucharist in the hand while standing was the most significant concern potentially contributing to a loss of faith in the Real Presence of Jesus Christ in the Holy Eucharist.[692]

The act of receiving the Holy Eucharist itself created considerable tensions and debate among Catholics and the clergy during the pandemic even though in the past "no evidence for transmission of any infectious disease has ever been documented."[693] Fear of contagion of COVID-19 was quoted as one reason to receive communion into the hand, although many Catholics rejected this suggestion and continued to receive the Holy Eucharist on the tongue.

Muslims, on the other hand, also require congregational prayer for men in the mosque (i.e., Sacred Friday Prayers, Ramadan night prayer). There are also communal obligations as part of strict religious observance, as well as the expectation of pilgrimages to the Holy Cities of Mecca and Medina. On another note, in Judaism, some prayers cannot be said if a minimum of 10 people are not present.

What were the key consequences of the unjustified government non-medical COVID-19 measures? Firstly, research confirms that in-person participation in religious services declined sharply. In the U.S., as found by Pew Research, in-person participation in religious practices across various religions declined to about 13 percent in July 2020 but grew steadily to around 28 percent by November 2022.[694] When restrictions subsided people did return to in-person services, which is evidenced by a declining participation in online or TV-based services. According to research, the most active and dedicated returnees to in-person religious practices were Jews and Catholics between the ages of 30 and 49. However, about 40 percent of individuals polled maintained their participation in religious services, whether online or in-person, during the same time period (between July 2020 and November 2022). The most significant decline in attendance was experienced among Protestants (a 7 percent decline from 53 to 46 percent), and especially Black Protestants. Poland similarly saw a decline in participation in religious practices, which fell from 31.2 percent pre-pandemic to about 11.9 percent early in the pandemic.[695]

There is also strong evidence confirming that church closures negatively affected parishioners' mental health. For example, Protestants had a higher chance of depression compared to other religious groups.[696] Additionally, over 60 percent of surveyed Catholics in the U.K. confirmed that their mental health was negatively affected by the church closures that lasted from March 2020 to July 2021.[697] These closures were often not supported by parishioners and were vocally and actively resisted by local clergy.[698] Also, "Catholic media sources and spokespersons described church closures as unjust."[699] As a result of their experiences, approximately 90 percent of Catholics sought to classify public worship as essential in any future pandemics.[700]

Considering COVID-19 response, church closures, and other associated restrictions, from evidence, it has been suggested that individuals' behavioural, spiritual, and emotional connection to local churches and religious communities was significantly undermined, which may have lasting effects.[701] This disconnection can most profoundly affect those whose religious ties to their house of worship was already strained or who did not engage in religious practices regularly. In some situations, the pandemic and COVID-19 response perhaps pushed individuals away from the church. Additionally, many religious people were disappointed with their religious leaders' support of closing churches and withdrawing religious services. Instead of re-assurance, consolation, empathy, and encouragement, they saw closed churches and cancelled religious services during the time of the most significant, profound, and worrisome event in their lives. As suggested by one survey respondent from Australia and in reference to the Catholic Church:

> I think it is a real shame that the Church hierarchy have kowtowed so much to the authorities in closing churches, stopping the sacraments and even refusing sometimes to give sacraments to the dying during this pandemic. Look at what brave Christians have done throughout the centuries to bring Christ to people–against all odds.[702]

On the other hand, there are also multiple examples of the local clergy and Catholic Church leadership offering Mass, administering the Holy Eucharist, and fighting against unjustified restrictions. Even in the first months of the pandemic, as evidence by research from different countries confirms, "a majority of priests (59%) continued the celebration only in presence, whether with a limited number of faithful (36%), alone without a public (21%) or with the usual faithful attendance (2%)."[703]

Of course, this section would not be complete without a reflection of the name calling that accompanied religious observance during the pandemic. Such name calling was levied against religious people who defied public orders, vocally opposed COVID-19 response restrictions, and desired to worship God in-person. For instance, in Canada, the actions of these Christians were described as a "tiny minority [who] make it appear that all Christians are selfish, self-righteous, anti-science, and don't care about others."[704]

And yet, despite these hardships, there are also some positives that arose because of COVID-19 response. Firstly, many religious people have returned to their faith since the onset of the pandemic and have even devoted more time to individual prayer and religious practices.[705] In other words, they may have experienced a moment of religious conversion or re-awakening. For example, more than 20 percent of Polish Catholics admitted to spending more time on religious life because of the pandemic, while over 43 percent confirmed that their religiosity and faith remained unshaken by the pandemic and COVID-19 response. Secondly, it appears that religious commitment post-COVID-19 response was correlated with religious vigour and dedication in pre-pandemic times. Thus, if religious people were devout prior to the pandemic, they became even more committed to their faith post-COVID-19 response, meaning that the pandemic and resulting events strengthened their faith. Lastly, research indicates some religious people are now more appreciative of their family, experience greater thankfulness, spend more time thinking about faith, feel closer to God and see His presence in their life, and value going to Mass.[706]

The impact of COVID-19 response on religious clergy

COVID-19 response also affected the physical and mental wellbeing of religious leaders. This part of the chapter will focus on the impact of COVID-19 response on Catholic priests and Protestant pastors as there was less research coverage of other religions, although it perhaps may be conjectured that pastors, clergy, and religious leaders from other denominations and religions were impacted in a similar manner.

Research confirms that the Catholic clergy and ministerial staff suffered from similar mental health afflictions to those that impacted the general population, including stress, anxiety, fear, depression, and loneliness.[707] In this case, their mental struggles were associated with the fact that they were not able to fulfil their pastoral duties, which normally includes holding Mass for the public, connecting with parishioners in a meaningful manner through spiritual guidance, ministering to the sick, and so on.[708] Interestingly, older priests appeared to suffer less than their younger counterparts under COVID-19 response.[709]

The most brutal manifestation of political power against religion was exhibited when Christian pastors in Alberta, such as James Coates (GraceLife Church near Edmonton) and Tim Stephens (Fairview Baptist Church in Calgary), were jailed for alleged violations of COVID-19 restrictions. Pastor Artur Pawlowski (Street Church in Calgary) was also repeatedly jailed. There are also numerous other examples of the persecution of pastors around Canada, including, to name just a few, Phillip Hutchings (His Tabernacle Family Church in New Brunswick), Aaron Rock (Harvest Bible Church in Ontario), Jacob Reaume (Trinity Bible Chapel in Ontario), and Stephen Richardson (Faith Presbyterian Church in Ontario).[710] These pastors were not only physically and mentally abused, but they also faced significant fines that could financially ruin them and their churches. These persecutions extended outside of Canada and were seen in the U.S. and around the world. This type of crackdown on religion leaders was unprecedented in the modern history of Western countries.

COVID-19 response and financial impact on churches

Churches were also affected in terms of increased financial challenges, as lockdowns resulted in fewer cash collections and financial contributions from parishioners, especially in cases when collections were only held during Sunday liturgy.[711] Research indicated a meaningful decline in collections early in the pandemic, with some Catholic churches, for example, seeing a decrease in collection revenue in excess of 10 percent.[712] Since some parishes were already experiencing financial difficulties pre-pandemic, it is conceivable that as a result of COVID-19 response, they could be facing bankruptcy and insolvency issues, forced to sell off church assets or lay off staff, or even close parishes and consolidate geographic coverage.[713] For example, initial research from the U.S. among Catholics indicates a decrease in weekly donations and corresponding increase in the number of people not making financial contributions.[714] Fortunately, it appears that collections are quickly returning to pre-pandemic levels.[715]

Online religiosity and the church

One of the most profound changes to religious practices during COVID-19 response was a rapid shift from in-person to non-in-person forms of worship. In some denominations, online, virtual, TV, and radio interaction with the faithful has been known and practiced for years. For example, online preachers and evangelists have built megachurches on the back of television ministries.[716] Catholics around the world have also relied on various television channels, radio stations, and online programming. Perhaps the best-known Catholic program, called *Life is Worth Living,* was hosted by Bishop Foulton Sheen and aired in the 1950s. It had a weekly audience of millions of Americans and even won an Emmy Award in 1953.

Various forms of digital worship can be seen as an expansion of existing religious practices, stretching the geographic reach of churches, and even increasing "attendance" or the presence of parishioners during worship. However, some parishioners are choosing to watch services at their convenience, rather than watching in real time when religious services are held. Some churches quickly adopted these online methods, as "up to 90 percent of Anglican churches were now doing online services" in Canada, while others were more sceptical.[717] In the latter case, for example, Archbishop of Winnipeg asserted that he thinks "technology will always be secondary to the face-to-face aspect of gathering together as a spiritual community."[718] Despite a history of digital engagement, the Catholic Church may not regard virtual forms of worship "as an effective substitute for face-to-face ritual contact."[719] Furthermore, the clergy prefer to verbally communicate with parishioners in-person.

However, the trend of online worship delivery seemed to grow in popularity for some congregations as a result of COVID-restrictions due to a combination of fear of contagion, convenience, and perhaps other reasons.[720] In the words of Neil Elliot from the Anglican Church of Canada, "God is giving us an unprecedented opportunity to change."[721] And yet, this form of worship carries significant disadvantages, and is even impossible for some religions like Catholicism due to the in-person requirements for sacraments.[722] In the first case, offering online services changes the relationship between parishioners and the church. It may even negatively affect the relationship between believers and God, especially for those whose physical presence in the church or place of worship is required. Secondly, as evidence suggests, many parishioners did not return to in-person worship but instead decided to rely on digital worship or a hybrid approach.[723] It is worrisome that online participation in worship may have contributed to weakening the connection between parishioners and their place of worship. For example, research from mid-2022 indicates that "only six in 10 previous weekly Mass-goers expect to be back to 'full time' in-person Mass attendance this summer."[724] The same research indicates that these Catholics have become accustomed to not going to church over the pandemic. However, many Catholics also find that substituting online participation in worship for the real experience was unsatisfactory.[725] It is unclear now whether COVID-19 response restrictions were severe and long enough to permanently break the regular patterns of religious practice and worship among religious people.

The legal struggle for religious freedom

The government imposed COVID-19 response appears to have interfered with the basic freedoms of religion, conscience, peaceful assembly, association, and liberty. The state and unelected public health officers prohibited people from acting in accordance with their religious beliefs, standards, and practices. In essence, the COVID restrictions interfered with people's ability to search for and worship God. These negative conditions led churches to file lawsuits claiming that state-led restrictions violated their religious rights; brief examples of such proceedings are described below.

COVID-19 response and its associated restrictions arguably represented the most unprecedented infringements upon civil liberties and human rights ever known. The state appears to have violated the rights to worship, practice religious beliefs, and freely assemble in the name of public safety. Churches experienced the brunt of this discrimination due to the length and severity of the restrictions placed upon them. For example, in-person church attendance was limited to a small number of parishioners, in some cases only 10, 25 or 50 attendees, regardless of the church's capacity. Simultaneously, non-religious venues (i.e., restaurants, casinos, libraries, shopping centres, etc.) were allowed up to 50 percent capacity and had fewer restrictions. Of course, there were limited restrictions for businesses and other venues that were deemed 'essential'. As it was described in one U.S. lawsuit:

> If the Archdiocese were to fill its churches with library books, washing machines, exercise bikes, restaurant tables, or shopping stalls instead of pews, the District would allow many more people to enter and remain for an unlimited amount of time … That is because for public libraries, laundromats, retail stores, restaurants, tattoo parlors, nail salons, fitness centers, and many other establishments, the District imposes capacity-based limits, rather than hard caps. For example, there is no hard cap on the number of people who can dine indoors in restaurants, where alcohol is commonly served, and patrons do not wear masks during meals.[726]

The government's behaviour in Canada was no different, as summarized by the Justice Center of Constitutional Freedom (JCCF) in its appeal to the Supreme Court of Canada:

> Through public health orders, Manitoba had closed churches while permitting businesses to continue to operate. Taxis, in-person

university classes, film and tv productions, law offices, and liquor stores were allowed to remain open. The Winnipeg Jets could meet and train indoors with their extended crew, and summer Olympic competitors were allowed to train indoors.[727]

Courts reluctantly engaged in considerations of the impact of state-led restrictions upon church activities. The following is an example from the Canadian judicial system based on the cases of *Ingram v Alberta* (2023, ABKB 453), *Gateway Bible Baptist Church et al v Manitoba et al* (2023, MBCA 56), and other legal disputes.[728] In the first instance, the Alberta court appears to have pled ignorance about the issues related to science, epidemiology, biology, and medicine. The court admitted that they did not want to engage in these areas and chose to simply follow the recommendations of local government, public health officials, and independent experts. The court blindly followed the opinions of public health authorities, giving limited weight to alternative opinions. This of course seems counterintuitive, since the court's task should be to resolve a case based on evidence. In abrogating this responsibility, it may be argued that judges wrongly used the notion of "judicial notice" to accept the state's assessment of COVID-19 and the lockdowns that plaintiffs questioned. Put simply, the courts did not implement appropriate checks and balances to counteract the state's overreach. It is also worrisome that the court argued that the government did not have to be held to a particular standard of scientific certainty and could make their own choice regarding its relevant standard, which effectively established a low quality of proof guiding its judgment as well as the behaviour of the government.

In terms of specific restrictions against churches, the court argued that the authorities never banned religious services and that alternative methods of religious expression were available to parishioners. Additionally, it was the court's opinion that restrictions had only an "incidental effect" rather than causing full-blown content-based restraints, arguing that individuals were merely prevented from attending church in their preferred or desired manner. Most significantly, the Alberta and Manitoba courts confirmed that violations of freedom of conscience and religion had occurred but argued that these restrictions were justified under Section 1 of the *Canadian Charter of Rights and Freedoms*. For example, in the case of *Ingram v Alberta*, the court ruling confirmed that "lockdowns did violate Albertan's fundamental freedoms of conscience, religion, association, and peaceful assembly protected in the *Canadian Charter of Rights and Freedoms*."[729] Furthermore, it was confirmed that these violations occurred without proper cost/benefit analysis or justification, and the case confirmed that "the Alberta government produced no comprehensive studies, reports or data analysing lockdown harms."[730] And yet, despite these acknowledgements, the judge "nevertheless concluded that lockdowns were justified violations of Charter freedoms because they produce more good than harm."[731] How could this be determined if no proper analysis was conducted? There was other worrisome behaviour exhibited in this court case, such as the court's exclusion of a study on the ineffectiveness of lockdowns from consideration, arguing that the study would somehow include the benefit of hindsight for contemplation. The court also excluded the testimony of Brian Peckford, a living signatory to the *Canadian Charter*.

In other legal cases involving the infringement of COVID-19 response on religious matters, it is not difficult to conjecture that the courts may have delayed reviewing these cases until restrictions, lockdowns, and other constraints were lifted for the purpose of stating that the consideration of these legal issues was "moot" since restrictions were already lifted and allegedly "no longer impacted the applicants' rights."[732] However, as it was argued, "one of the biggest, most important facts that was overlooked by Manitoba Court of Appeal in their written decision was that movie sets were allowed to be open while churches had to be closed;"[733] never mind the Walmart, liquor stores, cannabis stores, and other venues that remained open.

Religiosity and the requirement for the COVID-19 vaccine

There is also the matter of COVID-19 vaccine requirements and their impact on religiosity. For example, research indicates a significant degree of conflict in Catholic families in this area. Nearly 50 percent of Catholic families, as indicated by survey responses, had differing perspectives on COVID-19 or its vaccines, which led to family disagreements, with about a quarter leading to moderate or significant degrees of conflict.[734] Just as COVID-19, COVID-19 response restrictions, and the vaccine contributed to division within families, workplaces, friendship circles, and other relationships, so too did it affect religion, churches, and parishioners. Research from the U.S. indicates that 39 percent of church attendees were encouraged to receive the COVID-19 vaccine, with the highest percent rates reported by Catholics (42 percent).[735] In Canada, however, there was no uniform policy regarding COVID-19 vaccines in the Catholic Church. Most Catholic parishes did not require vaccination to attend Mass, but there were also some exceptions. One notable outlier was Bishop Robert Anthony Daniels of Grand Falls in Newfoundland, who required proof of vaccination to enter his church.[736] Similarly, Protestant denominations allowed local churches to decide on their own vaccination policies with respect to parishioners, clergy, and staff.

The Catholic Church and the COVID-19 vaccination

Catholic pastors have reflected upon state-induced restrictions from the Catholic point of view, which, in the U.S. for example, manifested in the form of official notes, letters, and documents from the Colorado Catholic Conference, Wisconsin Catholic Conference (signed by five Bishops and Archbishops)[737], and the Diocese of Tyler. In its note titled the "Statement of the Catholic Bishops of Wisconsin on COVID-19 vaccination and the protection of conscience," the Wisconsin Catholic Conference confirmed that in relation to the question of whether "the Church or any other organization [should] force a person to receive the COVID-19 vaccination," their answer succinctly stated that "nobody should violate the sanctity of conscience by forcing a person to do something contrary to his or her conscience."[738] The Conference further clarified that "someone who in conscience decides that he or she should not receive the COVID-19 vaccine should be granted an exemption based on his or her beliefs or convictions."[739] At the same time, in the absence of the COVID-19 vaccine injection, the conference recommended other means of avoiding or potentially spreading infection through social distancing, hand sanitizing, and periodic testing. The Colorado Catholic Conference stated in its letter that "there is no Church law or rule that obligates a Catholic to receive a vaccine—including COVID-19 vaccines."[740] Moreover, the Bishop in the Diocese of Tyler observed that "Christians are called to form their consciences in accordance with what is true as revealed in natural law and divine revelation and to act accordingly when deciding about the use of a COVID-19 vaccine."[741] These statements confirmed the voluntary nature of the COVID-19 vaccination and the right of an individual to rely on his or her properly formed conscience in their decision to receive it. In fact, the Colorado Catholic Conference said that "[v]accination is not morally obligatory and so must be voluntary."[742]

Some Catholic leaders in Canada also expressed significant concerns about the COVID-19 vaccine mandates. For example, the Bishop of Saskatoon noted that "vaccine mandates of the general population are becoming severe and perhaps ethically questionable in our current circumstances."[743] The Archbishop of Ottawa-Cornwall, who was generally more positive about the COVID-19 vaccination, unequivocally stated that "I will not force anyone to receive the vaccine if they are not willing."[744] The Bishop of Calgary also confirmed the relevance of "conscientious objection" in the context of COVID-19 vaccination mandates and requirements by stating that "there must also be on the part of legitimate authorities, the necessary provisions of reasonable accommodation which respects and promotes the dignity of the individual conscience and the decision of conscientious objection."[745] The Bishop similarly underlined the importance of religious conscience in personal decision-making. The Bishop also stated that "those who choose not to be vaccinated for whatever reason must do their utmost to ensure that they take all precautionary measures possible to avoid places and circumstances where they and others would be most vulnerable."[746]

Another reference to the freedom of conscience and the voluntary nature of COVID-19 vaccine injection was provided in the "Note on the morality of using some anti-COVID-19 vaccines" (dated December 20, 2020, paragraph #5), which was issued by the Catholic Church's Congregation for the Doctrine of Faith (CDF).[747] As the Congregation is one of the oldest congregations of the Holy Office in the Vatican responsible for defending and protecting Catholic religious teachings, their statement was a guiding authority on this matter. Therefore, the document issued by the CDF was the most authoritative document of the Catholic Church on the COVID-19 vaccines and was approved by Pope Francis. While the Congregation outlined that "the common good may recommend vaccination, especially to protect the weakest and most exposed", the note also underlined that "practical reason makes evident that vaccination is not, as a rule, a moral obligation and that, therefore, it must be voluntary."[748] Significantly, this official statement from the Catholic Church's CDF did not outline any requirements, mandates, or force that could or should coerce Catholics to receive the COVID-19 vaccine injection.

As noted in chapter 1, the COVID-19 vaccines were experimental and investigational since their long-term effects were not known or were poorly understood. In many countries, the vaccines were implemented with only interim approval. In this respect, the *Catechism of the Catholic Church* (#2295) specifically notes that "experimentation on human beings is not morally legitimate if it exposes the subject's life or physical and psychological integrity to disproportionate or avoidable risks. Experimentation on human beings does not conform to the dignity of the person if it takes place without informed consent of the subject or those who legitimately speak for him."[749] Interestingly, this quote from the *Catechism* comes from the article on the Fifth Commandment, "You Shall Not Kill."

It is also worthwhile to examine the words of Pope Francis, whose appeals in mainstream media for Catholics to receive COVID-19 vaccinations were framed as "acts of love."[750] The key context surrounding Pope Francis' appeals that the mainstream and social media missed or simply ignored is that his statements were offered when he was not speaking *ex cathedra* (i.e., not as the official magisterium of the Catholic Church). In this context, the Pope's remarks may be interpreted as personal opinions, viewpoints, judgements, or expressions and thus may be viewed as advice or reference (i.e., something to consider) to a person trying to decide within his or her conscience if they should receive the COVID-19 vaccine. Notably, his remarks were inconsistent with the CDF's authoritative document on COVID-19 vaccines. It is also important to state that, as reported by the mainstream media, there were other Cardinals in the College of Cardinals (i.e., an official senior body of the Catholic Church) who did not consent to the COVID-19 vaccine injection.

The principle of love, which was drawn upon by Pope Francis, is eternally important and applicable (particularly in times of crisis) within the Church, the family, workplaces, etc. First and foremost, love must be expressed to God, and then to one's neighbour. While love of God is primary and there are many means of manifesting love of and to God, there are equally as many ways to freely express love of one's neighbour; these may include acts of kindness, prayer, financial assistance, emotional support, loving gestures, and other behaviours. When a person chose not to consent to the COVID-19 vaccine injection, the Church recommended other measures to protect one's neighbour (as outlined above in the note from the Wisconsin Catholic Conference).

Douglas Farrow, a professor of theology and ethics, also reminds that "as Aquinas insists, 'that a man should not give way to his neighbour in evil, but only in good things, even as he ought to gratify his will in good things alone, so that his love for his neighbour may be a righteous one'."[751] Farrow also draws upon the words of Augustine, who said "'it is not kindness to cooperate in the loss of a greater good, nor blameless to acquiesce and to permit a slide into greater evil'."[752]

When reflecting on the conduct of many churches in the West during the pandemic, Farrow has concluded that:

> In short, many churches in the West have failed their spiritual covid test. They carried a high viral load of fear–fear of sickness, fear of man, fear of death–and displayed low levels of spiritual antibodies. The gospel of freedom from fear was rarely preached in a way that challenged secular powers or popular sentiment.[753]

Farrow further observed that this failure stems from a combination of reasons, including "a lack of spiritual alertness", the "corporate grooming" of churches, some clergy being "more solicitous of the para-liturgies of masking and hand sanitization than of the divine liturgy itself", and "the failure of many Christians to resist the spirit of fear", among others.[754] Farrow forewarns that "only when the diabolic drive to suppress both human and ecclesial fecundity is clearly identified will we understand what we are up against in the contests that has overtaken us."[755] He also cautions that "our elites' colours are showing clearly, as is their admiration for socialism with Chinese characteristics."[756]

6

COVID-19 response and the assault on small business

The unprecedented assault on small businesses was inflicted by COVID-19 response, lockstep actions of various levels of government (i.e., municipal, local, and federal), unelected public health officers, law enforcement, and others. It is perhaps true that small business owners would have not voluntarily closed their businesses for a long period of time because they implicitly understood that it would lead to catastrophic financial and operational problems such as insolvencies, bankruptcies, and even outright ruin. Owners instinctively recognized that closing their business would mean the destruction of what, in many cases, they worked for their entire lives to achieve, in only a matter of weeks or months.

So, why did small business owners not object to forced business closures, mass restrictions, lockdowns, and stay-at-home orders? This may have been for a combination of reasons, including being fearful of the coronavirus contagion (for themselves, family members, and especially the elderly), succumbing to broad mass panic and groupthink, or trying to do what they saw as the right thing or the broadly defined "public good." It is also possible that many small business owners were simply directed or even deceived into thinking that their business closures would only last for a two-week period to "flatten the curve." [757] Many of them believed that they could sustain themselves for this short-term closure and did not anticipate prolonged lockdowns.

Areas of impact on small business due to COVID-19 response

Small and medium size enterprises (SMEs) are critical to many national economies for four reasons. Firstly, they generate a significant proportion of private sector employment. In the United States (U.S.), for example, small firms (defined as those with less than 500 employees) account for about 50 percent of private sector jobs and around 45 percent of gross domestic product (GDP).[758] In Canada, SME businesses account for approximately 98 percent of all employer firms and 64 percent of the total labour force (9.7 million employees) while medium-sized firms alone employ 3.2 million individuals and account for about 21 percent of the labour force.[759] Secondly, small businesses are significant new job creators. For example, small firms in the U.S. have produced over 70 percent of new private sector jobs since 2019.[760] Thirdly, SMEs are responsible for innovation, invention, and creative new solutions and ideas, rather than large firms as it is generally believed.[761,762] Lastly, as noted by Richard Bliss from Babson College, SMEs also serve niche and local markets and communities, which are often not served by large corporations.[763]

COVID-19 response and associated restrictions affected both the supply and demand side for both SMEs and large businesses alike. On the supply side, there were many interruptions to global supply chains, the supply of labour, and production capabilities. Supply chain issues were particularly connected to China due to their more severe lockdowns and included high shipping costs, delays, and disruptions. On the other hand, the demand for goods was reduced due to high unemployment and increases in precarious employment (i.e., part-time and gig-jobs), the reduction of family incomes, and cash hoarding due to economic uncertainties, all of which resulted in low consumption. Other factors that may have contributed to the reduction in demand were restrictions on business hours, limited numbers of customers permitted inside establishments at any point in time, legal requirements to confirm one's vaccination status, and so on. These challenges also coincided with increases in sub-contracting and outsourcing.[764]

Public restrictions created significant turbulence to the SME sector specifically because "regulations were often a binding constraint for firms' operating decision."[765] As a business owner from Alberta in Canada notes, "I am going to lose my business if the restrictions in Alberta aren't lifted soon. As it is, I have accumulated over $90,000 in debt and that number keeps going up. It will take me years to pay it off."[766] Small firms were disproportionately affected by COVID-19 response due to weaker financial resources and standing (i.e., less cash, fewer liquid assets, limited opportunities to generate new revenue streams, restricted access to debt financing, less savings, etc.), limited operational resources (i.e., fewer staff, smaller network of contacts, reduced customer base, undeveloped supplier base, restricted expansion opportunities, etc.), and constrained strategic management considerations (i.e., limited access to expensive external advisors). Furthermore, different segments of the economy in which SMEs operate were affected by COVID-19 response to varying degrees. For example, small businesses operating in retail, hospitality, accommodations, food services, arts and entertainment, leisure, and recreation were severely affected.[767] Small firms that relied on personal, face-to-face interactions were undeniably hit the hardest.[768]

In contrast, the clear beneficiaries of COVID-19 response were big-box stores, social media firms, online shopping operators and platforms, and other large businesses. More sizeable ventures, larger corporations, and multinational firms had more cash on hand and short-term assets that could be easily liquidated, in addition to easier access to capital markets. Conversely, smaller firms with some debt faced stricter barriers when attempting to access finance.[769] Larger firms also have pricing power in their ability to pass price increases on to customers while price-taking sectors such as retail do not have this same pricing power in the marketplace. Similarly, large firms' higher levels of profit can be reduced or supressed for a considerable period without unduly threatening the firm's survival, operations, or financial standing. Furthermore, the attack on small firms through lockdowns, COVID-19 response, and their resulting restrictions was profitable for selected large corporations, which experienced a record level of online commerce.[770,771] The pandemic effectively redirected revenue from SMEs to these large firms,[772] thereby beginning the process of smaller entrepreneurial firms' elimination from the marketplace. In short, it was not too difficult to see that the "pandemic [could] threaten to deepen divide between big and small businesses"[773] since the SME sector was unprepared to withstand a "black swan" event when COVID-19 response was implemented.[774]

There were at least six major aspects of small firms that COVID-19 response directly or indirectly impacted, with the first being a severe decline in, or even complete loss of, revenue and massive dislocations in business operations.[775] Different studies indicate that between 50 and 85 percent of SMEs were affected by the pandemic, with about 45 percent of these impacted in a severe manner.[776] For example, a study by the Canadian Imperial Bank of Commerce (CIBC) found that 81 percent of Canadian small business firms were affected by the pandemic, while "the majority (85 percent) agree that uncertainty of how long COVID-19 measures will last is currently the hardest aspect to manage."[777] Firms from the SME sector not only had to deal with uncertainty regarding the future of their venture, but also with immediate cash flow issues. Research confirms that the level of operational and financial harm to the SME sector was proportional to the firm size defined in terms of revenue and number of employees. In other words, evidence is clear that large firms and major corporations were less impacted by COVID-19 response.[778] Revenue declined by about 50 percent for smaller firms and only about 30 percent for more sizeable ventures. These declines in revenue reflected smaller firms' inability to cover capital expenditures related to the establishment of and transition to online operations. For many small firms, revenues fell faster than their ability to reduce cost, resulting in cash flow challenges, which was compounded by poor access to new leads and trouble retaining customers.[779]

A second area in which small businesses were impacted was their inability to cover fixed financial obligations, including rent, loan payments, utilities, and other costs. They also struggled to pay the increasing costs associated with disruptions to supply chains (i.e., shipping costs). While many small firms initially aimed to maintain staffing levels, between 30 to 40 percent of small firms eventually resorted to layoffs, which often affected the youngest individuals (employees between 25 and 44 years old). There were also additional expenses related to COVID restrictions, such as plexiglass dividers, masks, sanitation accessories, stickers, and so on. Many small firms could not afford these unexpected and unbudgeted expenditures but were forced to make such purchases to keep their business open in an often-limited capacity. These restrictions changed with considerable short notice, thereby making medium- and long-time planning virtually impossible. As noted by a small business owner from Ontario, Canada, "the rotating lockdowns have hampered any ability to plan. We have a large winter stock that did not sell because we went into lockdown. Now we are trying to plan for summer with no money left and potentially entering another change to red status."[780]

The combination of both declining revenues and fixed obligations resulted in significant financial losses and cash flow issues for SMEs. Although cash flow was a perpetual issue for small businesses prior to COVID-19 response (i.e., small firms struggle in this area by definition), many firms struggled to achieve stability and repeatability of cash flow. Under normal circumstances, small business owners understand temporary cash flow interruptions and, barring unexpected circumstances, can manage liquidity issues. This adept management of cash flow is possible when entrepreneurs can rely on the relative stability of incoming revenue, even if their available cash resources can only cover a short period of time.

However, COVID-19 response eliminated this stability for SMEs. Research from the U.S. confirms that many small businesses only had cash resources equal to less than two months of expenses in the period following COVID-19 response. Under these abnormal COVID-19 response circumstances, entrepreneurs were forced to combat liquidity issues by selling inventory at reduced prices, disposing of some assets, reducing employee wages, cutting work hours, limiting planned capital expenditures, and engaging in other measures to extend cash runways (i.e., the amount of time the firms can rely on existing financial resources). Thus, small firms resorted to alternative tactics of desperation, including using personal savings, relying on credit cards, and remortgaging personal assets. Many business owners were forced to use personal savings to keep their business afloat, which had devastating psychological and financial impacts. In addition to these limited financial resources, small firms also had a truncated amount of time in which to strategize, plan, prepare, or develop any back-up plans in view of the quickly mandated public restrictions.

The next area of small firms impacted by COVID-19 response was the redefinition or destruction of existing business models and structures. While the concept of creative destruction is often romanticized in management literature, it can lead to the complete decimation of specific sectors of the economy, such as hospitality and the entertainment industries, to name a few. These segments of the economy were given weeks or even days to alter their modes of operation, which would normally take years to optimize and perfect. As previously noted, the severity and speed with which COVID-19 response measures were enacted left many entrepreneurial firms with no true opportunity to viably adjust their operations. In some cases, unanticipated changes to the business model resulted in firms catering to a different segment of the market and contending with new competitors, in addition to dealing with new customers' consumptions patterns, perceptions, choices, and preferences. Many firms were also forced to offer online business delivery even if they were not designed to operate in this manner. Due to their limited protections against external shocks, rapid revisions of existing business models became critical to the SME sector's prosperity. While their small size means that SMEs are normally flexible and agile, their capacity to respond in this case was thwarted by the speed and strictness of government restrictions. Although most firms attempted to adjust their operations, they lacked the financial, managerial, technological, and human resources necessary to effectively implement these drastic changes. For example, some small firms successfully shifted to other modes of business delivery (i.e., online ordering, curb-side pickup, and delivery) only to realize that the new business model they created overnight may not be financially sustainable even in the short-term. Thus, while these firms tried different creative tactics, they proved difficult to implement on a dime and with a small scale of business operations. At the same time, business experts and consultants promoted business solutions grounded in digitization (i.e., online ordering and delivery) as viable solutions to small business development and survival. Unfortunately, these solutions were only viable for larger and more established businesses that already had online platforms, could implement them quickly on short notice, and had a scale of operations large enough to be able to benefit from these recommendations. As one business owner from Ontario noted, "[our business is a] home decor small business, 4 years old. Eclectic one of a kind ... [We] created a reputation of very unique shopping experience and destination. [We] pivoted many times during the last year ... created an online store but the business model was always one of the customer experience while in the store."[781]

COVID-19 response also changed patterns of value creation for entrepreneurial firms across different phases of development (i.e., value uncertainty, progression, perpetuation, and realization). In the past, small firms were able to embark on a systematic pattern of value creation that allowed for the proper development of solid management teams, the establishment of superb organizational structures, and a focus on a unique part of the market (i.e., market niche). While younger firms normally struggle with access to finance, small businesses were able to rely on "bootstrapping" techniques to finance their continual development and expansion. The stability of the external environment also allowed these firms to experiment with new products and services. As a result of COVID-19 response, however, the regular pattern of business development and value creation became choppier, zig-zag-like, and uncertain due to severe fluctuations in revenue, profitability, and cash flow. An increase in risk, additional state constraints, prolonged operational uncertainty, and sporadic access to finance similarly interrupted normal patterns of value creation and even led to value destruction. These factors culminated in high levels of stress, frustration, and anxiety for small business owners. In other words, entrepreneurship is difficult enough in stable economic and business environments but is much harder in unstable and ever-changing external environments created by unconsidered and kneejerk reactions by the state and its associated stakeholders.

Lastly, COVID-19 response fundamentally changed the dynamics of business survival among SMEs. Research indicates that in the U.S., for example, over 90 percent of newly formed ventures fail, with less than 50 percent surviving beyond the five-year mark. Furthermore, only about one-third of newly created entrepreneurial firms reach the ten-year mark, with merely 10 percent of small firms surviving in the long-term. The most common reasons for business failure are tied to small firms' inability to generate adequate levels of revenue, a weak and uncertain market demand, broad financial mismanagement, excessive costs, and poor access to finance. It is easy to see that, even when accounting for normal business failure, COVID-19 response amplified existing problems and even created new ones in many key areas. While the confirmation of survival statistics post-COVID-19 response will be studied in years to come, currently available data already points to major problems. To provide just one data point as an example, the Organization for Economic Co-operation and Development (OECD) estimated a 20 to 40 percent increase in small business insolvencies compared to pre-COVID-19 response. In the U.S., for instance, various estimates confirmed that there were between 500 and 1,500 business closures per day in the initial stages of COVID-19 response. In comparison, business closures in Canada averaged 1,300 per day between January and March of 2020.

Timing of events and the impact on the entrepreneurial sector

The assault on the SME sector did not come in one swoop, but in stages (see table 6.1). The first phase, which included lockdowns, stay-at-home orders, quarantines, and other restrictions, occurred immediately after the onset of the pandemic in March 2020 and lasted for a period of about 18 months. In the U.S., for example, about 50 percent of the population lived under stay-at-home orders or shelter-in-place restrictions. COVID-19 response resulted in major macroeconomic dislocations, resulting in high unemployment, a reduction in GDP growth, and so on. As described earlier, this in turn translated into significant operational problems for SMEs due to the fluctuating nature of business operations, limitations when accessing finance, and financial underperformance. During this time, many SMEs closed their doors either temporarily or permanently,[782] which was identified early by academics who forecasted that COVID-19 response restrictions would "shutter many small businesses and entrepreneurial ventures."[783] In this phase of the pandemic, businesses also faced many legal and legislative uncertainties.

The second phase of difficulty for the SME sector came within the period between 18 and 24 months after the onset of the pandemic. This relatively short period was filled with considerable uncertainty and anxiety. Due to the speed with which vaccination mandates were pushed by governments and unelected public health officers, economies began to open in the fall of 2021 while many restrictions continued until at least the spring of 2022, with mask, vaccine mandates, and testing requirements. Also, there was also a prevailing climate of uncertainty that restrictions could be brought back at any time. This uncertainty could have been just as harmful.

Table 6.1: Stages of impact of COVID-19 response on the SME sector

Areas of impact	Immediate impact (0 – 18 months)	Intermediate impact (18 – 24 months)	Longer term impact (> 24 months)
Events and timing	• Introduction of mass lockdowns, stay-at-homer orders, vaccination mandates, mask requirements, etc.	• State restrictions lifted in spring of 2022 • War in Ukraine began	• Conflict in Gaza started in October 2023
Macro-economic	• Significant drop in GDP • Mass layoffs • Deferral of consumption due to vast uncertainties • Massive increase in money supply and government spending • Disruptions of global supply chains • Rapid increase in official and unofficial business closures	• Acceleration of inflation • Rapid increases in interest rates • Recovery in GDP growth rates due to government spending • Decrease in private sector employment • Significant increase in energy costs for European firms	• Continuation of high interest rates and inflation rates • Slowdown in economic growth
Operations	• Operational challenges due to COVID-19 response restrictions • Adjustment to business model (i.e., digitization, curb-side delivery, etc.)	• Continued supply chain issues, but slowly being resolved • Problems with supply of labour • Elimination of certain products from offer due to high cost • Reduction of workers also meant transition to sub-contracting and outsourcing	• Continued problems with labour supply • Inability to automate and digitize business operations • Some workers prefer to work on remote basis, which prevents return to normal functions
Finance	• Decline or loss in revenue • Necessity to incur extra costs • Cash flow problems • Poor access to finance • Financial institution unwilling to extend credit	• Rapid inflation increases operational costs • Loss of customers due to rising costs and prices • Increase in pandemic debt	• Revenue levels return to pre-pandemic levels for many firms • Business unable to return government loans • Continuation with pandemic debt

At the same time, fears of coronavirus began to yield to fears of a war in Ukraine, especially within Europe. In the months to come, the war in Ukraine had a severe impact on the European SME sector. Throughout this period, SMEs generally continued to experience an acceleration in the pace of input cost, paired with slow consumer demand and some improvement to global supply chains. However, SMEs also began to recover revenue, reduce COVID-19 response costs, improve cash flow, and slowly normalize operations. Evidence from Canada, for example, confirms that in 2022 about 35 percent of small businesses returned to normal revenue.[784] Of these, only 11 percent were in the arts and recreation sector, 12 percent in hospitality, and 15 percent in personal services. At the same time, one in seven firms (or around 15 percent) were still contemplating shutting down, orderly winddown, or bankruptcy. In Canada, the average levels of pandemic debt were more than $150,000, with the highest levels noted in British Columbia at more than $220,000. This period also evidenced a shortage of labour, which in turn influenced wage growth.[785,786] There was also what came to be known as the "great resignation" or "the big quit", a mass exodus of employees caused by a combination of wage stagnation, increase in cost of living, poor opportunities for career advancement, excessive workloads, unrealistic expectations, and perhaps additional work pressures and frustrations related to COVID-19 response. This trend also coincided with the improvement of social assistance programs from the government.

The third stage resulted in different challenges for the SME sector even though they continued to normalize operations and return to more stable financial footings. For instance, inflation continued to increase during this period, albeit at a slower pace than previously, and labour shortages persisted. Interest rates also rose quickly and remained at elevated levels for a longer period, which negatively impacted existing debt levels and opportunities to raise additional financing. In Canada, for example, over 50 percent of small firms still carried "pandemic debt" equal to more than $100,000.[787,788] While some SMEs operations returned to normal levels, "many businesses continue[d] to feel the burden of years of subpar business conditions."[789] The key concerns continued to be rising prices and the overall cost of doing business.[790] When reflecting on the state of Canadian businesses, the chief economist at the Conference Board of Canada conceded to tell "a story that we've been a little concerned about, and that is essentially that we're seeing a very tough economic climate for a lot of businesses."[791]

The inability for SMEs to repay "pandemic debt", including loans from the state, is the true reflection of their ongoing financial challenges. In Canada, for example, more than 10 percent of SMEs perceive their debt "as heavy and threatening their long-term viability."[792] Put simply, "many businesses are already on a razor's edge. The additional costs to service their debts will mean even less room to cover increasing costs of business going into 2024."[793] It is estimated that some 900,000 of Canada's small firms and non-profit institutions received financial assistance of up to $60,000 from the Canada Emergency Business Account (CEBA), which dispersed about $50 billion in total. Of these firms, nearly 21 percent of Canadian SMEs took up to $40,000 while 68 percent of firms took up to $60,000.[794] All in all, about 90 percent of Canadian SMEs accessed the CEBA program.

Small firms in Canada have continued to struggle with debt repayment even though the deadline for repayment was already pushed back to the end of 2023. Surveys suggested that approximately 72 percent of firms that obtained CEBA loans desired their payments to be further deferred, claiming that this would significantly increase survival chances; of these, 30 percent sought a deferral of one year and 42 percent wanted up to two years.[795] As of June 2023, only about 10 percent of firms had repaid these loans, with an additional 47 percent intending to pay by the deadline in order to claim the forgivable portion (33 percent or up to $20,000), even though they still faced significant operational and financial challenges. There is evidence that some of these small firms paid off their CEBA loans by borrowing elsewhere. The remaining 43 percent (i.e., about 250,000 SMEs in Canada) were unsure of making the deadline. About 60 percent of SMEs which were likely to miss the deadline also planned to borrow to repay. Thus, the repayment of loans became a significant source of financial burden for the SME sector because of COVID-19 response.

Mental health of business owners

Operating a small business is a stressful undertaking. The commitment to entrepreneurial ventures commonly involves workweeks more than 80 hours and is often accompanied by out-of-town travel and missing parental and spousal responsibilities, household commitments, and other familial duties. Constant cell phone usage, active mental problem solving, and constant decision making takes its toll on business owners over time. Therefore, chronic market, competitive, financial, and operating pressures can easily lead to bursts of stress, anxiety, and frustration. As noted above, small firms are very sensitive to business turbulence, which can translate into operational chaos and can in turn amplify levels of stress and anxiety, causing a perpetual circle of turbulence, chaos, and stress.[796] These emotional states often extend to business owners' personal lives by affecting their marriages and relationships with children, family members, and friends.

The consequences of COVID-19 response have been dire for entrepreneurs in terms of their mental health. For example, research confirms that about 45 percent of business owners in Canada experienced mental health challenges (which increased from 38 percent in 2022), with nearly a third contemplating seeking counselling (up from 21 percent in 2022).[797] As one business owner from Quebec reflected on the first year of the pandemic, "there was stress associated with guiding my staff with all the different measures, adjusting each time, and explaining everything to the customers. It is a year full of stress, continuous adjustment and uncertainty, combined."[798]

The key impacts of stress and anxiety include feeling tired, having low energy, or experiencing depression. Entrepreneurs also felt that these mental health challenges and manifestations of chronic stress and anxiety interfered with their ability to work and concentrate. The main sources of stress included inflation, improper work-life balance (due to working excess hours as a result of labour shortages or attempts to reduce labour cost), and financial challenges.[799] The culmination of both mental health and business issues also resulted in burnout.[800] These effects are perhaps no surprise since "tens of thousands of businesses were unable to open their doors for 430 days,"[801] which is well beyond the period of two weeks initially imposed by the state and unelected public health officials to "flatten the curve". These mental health challenges may only be getting worse and affect not only business owners but also their employees. As discussed in chapter 4, others also suffered from mental health issues, most notably children and adolescents.

There are no official statistics related to entrepreneurial suicide rates, but it has been suggested that small business owners are at twice the risk of suicide compared to the average person.[802] Entrepreneurs in the U.S., for example, likely account for a significant percentage of the 75,000 "deaths of despair" that occurred post-COVID-19 response.[803] There is also some evidence of the impact of COVID-19 response restrictions on suicide in India, which increased by 29.4 percent among small business owners, vendors, and tradesmen in 2020. Local economics professor Vibhuti Patel noted that these individuals "were self-made people who couldn't step out to earn their living. If they did, they were brutalized by the police."[804] As seen elsewhere, "any advantage was only to industrialists and the corporate world, leaving small shopkeepers with no option but suicide as they couldn't pay loans and rent."[805] Suicides also rose in 2021, but only by 2.9 percent. Some states in India, such as Karnataka, Maharashtra, and Madhya Pradesh, experienced a more than 10 percent growth rate in suicide. The key reasons "behind the suicide cases are bankruptcy and indebtedness."[806]

Amplification of small business risks by the state

Historically, small business owners have been cognizant of the risks inherent to their entrepreneurial journey and are often successful in devising some, albeit imperfect, protections and solutions against such risks. While some risks can be expected, such as facing more formidable competition, experiencing financial difficulties, or losing key accounts or personnel, entrepreneurs could count on a relatively stable external environment. Specifically, small business owners could rely on the stability of decisions made by political apparatuses, taxes, and business regulations in conjunction with their long-tested business model. All of this changed with COVID-19 response because the external environment for most business owners was severely disrupted. Under state restrictions, bans, and limitations, small business owners began to face a continuously unpredictable and evolving external environment driven by the state. During the pandemic, the state emerged as one of the most unstable components of the external environment for small businesses not only in the short-term but also over the medium-term (restrictions in Canada, for example, lasted from March of 2020 to around the spring of 2022).

It is becoming increasingly clear that governments, political leaders, and unelected public health officials enacted public policies and restrictions without proper consideration of the impact of their decisions on the entrepreneurial ecosystem. Political actions were taken without any cost-benefit analysis, an understanding of potential long-term economic and human consequences, or even basic and rational assessments of risk. There was also a failure to perform any independent verification of the initial model provided by Neil Ferguson from Imperial College, which led to the lockdown of entire countries.[807] However, Ferguson was no exception in providing inaccurate epidemic forecasting models that were taken at face value without appropriate vetting and verification, resulting in mass panic. It was already known by the fall of 2020 that "forecasting for COVID-19 has failed." [808] Furthermore, it is undeniable that this COVID-19 response enacted by federal, state, provincial, and municipal governments, and their associated public health officials, broke the back of entrepreneurialism.[809] In addition to basic restrictions, governments also ordered business closures based on essentiality (i.e., dividing businesses into essential and non-essential categories), which they pre-determined for their citizens.[810] For example, Public Safety Canada designated 10 sectors of the economy as essential, meaning members of these sectors could freely travel abroad and back. Most interestingly, the financial sector was among the ten pre-selected sectors, thereby allowing finance executives to travel back and forth.[811] The state effectively decided which products, goods, and services were essential for human beings' existence, survival, and prosperity. One inadvertent consequence of this division was the state's simultaneous determination of which firms were essential, and which were not. Of course, the demarcation between essential and non-essential businesses was also deeply flawed because various parts of the economy are inter-connected. In other words, it is unlikely that politicians and unelected public health officials understood that restrictions on some parts of the economy would have profound spillover effects. How did this delineation between essential and non-essential work in practice? While shopping in one store, an individual would be able to purchase groceries, milk, and flour, as these items were deemed by the state essential, but they would be unable to purchase a birthday card or bouquet of flowers, located only a few meters away, because these items were deemed non-essential. In another example, access to the underwear section remained open while shoe sections were closed. The multiplicity of such examples will not be listed here for the sake of brevity. Most important to note, however, is that these are prime examples of central planning of the economy.

It is also becoming clear that COVID-19 response not only affected existing business owners, but also the future generations of entrepreneurs. For example, evidence from Canada confirms that most individuals do not intend to start a business. This trend may be difficult to forecast, but people's negative propensity toward entrepreneurialism may be sustained in the long-term, thereby decimating entrepreneurial ecosystems in many countries. If this were to occur, it could prevent new business formation and entrepreneurial migration, thus hindering small firms from becoming larger firms, and medium-size firms from becoming even bigger.[812] This migratory pattern of entrepreneurial development, which has been one of the focal points of entrepreneurial ecosystem development, would be permanently dislocated. On the other hand, the trend seems to be reversed in the U.S. There has been a significant surge in new business applications since the onset of the pandemic in 2020 and they continue to be above the pre-pandemic levels. Reflecting on this surge in business formation as reflected in new business applications, Haltiwanger noted that "the pace of applications since mid-2020 is the highest on record (earliest data available is 2004). The large increase in applications is for both likely new employers and non-employers."[813] Haltiwanger also added that "dominant industries include non-store retail (alone accounting for 33% of the surge), professional, scientific and technical services,"[814] which may reflect individuals' desire for work-from-home and online employment settings. Moreover, the MetLife and U.S. Chamber of Commerce report growing optimism among U.S. small firms: over 70 percent of small firms expect revenue growth, but inflation remains their most significant challenge.[815] While new business formation is advantageous to the economy, it needs to be reiterated that self-employment may pay less and be less stable. Also, it is also unclear whether individuals started new businesses because of their desire to become entrepreneurs or due to their inability to secure stable employment. The actual personal motivation of entrepreneurs is important to the long-term survival and success of these newly created firms.

Lastly, governments around the world attempted to address some challenges of small businesses, but these remedies were often mistargeted and misguided. In fact, it is suspected as to whether these policies were even grounded in research and actual evidence. However, one can argue that state programs proved helpful in reducing the speed of bankruptcies by perhaps delaying the inevitable.

Oppression of entrepreneurs by the state

It appears that governments not only negatively affected entrepreneurialism, but they also actively persecuted entrepreneurs with the use of the police, law enforcement, the judicial system, and other means at their disposal. While one could cite examples of small business owners being oppressed and persecuted by the state in Canada and the U.S., this brief section describes the case of Chris Scott, owner of the Whistle Stop Café in the small town of Mirror in Alberta.

During the pandemic, Chris Scott chose to keep his business open, thereby disobeying the provincial government's orders and restrictions. He also spoke against public health orders at a peaceful rally outside of his restaurant at the time when the province banned both gatherings and in-person dining. Around this same time, Premier of Alberta was caught dining with some of his cabinet members without wearing masks on the balcony of the "Sky Palace" at the height of the pandemic, thereby violating his own government's provincial restrictions.[816] However, it was small business owner Scott who was charged with breaking public health regulations. Reflecting upon his experience with the local provincial government, Scott noted that he was

> forced to stand up to the might of the administrative state in the face of Alberta Health Services illegally seizing my business at gunpoint, dragging me away in handcuffs, throwing me in jail and padlocking the enterprise that feeds my family … I was assaulted, jailed and my liberty violated under the guise of phony Public Health Orders that had no business being issued in a free and democratic society … I was slandered, libelled, and defamed by Government propaganda, including having 'teachers' telling my child I was comparable to a Nazi.[817]

After two years of legal battles, Scott was acquitted of all charges in light of the *Ingram v Alberta* decision, which found that public orders were illegal because they breached Alberta's Public Health Act.[818] In short, public orders of the Public Health Officer were found to be *ultra vires* (in Latin, "beyond the powers", not lawfully authorized, outside of the law).[819] Similarly inspired by the *Ingram v Alberta* case, an Alberta law firm filed a class action lawsuit against the provincial government "on behalf of owners who faced operational restrictions due to, now deemed illegal, Public Health Orders."[820] John Carpay, president of the Justice Centre for Constitutional Freedom (JCCF), noted that "this is an important case about government actions and overreach during a time when owners were unlawfully mandated to close their businesses at a moment's notice."[821] Consequently, "the proposed class action lawsuit targets the financial losses for business in Alberta that were either fully or partially restricted due to the public health orders during the pandemic."[822] It is perhaps not surprising that there was a 70.5 percent rise in business bankruptcies in Alberta in 2022. However, Canada is no exception; similar behaviour of the state is also evident in other countries.

Impact of COVID-19 response in numbers

There are different measures of assessing businesses in trouble, with the main ones being business insolvencies and bankruptcies. Business insolvency is defined as the inability to pay debt as it comes due. Business bankruptcy, on the other hand, is a formal legal process where a debtor who is unable to pay their debts signs over their assets to a trustee, whose role is to liquidate these assets to satisfy outstanding debts. Similar measures can be applied to individuals. This part of the chapter has a closer look at the impact of COVID-19 response on businesses in Canada. It is also important to analyse the situation in Europe because the continent was not only affected by COVID-19 response, but also the war in Ukraine, the attack on the Nord Stream pipeline, and sanctions on Russia, which had a significant impact on SMEs collectively.

Business insolvencies in Canada

There are about 1.35 million registered employer firms in Canada as of June 2023, of which about 930 thousand are active. Canada also has approximately 3.1 million non-employer businesses (no employees hired beyond one owner/operator). While there are different measures as to what defines a small business (in terms of the number of employees, assets, or revenue levels, etc.), in Canada small businesses are defined as those employing less than 100 employees. About three quarters of firms in Canada fall in this category and employ less than ten people while nearly 50 percent of these firms have less than five employees. On aggregate, small firms employ about 10.3 million people, contribute about 40 percent to GDP, and create about 150,000 new jobs annually. Of these, nearly 80 percent of them operate in service sectors. It is estimated that more than 90 percent of SMEs (and particularly small firms) in Canada were affected by COVID-19 response while many were outright devastated by the unprecedented measures.[823,824]

The trajectory of growth for Canadian firms was steady between 2014 and 2019, with an average of about 100,000 newly created firms while 90,000 disappeared on an annual basis, which contributed to a net growth of about 10,000 firms per annum.[825] Between 2015 and 2023, there were approximately 12,000 newly created firms and an average growth in the number of firms of less than one percent. Figure 6.1 presents these growth dynamics in Canadian firms between 2014 and 2023 and confirms a steady increase in net growth in the number of registered employer firms, except for 2020 and 2021. While dynamics in the number of registered firms appear stable, more worrisome is the trend of active businesses, which declined by 11.8. percent in 2020 (June to June) and recovered by about the same percentage the following year. This is still below the pre-pandemic levels seen in 2018 and 2019. While a trend in the number of active businesses was stronger in 2022, there has been a steady decrease in the percentage growth of new openings.[826]

It is also worth noting that the businesses which close and those that open are different. In essence, opening and closing the same number of firms per annum is not equal, as in the first case, the risk profile of newly created firms is different than established firms. Newly created firms have higher chances of bankruptcy and lower chances of survival, while small businesses that have been in existence for a while have already gone through some of the most difficult teething problems. Secondly, new firms normally start small in terms of the number of employees, so their contribution to job creation is small compared to more developed firms. Thirdly, the closure of more mature firms, with a higher number of employees, has a disproportionate impact on the economy compared to smaller firms with fewer employees.

Figure 6.1: Employer firms in Canada between 2014 and 2023

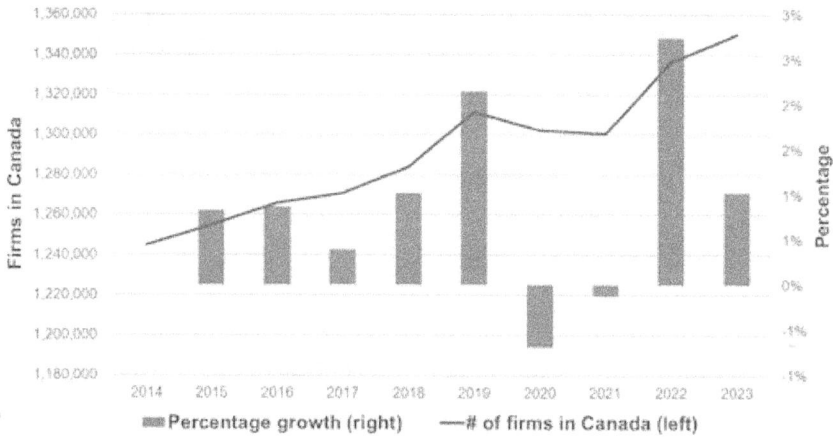

Source: Statistics Canada.

Figure 6.2a presents statistics related to business insolvencies in Canada and confirms that there was a steady decline in business insolvencies over the last ten years, with even more profound declines in 2020 and 2021. The explanation for a rapid decline of insolvencies (and bankruptcies) is that business owners often chose to close their business rather than declare insolvency or bankruptcy and undergo formal legal proceedings.[827] However, this trend is now on the uptick as the number of business insolvencies increased from 2,480 in 2021 to 3,402 in 2022, which represents a 37.2 percent increase. In 2023, the number of insolvencies rose to 4,810, which is an alarming 41.4 percent increase, the level of which has not been seen for ten years (2011–4,775). It also appears that insolvencies are backloaded, meaning that the extent of the full pandemic damage to businesses may only now be visible and will be seen in full force in the future. In other words, there may be many more business insolvencies in the coming years.

Figure 6.2: Business insolvencies and bankruptcies in Canada

a) Business insolvencies in Canada between 2011 and 2023.

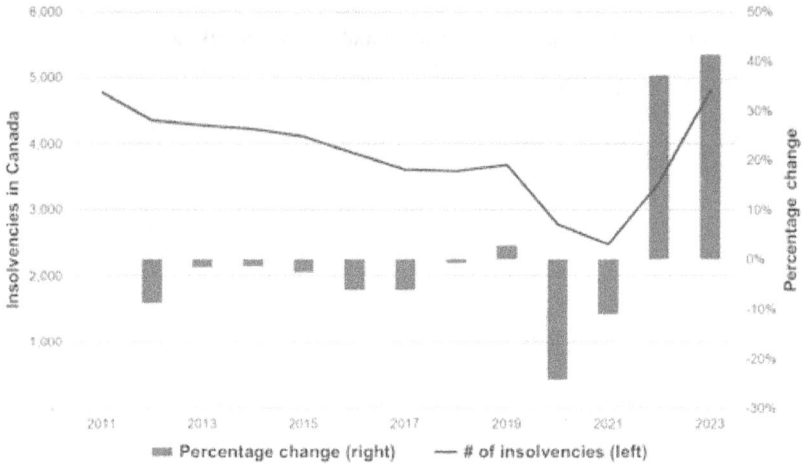

b) Business bankruptcies in Canada between 2001 and 2023.

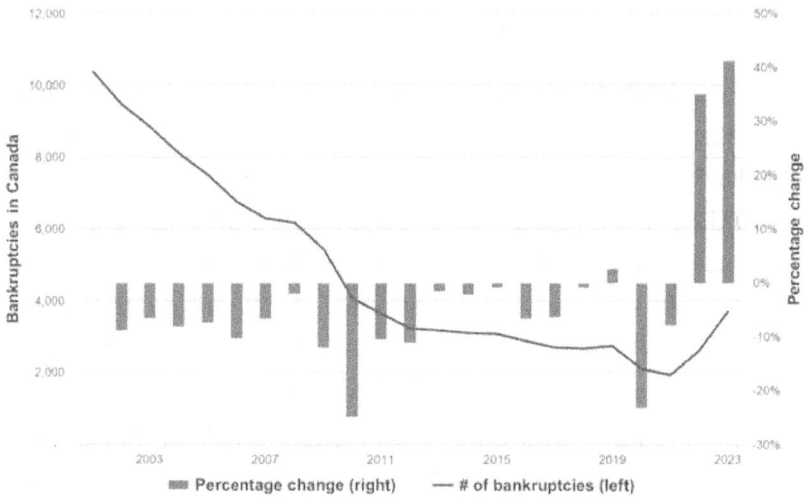

Source: Government of Canada.

However, insolvencies did not affect all sectors of the Canadian economy uniformly. Sectors which experienced the highest increase in insolvencies included healthcare and social assistance (an increase by 54.5 percent in 2022), transportation and storage (52.1 percent), retail (46.7 percent), construction (40.7 percent), and accommodations and food services (36.2 percent). Industries that enjoyed a reduction in insolvencies included mining/oil and gas extraction (-25.6 percent), as well as finance and insurance (-24.5 percent). In terms of geographic coverage, most insolvencies in Canada occurred in Ontario, British Columbia, and Alberta.

Figure 6.2b presents the trends in business bankruptcies in Canada between 2001 and 2023, which show similar dynamics to insolvencies. The graph also confirms a steady decrease in bankruptcies since 2001, which bottomed out in 2021 and began to reverse sharply in 2022. The number of bankruptcies in Canada increased to 2,621 in 2022 (a 35.0 percent increase) and reached 3,702 in 2023 (41.2 percent). A similar trend is seen in the U.S. as business bankruptcies have been on a steady decline since 2009 (when the number of bankruptcies reached about 60,000 case filings). During the pandemic, the number of bankruptcy cases declined from 22,482 cases in 2020 to 12,748 cases in 2022. However, the U.S. has seen a steady increase in bankruptcy case filings reaching 15,724 cases in 2023, and 22,060 cases in 2024 (in the year ending June 30), which represents a 40.4 percent increase.

Lastly, it is important to note that the insolvency and bankruptcy statistics seen above do not illustrate the full and complete picture of the total damage to the SME sector caused by COVID-19 response. This is because the figures do not include small businesses that could have gone through shutdown or orderly winddown of operations, which would have especially affected micro and owner/operator firms. It is estimated that for every one bankruptcy, nine firms could have closed their operations in this manner (i.e., winddown or shutdown).[828] There are also "business failures that actually haven't been reported."[829] As stated by the chair of the Canadian Association of Insolvency and Restructuring Professionals

(CAIRP), "often, we see business owners close up shop and simply walk away rather than taking formal steps to wind the business down or get restructuring advice."[830] When the business owners decided to toss the keys behind their back, such actions are not reflected in officials statistics or may be reported with a considerable delay (i.e., when a firm stops submitting taxation filings). Chief economist of the Canadian Federation of Independent Businesses (CFIB) has further concluded that "official Canadian data on small business bankruptcies doesn't account for zombie companies or businesses that would rather wind down than file for bankruptcy."[831]

The European SME sector in trouble

Trends visible in Canada are also visible in Europe, which is evidenced in the summary of bankruptcy declarations in Europe between 2015 and 2023 (estimate) found in figure 6.3. Similar to Canada, the graph also presents a noticeable decline in bankruptcies between 2015 and 2018, with an increase of 2.9 percent in 2019. Following the implementation of COVID-19 response restrictions, Europe experienced a 26.1 percent reduction in bankruptcy declarations in 2020 and reached 105,717 cases. But compared to general trends in Canada, bankruptcies in Europe began to rise earlier in 2021. They increased by 16.4 percent in 2021, 14.0 percent in 2022, and an estimated 8.4 percent in 2023, which represents a steady increase from quarter-to-quarter.[832] The estimated bankruptcy levels also reached 152,090 cases in 2023, which was about equal to the 2015 level (i.e., 155,791 cases). This upsurge reflects a combination of reasons, including the end or rollback of public support measures (equal in Europe to about €8 billion), the cumulative effect of price increases, the aggregate effect of rising energy costs, increased debt cost in view of higher-for-longer interest rates, sanctions on Russia, and increasing cost of living for consumers (thereby reducing consumption).[833]

The most affected sectors of the European economy were retail, small retail (i.e., jewellery stores, bakeries, clothing boutiques, bookstores, etc.), retail trade (i.e., automotive repair, repair and maintenance, and other professional services), accommodations, tourism, food services, construction, transportation, and storage.[834,835,836] In terms of geographic coverage, the countries which experienced the greatest acceleration of bankruptcies between 2020 and 2022 were Spain (139.3 percent increase in bankruptcies), Austria (58.5 percent), Denmark (45.7 percent), Croatia (44.5 percent), and France (32.9 percent). European economists are beginning to realize, as noted in the case of France, that "we need to bear in mind the economic reality of tomorrow will not be as good as what it was pre-COVID."[837] It is clear that "the rapidly increasingly numbers of bankruptcies are alarming"[838] and that a rise in bankruptcies may be "the beginning of a longer, more painful trend."[839] It is already expected that Germany and France will be two of the most affected countries in the future.

Figure 6.3: Business bankruptcy declaration across Europe between 2015 and 2023

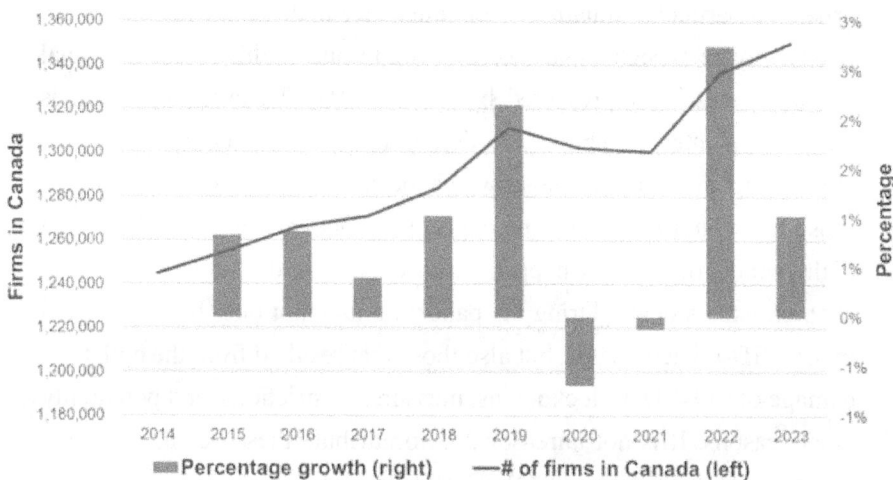

Source: Eurostat, 14 November 2024.

7

Excess deaths

Excess mortality: definitions and background

The term excess mortality has been traditionally used in the fields of public health, epidemiology, health management, healthcare economics, and other similar disciplines. Excess mortality is used to describe the number of deaths from all causes, often called all-cause mortality, that arise in a particular situation or circumstance and are above what could reasonably be expected under normal conditions. In this case, the special circumstances are represented by the COVID-19 pandemic, which is an event of interest. The key to determining excess deaths during this event is to differentiate those which occurred due to COVID-19 and those that could reasonably be expected to occur over the same period if the pandemic had not happened. Of course, as discussed later in the chapter, excess death during the pandemic may not only be represented by COVID-related deaths, but also those that resulted from the collateral damage of COVID-19 lockdowns, measures, restrictions, and potentially other reasons. It is not unreasonable to attribute these deaths to policy choices, which are termed COVID-19 response.

In practical terms, excess mortality can be captured in two measures, which can both be reported on a periodic (i.e., time specific) and cumulative basis. In the first instance, excess deaths or mortality may be expressed in terms of raw numbers or data and measured as the difference between actual (i.e., reported) deaths and an estimated number of deaths.

Projected mortality in statistical models is estimated with the use of statistical methods based on historical data from pre-selected periods; this is often called a baseline. These estimates may be further adjusted for any number of demographic factors. Alternately, excess deaths can also be expressed as a percentage (often called the P-score), which is calculated as the difference between actual deaths and projected deaths divided by the number of projected deaths (i.e., [actual or reported deaths – projected deaths] / projected deaths x 100). This metric measures the percentage increase in actual or reported deaths above the projected baseline figures. For example, if the value is equal to 50 percent, it means that the reported death count over a specific period was 50 percent higher than the projected death count. This type of data allows for better comparison between countries since it is expressed in percentage terms rather than raw numbers of excess deaths.

However, there are some challenges related to excess mortality statistics which are important to note. Primarily, excess mortality is an estimate. It may also be subject to change from year-to-year although longer-term and consistent trends may offer persuasive evidence. It is critical to consider several demographic parameters around which excess mortality is measured, such as population growth (i.e., births, deaths, immigration), demographic shifts (i.e., aging of the population, males versus females, size of the family, etc.), and other factors (for example, "duration of test positivity, diagnostic time window, and testing practices close to and at death"[840]). Other issues pertain to complications of accurate record keeping, proper evaluation of medical records, robust dissection of "the relative contribution of each disease/condition to death," and appropriate classification of deaths.[841] In simple terms, there is likely a difference between dying *from* COVID-19 and dying *with* COVID-19, especially in relation to the frail, the elderly, and individuals with a substantial list of underlying comorbidities and medical conditions.

As noted in chapter 2, testing for COVID-19 is highly imperfect and may significantly impact the ability to estimate COVID-19-related deaths. The estimates may be under-reported or over-reported. As Ioannidis noted "under-counting of deaths may occur when no testing is done or testing is false-negative; and over-counting may ensue from false-positive testing."[842] On one hand, a lack of proper testing, access to testing facilities, and other hurdles may lead to under-reporting on the number of COVID-19 associated deaths. On the other hand, due to problems with using amplified C_t values used in the PCR test, COVID-19 deaths may be over-reported. Also, exceedingly broad definitions of COVID-19-related deaths may have prompted over-reporting through the inclusion of *probable* COVID-19 cases. While the debate on over- and under-estimation of COVID-19 deaths is likely to continue, the initial estimate by Ioannidis suggested potential over-reporting in the number of deaths associated with COVID-19 in developed countries and under-reporting in developing or emerging countries.[843] A study by Alegria and Nunes focusing on the United States (U.S.) also confirms "a systematic over-reporting of COVID-19 when reported as the underlying cause of death compared to influenza and pneumonia."[844]

An additional factor that may have driven over-reporting could be "the financial incentives for hospitals to attribute deaths to COVID, though we can't measure to what extent that may have affected reported numbers."[845] As noted by Mulligan, there are concerns whether "the 2020 CARES Act's financial incentives are affecting COVID death accounting. Specifically, the CARES Act created a 20 percent add-on payment for Medicare reimbursement that involved COVID."[846] This is worthwhile to consider since financial incentives can be a powerful motivator of human behaviour.

In terms of financial motivation in the medical field, according to a report from the Office of the Auditor General of Ontario, the total billing from physicians for vaccination, supervision, and monitoring between March 2021 and May 2022 was equal to over $200 million, with an average of $30,488 billed per physician working at a "vaccination site or assessment centre operated by a hospital", and an average of over $22,124 per physician for those at a "vaccination site or assessment centre operated by a public health unit."[847] Physicians also vaccinated in their own offices, for which they billed an average of $2,565 per physician.[848] In another example of a incentivization program, the government in Manitoba dedicated $14 million "in community-focused and one-on-one outreach programs to improve access to the COVID-19 vaccine and to boost vaccine uptake."[849] Part of this program included outreach to patients who were not vaccinated to allegedly address their concerns. It is apparent that Canadian family physicians were keen to get involved in these vaccination initiatives. There is also evidence from the U.S. that Anthem Blue Cross and Blue Shield Medicaid offered a "provider incentive program" under which physicians could qualify for bonuses calculated on the basis of timing of vaccination (prior to September 2021 or after) and the percentage of members vaccinated.[850] For example, vaccinating 30 percent of patients would allow a physician bonus of $20 per patient, while vaccinating 75 percent of patients was rewarded with a bonus of $125 per patient. Vaccinating new patients in the period between September and December 2021 would yield an even greater bonus of between $100 to $250 per newly vaccinated patient. A basic simulation of the number of patients, vaccination percentages, and timing of delivery (prior to or after September) illustrates that physicians could receive bonuses starting at $56,000 to over $250,000. While it is unclear to what extent these financial structures affected physician decisions and modes of action, the simple fact is that physicians were incentivized and well compensated for performing COVID-19 vaccinations.

Another challenge with excess mortality calculations is that death reporting may not be consistent across countries, which can make international comparisons difficult. International reporting can differ in terms of time delays (i.e., differences between when deaths occur and when they are reported), defining the beginning and the end of the week, methods of assigning cause, the application of alternate statistical methodologies, and so on. There is also variety in data sets themselves, as they can varyingly include regional, national, and international numbers. Lastly, there may be other unanticipated complications, circumstances, events, shifts, and adjustments. For example, the deaths of already sick or frail individuals "that were expected to occur during the observation period, but were brought forward by COVID-19, [hastened] a temporary surplus in mortality followed by a deficit, and [was] consequently ignored when calculating cumulative excess deaths."[851]

Understanding excess deaths is critical for interpreting public policy and the actions of unelected public health officials and governments. Excess mortality is regarded as a comprehensive measure of the total impact of a special event, circumstances, or conditions. In the case of the COVID-19 pandemic, excess mortality can be used to evaluate the effectiveness of lockdowns, restrictions, and other measures. While this metric can identify the benefits of a specific policy, it can also highlight any unintended collateral damage. Furthermore, this statistic can be used to illuminate differences between countries that may have implemented alternate public health and management policies to gain a greater understanding of their respective efficacy.

Early signs of elevated excess deaths

One of the early signals related to elevated excess deaths came from the insurance industry, both in Europe and the United States (U.S.), which pointed to two significant problems. Firstly, in early January 2022, a CEO of OneAmerica, observed a significant increase in death rates among working age individuals (i.e., 16- to 64-year-olds), rather than in the elderly who should be more affected by COVID-19. To contextualize this increase, the CEO stated, "just to give you an idea of how bad that is, a three sigma or 200-year catastrophe would be a 10 percent increase over pre-pandemic levels … so, 40 percent is just unheard of."[852] This observation was significant because it effectively translated into millions of dollars of short- and long-term liabilities for the insurer. Secondly, German insurer BKK ProVita observed "very significant under-reporting of suspected cases of COVID-19 vaccination side-effects."[853] A board member of BKK noticed that, based on the insurer's internal analysis, "we consider 400,000 visits to the doctor by our policyholders because of vaccination complications to be realistic to this day. Extrapolated to the total population, this value would be three million."[854] Interestingly, German Health Minister Karl Lauterbach, who pushed for mandatory vaccinations, lockdowns, and other restrictive measures, officially admitted that people were suffering from adverse COVID-19 vaccine-related side effects.[855] The insurance industry has continued to raise these concerns in 2024. For example, Swiss Re Institute noted that "four years on, many countries worldwide still report elevated deaths from their populations."[856] The institute also observed that

> We find evidence of inconsistency in the cause of death recorded in this period, with signs that other causes of death were misclassified as COVID-19. The UK and US data shows a large, unexplained jump in deaths attributed to cardiovascular diseases (CVD) since 2020. Some countries also reported excess mortality over a pre-pandemic baseline for other major causes of death, such as cancer.[857]

There have also been four other health-related issues, which received minimal coverage from social and mainstream media, that need further investigation. The first is the prevalence of a medical condition called Sudden Adult Death Syndrome (i.e., SADS), which is a life-threatening medical condition often resulting in the unexplained and sudden death of healthy young adults who are usually under the age of 40. While the cause of SADS-related death may be unexplained, the condition may be aggravated by subclinical heart abnormalities that result in the disturbance of the heart's normal pattern, ultimately leading to an abrupt cardiac arrest.[858] This relationship between the condition and cardiac anomalies is supported by the acronym's secondary meaning, Sudden Arrhythmic Death Syndrome, which also represents a disturbance of the heart's electrical impulses resulting in a wide range of arrhythmic disorders, although this syndrome adversely affects adults and newborns.[859] Concerns related to SADS have been raised in the context of vaccinated individuals, and particularly regarding cases of myocarditis in adolescent and young adults, although SADS can strike anyone regardless of their vaccination status. One such concern was voiced by Canadian conservative politician Leslyn Lewis, who aimed to shed some light on the issue. Another key unanswered concern relates to an increase of so-called "ill-defined and unspecified causes of mortality." [860] In Canada, for example, this category of mortality increased from 3,389 cases in 2019 to 16,043 cases in 2022; the acceleration of deaths in this category is worrisome. There is also the matter of a decrease in life expectancy, seen across the globe, which has been unparalleled for at least the last fifty years. In just one example, a newly born child in Canada can expected to live one year less compared to those born in the pre-pandemic era. [861] Of course, this can be driven by multiple factors. Lastly, there is also a matter of economic displacement and its impact on excess deaths. When reflecting on the impact of COVID-19 in the United States, Polyakova et al. have noted that "employment displacement was positively correlated with excess mortality."[862]

It is important to note that the topic of excess deaths was placed to the side during the pandemic since the spotlight was on COVID-19 cases and deaths. Now, however, it appears that most social media platforms, mainstream media outlets, politicians, medical doctors, academics, and medical health officers do not wish to pursue this topic, with some notable exceptions. This is certainly true in Canada, for although COVID-19 cases were on the minds of everyone during the pandemic, "excess deaths no longer occupy the attention of politicians, public health officials, media, or the broader Canadian public. Excess deaths appear to be 'out of sight, out of mind'."[863] As noted by Mulligan and Arnott, "there was little curiosity about testing whether public or private Covid-policies were aggravating previous health problems."[864]

It is easy to imagine that the topic of excess mortality is uncomfortable for the politicians, political leaders, unelected public health officers, medical doctors, academics, and public administrators whose policies may be inherently connected to adverse health outcomes. However, and as noted in chapter 3, there were attempts at formal investigations into the causes of excess deaths, even though they were side-lined, ignored, and swept under the carpet in most countries. A good example is the United

Kingdom (U.K.), which is discussed later in this chapter. Some articles have even been trickling in from mainstream media, such as an article from Canada that quoted a local professor as saying, "We absolutely need to know why we have historically high levels of death."[865]

As noted in chapter 2, excess deaths have been investigated by some academics from diverse viewpoints, including economics. For example, Mulligan and Arnott, who focused on the U.S., concluded that during the period from April 2020 to the end of 2021, "Americans died from non-COVID causes at an average rate of 97,000 in excess of previous trends" in the period "from April 2020 through at least the end of 2021."[866] The authors further observed that "the first indicator of abnormalities comes from the 46 percent of the adult population who had not yet reached age 45. While largely unharmed by Covid, their aggregate mortality rates increased by 26 percent above previous trends."[867] The mortality rate for the elderly also increased by 18 percent, although this was chiefly driven by COVID-19 deaths. In another study, Arnott et al. catalogued multiple areas of collateral damage resulting from the COVID-19 pandemic which they termed "deaths of despair"; these may arise as a consequence of drug and alcohol abuse, divorce, disrupted or outright cancelled career paths, child abuse, poverty, severe depression, and other circumstances.[868] These are all human costs that are likely to affect individuals in the long-term, although their impacts are yet to be captured in official statistics, in part because they may not be properly attributed to their key source. In more specific terms, COVID-19 symptoms generally resemble those of flu and pneumonia. Since there is a considerable decrease in deaths from these diseases during the pandemic, which is visible in the data, is it possible that flu and pneumonia deaths were simply mis-labelled as COVID-19 deaths, especially in view of a problematic PCR test?

Another way in which to measure the collateral damage of the pandemic is through an analysis of what is commonly referred to as the "years of life" and is perhaps a difficult and sensitive topic. In this case, Arnott, Kalesnik, and Wu drew an important distinction between "years lost" and "lives lost,"[869] and is best described by the authors' own example:

> For an octogenarian in a nursing home, with stage four cancer, dying a few months early from Covid is still a personal and family tragedy. But most would agree that it's a greater loss when a child or sibling in their 20s, struggling with depression after their career has been derailed, gives up on that career, runs away from their family, overdoses, or commits suicide.[870]

The authors, while making basic assumptions about life expectancy, loss of life, and demographic composition, estimated that "COVID cost us far more lives than the surge in unnatural and Big Four deaths [heart disease, lung disease, cancer, stroke], mostly in the lowest-quality end-of-life years, but this 'collateral damage' may have cost twice as many years of life as COVID."[871] The value of years lost in the U.S. has been estimated to be equal to about 1.6 million years of life.[872] A study by Ruhm in the U.S. further underlines that while the majority of excess deaths early in the pandemic occurred due to COVID-19, there were also numerous non-COVID-related deaths attributed to drugs, suicide, and homicide.[873] Mulligan's study observed that "the demographic and time patterns of the non-COVID excess deaths (NCEDs) point to death of despair rather than an undercount of COVID deaths."[874] Arnott, Kalesnik and Wu determined that "non-COVID deaths caused by the pandemic and possibly by our policy choices, are likely to total at least this 151,000 difference."[875] Other research focusing on life years lost has confirmed that "non–COVID-19 excess mortality is much more common among males, minorities, and the young."[876] In a recent study from Australia, researchers compellingly argue that

> most COVID-19 related deaths in Australia occurred between September 2021 and September 2022. Prior to this, COVID-19 related deaths were below 1000 for 2020 and only 1300 for 2021. Yet over 10,000 excess deaths occurred in the country in 2021 (for a population of 25.5M). Therefore, around 90% of excess deaths were non-COVID deaths.[877]

Possible causes of excess deaths

Discerning the reasons for excess mortality is an inherently difficult and complex matter since causes of deaths may be difficult to precisely pinpoint and "are likely to be multiple."[878] Getting to the bottom of this issue may take time and considerable resources, and it is possible that we may not be able to resolve this matter with the desired level of precision. There may also be numerous socioeconomic issues surrounding these deaths that contribute to medical causes. Alternatively, it is possible that various trends which started well before the pandemic were effectively accelerated or exacerbated during the pandemic and are now more obvious. Examples of these adverse trends may include a "toxic drug crisis and other public-health crises."[879] As noted by Mulligan and Arnott, between April 2020 and December 2021, there was a 28 percent increase in excess deaths related to alcohol-induced causes, a 27 percent increase in homicide-related deaths, and a 13 percent increase in drug-related causes.[880] Patrick et al. have confirmed that various substances are being used to deal with various challenges associated with, caused by, or related to the COVID-19 pandemic. The authors specifically state that "in Fall 2020, 15.7% reported using marijuana, 8.9% increased vaping, and 8.2% increased drinking to cope with social distancing and isolation."[881] Moreover, Patrick et al. found that the use of marijuana was positively correlated with the level of isolation, stress, and economic challenges an individual was experiencing. Beyond these causes of excess deaths, there is also a possibility that people could have died "from the virus prior to getting tested or treated."[882] A lack of social support for the elderly during the pandemic due to stay-at-home orders and other public measures is another potential reason.[883]

There may also be behavioural causes that contributed to excess deaths. For example, some individuals did not to go to the hospital to obtain necessary or even emergency treatments because they believed they were at an increased risk of exposure to COVID-19 in a healthcare setting.[884] There was a similar reluctance of some to attend their local medical clinic to obtain a prescription for necessary medications.[885] To this end, evidence confirmed that "1 in 5 adults (20%) in the U.S. reported their household members were unable to get or delayed getting medical care for serious problems. Among those reporting delayed care, more than half (57%) said they experienced negative health consequences as a result."[886]

Furthermore, deaths may also be attributable to mental health issues which arose because of the pandemic and lockdowns, and delays in receiving diagnostic tests and medical interventions (i.e., surgeries, treatments). To this end, Ruhm has confirmed "substantial delays between the timing of screenings or treatment and deaths."[887] With respect to screening problems, for example, "Massachusetts General Brigham hospital reported a 74 percent reduction in cancer screens in March, April, and May 2020 as compared to the prior year."[888] A further complication in this area has been identified by Mostert et al., who observed that "deaths caused by restricted healthcare utilization and socioeconomic turmoil are difficult to prove."[889]

There were also elevated deaths related to Alzheimer's disease and obesity. In the latter case, Lin et al. interestingly observed an increase in weight gain of about 1.5 pounds per month of lockdowns.[890] Other studies, like that conducted by Bhutani et al., confirmed these weight trends with respect to the entire population.[891] Most worrisome are the trends in weight gain seen in children and adolescents, which has been confirmed by Chang and colleagues.[892] These tendencies indicate populations may be on the verge of creating another epidemic, this case of obesity, which will impact the entire society with dire long-term physical and mental health consequences post-COVID pandemic.

Finally, on the other hand, a study by Paglino et al. informed that their investigation "suggests that many excess deaths reported to non-COVID-19 natural causes during the first 30 mo[nths] of the pandemic in the United States were unrecognized COVID-19 deaths", suggesting there were more deaths related to COVID-19 that were not properly recorded as such. [893] Paglino et al. also raised a concern, noting that "deaths could also be indirectly related to the pandemic as a result of healthcare delays and interruptions and/or social and economic impacts of the pandemic such as housing instability, employment loss, food insecurity, social isolation, and increases in poisonings, suicide, homicide, and accidents."[894] The authors concluded that medical interruptions and health care delays were not a significant contributor to deaths.

The Peltzman effect

It is also worth considering the so-called "Peltzman effect". In the mid-1970s, Sam Peltzman, an economics professor from the University of Chicago, investigated unintended consequences of highway and traffic regulations introduced in the 1960s (i.e., seat belt requirements, stronger windshields, dual braking system, and so on) and their potential impact on fatalities, injuries, and individuals' decision-making and behaviour.[895] While there has been some criticism of Peltzman's model in terms of its theoretical underpinnings, methodology, model validity, predictive abilities, level of impact, consistency, and so on over the years, (see Robertson,[896] for example), Peltzman proposed that when cost of risky behaviour is lowered, people engage in more of it. In essence, Peltzman argued that when new safety measures are introduced and implemented, individuals may choose to engage in more risky behaviours due to their lower perception of risk arising from these regulations. This is termed "risk compensation", which is a model of self-adjustment on behalf of individuals in response to different levels of perceived risk. This occurs because individuals that engage in risky behaviour can undo benefits arising from certain measures or restrictions implemented by the state. In short, while Peltzman conjectured that safety measures could be offset by incremental human risk taking, it is not clear whether "offsetting" risky behaviour would be substantial enough to undo all the benefits of certain measures or restrictions, or only some.

One, of course, could ask: can the Peltzman effect be applied to the COVID-19 pandemic? Are there any unintended consequences of lockdowns or other measures introduced by the state, which can be explained by the Peltzman effect? On one hand, vaccinated individuals (feeling fully protected by the COVID-19 vaccine) could begin to engage in "potentially risky" behaviours such as skipping personal hygiene measures (i.e., handwashing), sanitation regimens, taking fewer safety precautions (i.e., avoiding large crowds), ignoring early symptoms of diseases not related to COVID-19 (i.e., pneumonia, flu), and so on. Additionally, "some people may feel protected by just looking at the vaccination numbers",[897] thereby drawing conclusions that the society is sufficiently protected through vaccination and feel safe to engage in risky decision making and behaviours. Consequently, it is not surprising that in some countries the Peltzman effect was viewed as the source of increased cases of COVID-19.[898,899] The Peltzman effect could also work in such a way where fewer or more subtle restrictions (like those in Sweden) could lead to more precautionary actions taken by individuals as they self-adjust their behaviour in view of freely perceived risks. In simple terms, individuals could easily adjust their behaviour to minimize risks and act in a more cautious manner due to lower vaccination rates or in the absence of the state's restrictions and its light-touch "nudge" or heavy-handed push. Individuals could use safer substitutes or alternatives for what they perceive as risk-ridden actions of the state and unelected public officers.[900]

However, it is unlikely that the Peltzman effect could serve as the only plausible explanation, as some studies suggest, [901] of different behaviours and outcomes post-COVID-19 response (including excess deaths). Without a long discussion, one can offer three basic arguments here. Firstly, it may be difficult to argue that outcomes of the pandemic (including excess deaths) solely arose from "irresponsible", reckless, or risky behaviours of individuals which occurred *en masse*. Secondly, it is important to note that the effect of COVID-19 vaccines on the population was not zero. COVID-19 vaccines may have been perceived as risk-free but there were adverse events of interest associated with them, as demonstrated in chapter 1. Lastly, one may argue that if the COVID-19 vaccine was so effective, other precautionary measures should not have been necessary or have mattered. In fact, pre-pandemic normal human behaviour should not be viewed as too risky in the face of an allegedly effective medical intervention. Furthermore, when individuals are persuaded through mainstream media, social media, and official communications from the state, its associate stakeholders, and manufacturers that COVID-19 vaccines are effectively "bullet-proof" against the disease and transmission (which was not the case, as demonstrated in chapter 1), they may rationally choose to consume the benefit of this promise by returning to normal life.

The elephant in the room: Deaths potentially associated with COVID-19 vaccines

The topic of vaccine death is no doubt contentious, and it may again be uncomfortable for governments, unelected health officials, pharmaceutical firms, physicians, academics, and even the public. In this case, the "elephant in the room" is whether some excess deaths could have been potentially associated by COVID-19 vaccines. It is unlikely that one will be able to affirmatively resolve this matter since "consensus is also lacking in the medical community regarding concerns that mRNA vaccines might cause more harm than initially forecasted."[902] As noted in chapter 1, researchers are currently documenting the mechanisms of pathogenicity potentially associated with COVID-19 vaccines. While some researchers seem to reach cautionary conclusions, others are firmer in their convictions about the possible contributions of COVID-19 vaccines to excess death and injury. As an example, Rhodes and Parry concluded that "we have experienced a pandemic of viral illness, followed by a pandemic of vaccine injury."[903]

This topic is complicated for several reasons. Researchers point out that "most of these serious adverse events concern common clinical conditions, for example, ischemic stroke, heart attacks, acute coronary syndrome, brain haemorrhage, neurological disorders, and so on. This commonality of symptoms and clinical manifestations may hinder clinical suspicion and consequently detection as adverse vaccine reactions", especially when reporting adverse events is generally discouraged.[904] Moreover, "many of these persistent post-vaccine symptoms are similar to symptoms associated with post-acute sequelae of COVID (PASC), or long COVID."[905] Thus, it may be difficult for physicians or researchers to make such clinical attributions despite some official notes and warnings from the U.S. Food and Drug Administration that may potentially associate pulmonary embolism, acute myocardial infraction, thrombocytopenia, intravascular coagulation, and other adverse outcomes with COVID-19 vaccines.[906]

Let's cite a few studies here. For example, Aarstad and Kvitastein concluded that they "cannot rule out that COVID-19 vaccination uptake in Europe has led to increasing 2022 all-cause mortality."[907] They also specifically noted that "a one percentage point increase in 2021 vaccination uptake was associated with a monthly mortality increase in 2022 by 0.105 percent."[908] Alessandria et al. found that "all-cause death risks to be even higher for those vaccinated with one and two does compared to the unvaccinated."[909] They also found "a slight but statistically significant loss of life expectancy for those vaccinated with 2 or 2/4 doses."[910] Also, as quoted in chapter 1, a paper by Hulscher et al., which was based on a review of autopsy studies, independent medical adjudication of autopsy cases, and application of the Bradford Hill criteria concluded that "there is a high likelihood of a causal link between COVID-19 vaccines and death from myocarditis."[911] Note that a critical commentary of the Hulscher et al.'s analysis was provided by Van Wyk and colleagues.[912] Some quantitative analysis is provided by Skidmore[913] as well Pantazatos and Seligmann.[914] There are also more provocative (but not peer-reviewed) quantitative studies (see, for example, Rancourt, Hickey, and Linard).[915] In yet, another example, focusing on the elderly, Wong et al. noted the following:

> This early warning system is the first to identify temporal associations for PE [pulmonary embolism], AMI [acute myocardial infraction], DIC [disseminated intravascular coagulation], and ITP

[immune thrombocytopenia] following BNT162b2 vaccination in the elderly. Because an early warning system does not prove that the vaccines cause these outcomes, more robust epidemiologic studies with adjustment for confounding, including age and nursing home residency, are underway to further evaluate these signals.[916]

In any case, it is also encouraging that the potential harm from COVID-19 vaccines is being recognized by mainstream media, which only a few years ago advocated for mass vaccination and vilified the unvaccinated. One example of increased interest in the topic is an interview with a nurse practitioner from New York by a former anchor of CNN, who, while at CNN, advocated for COVID-19 vaccines.[917] After reaching out to his colleagues at the FDA, the CDC, and the NIH as well as local politicians, the nurse admitted that the topic was uncomfortable for many and "no one wanted to touch it."[918] Similarly, a recent article in *The New York Times* published at the end of April 2024 openly admits that there may potentially be serious problems with COVID-19 vaccination, citing the case of a 37-year-old woman who, within minutes of receiving the vaccine, felt pain, became sensitive to light, and had problems recalling basic facts. As reported in the article, this individual "has a Ph.D. in neuroscience, could ride her bicycle 20 miles, teach a dance class and give a lecture on artificial intelligence, all in the same day."[919] A few years following this incident, the individual was officially diagnosed with brain damage. Importantly, the article also claims that "thousands of Americans believe they suffered serious side effects following Covid vaccination. As of April [2024], just 13,116 COVID-19 vaccine-injury compensation claims have been filed with the federal government–but to little avail."[920] From this set, only 19.2 percent of the applications have been reviewed, of which 47 were deemed eligible for compensation and merely 12 were paid out an average sum of about $3,600.[921] Of course, this number of people who have received compensation so far in the U.S. is low given data from available surveillance systems. As previously stated, the VAERS surveillance system recorded over 1.6 million adverse events, with varying degrees of severity that were suspected of being associated with COVID-19 vaccines, and an additional 700,000 adverse events were self-reported through the V-safe program. However, as one immunologist from Yale University has observed, these COVID-19 vaccine injuries are "just completely ignored and dismissed and gaslighted."[922]

Excess deaths data in selected countries

Many countries around the world have experienced significant increases in excess deaths, which occurred, peaked, and oscillated at different time intervals. These excess deaths have "remained high in the Western World for three consecutive years, despite the implementation of containment measures and COVID-19 vaccines. This raises serious concerns."[923] Some countries, like Finland and Germany, experienced low excess deaths early in the pandemic, although they accelerated in later years. This pattern of excess deaths does not follow the three or four major waves (i.e., initial spring 2020 wave, Alpha, Delta, Omicron, etc.) in the pandemic, so in the cases of these countries it may be conjectured that excess deaths arose due to reasons other than from COVID-19. Other countries, such as Poland, experienced consistently elevated levels of excess deaths from the start of the pandemic in 2020 until 2023. This pattern of excess deaths is also unnatural as it does not reflect the most common three or four wave patterns of SARS-CoV-2 and its variants. In other words, excess death continued despite the decline in severity but increased transmissibility of SARS-CoV-2.

To further examine the trends of excess deaths, table 7.1 below presents the patterns of excess deaths for selected countries based on data from the Organization for Economic Cooperation and Development (OECD).[924] Note that the data included in the table may differ from statistics gathered within the countries listed by local agencies or international institutions. The table includes countries which instituted some of the most severe restrictions (i.e., Australia, Poland, U.K., and Germany) and countries that initially enforced restrictions but reduced their severity over time (i.e., Denmark). Table 7.1 also includes data from Sweden, the country with the loosest restrictions in Europe, as previously stated in chapter 2.

When analysing the European perspective, both Germany and Poland had significant excess mortality,[925] which is surprising since the peaks of SARS-CoV-2 and its associated variants had already passed in 2020 and 2021.[926]

Table 7.1: Excess deaths in different countries between 2020 and 2023

	2020		2021		2022		2023	
	Excess deaths	P-score	Excess deaths	P-score	Excess deaths	P-score	Excess deaths	P-score
Australia	1,325	1.1	11,130	7.1	29,738	18.7	15,063	13.1
Denmark	982	2.0	3,638	7.2	5,871	11.1	3,052	6.9
Finland	1,603	3.2	4,105	8.0	9,574	17.9	4,674	10.5
Germany	52,973	5.8	89,400	9.9	134,579	14.9	59,039	7.7
New Zealand	(71)	0.3	2,112	6.7	5,787	17.8	3,971	14.6
Norway	(297)	(0.5)	1,330	3.7	4,981	12.5	1,885	5.7
Poland	76,720	19.1	118,208	29.0	46,561	11.4	104	0.1
Sweden	6,454	7.3	(27)	(0.1)	2,288	2.6	(530)	(0.6)
U.K.	80,684	13.4	62,570	9.6	52,515	9.3	49,398	9.4
U.S.	599,477	21.3	674,983	24.2	495,749	17.5	155,763	7.8

Source: OECD. Own compilation.

In addition to the excess deaths that occurred in elderly populations, there was also a devastating loss of life among children, adolescents, young adults, and the middle-aged. As Mulligan and Arnott observed that "even including our estimate of 2,000 unmeasured Covid deaths ages 18-44, excess non-Covid deaths exceeded Covid deaths for that group. Overall, the excess deaths aged 18-44 amount to a 26 precent increase in the age group's mortality."[927] The authors further concluded that "although about three-fourths of Covid deaths were among the elderly, more than half of excess non-Covid deaths are among non-elderly adults."[928] Such statistics, particularly when these deaths occurred during non-peak periods of SARS-CoV-2 outbreaks, require additional analysis.

It is important to discuss the case of Scotland at length because it serves as a good example of the nature of possible government investigations into excess deaths. In September 2022, the Scottish government decided to review neonatal deaths (i.e., death of babies under the age of four weeks) following two unprecedented spikes. The first spike occurred in September 2021 when at least 21 newborn babies died, which equated to 4.9 neonatal deaths per 1,000 (note that the average mortality in Scotland was equal to about 2.2 deaths per 1,000).[929] The second spike in neonatal deaths occurred in March 2022 with the loss of at least 18 newborns (4.6 deaths per 1,000). Although the preliminary investigation into the deaths determined they were not related to COVID-19, further research suggests there may be more to the story.

Excess deaths in the United Kingdom

As seen in table 7.1, there have been a considerable number of excess deaths in the U.K. since the onset of the pandemic: excess deaths increased by 13.4 percent in 2020, 9.6 percent in 2021, 9.3 percent in 2022, and 9.4 percent in 2023. These numbers led to a formal government inquiry of excess deaths spearheaded by Andrew Bridgen, a former member of Parliament, who was incidentally ousted from the Conservative Party in April 2023 for raising concerns about the efficacy and safety of COVID-19 vaccines. During the debate in parliament on January 16, 2024, which occurred in a nearly empty house, Bridgen made several rather self-explanatory points. Most importantly, Bridgen asserted that "we bypassed the procedures, protocols, and science to inflict on a healthy population a brand new and untested product that had never been used outside of clinical trials, never mind approved."[930] With regard to excess deaths, Bridgen reminded parliament that "for two years we have turned society upside down so as not to 'kill granny'. Now that mum and dad are dying, it appears that no one cares."[931] Furthermore, Bridgen was critical of public policy's complicity in the nation's excess deaths, stating that "the excess deaths are the tip of a very ugly iceberg, and we have not even mentioned the world-shaking scandal of jabbing people who had already had covid, at a stroke, almost entirely demolishing the credibility of our public health policies."[932] Finally, Bridgen concluded by pointing to excess deaths in the younger population, since "particularly for cardiovascular deaths, there has been incessant week-on-week excess mortality for months and months in the young and middle-aged. Every age group is affected, but 50 to 64 age group has had it worst."[933]

Importantly, other conservative members of the U.K. Parliament contributed to this debate, such as Philip Davies, who spotted that "many of these excess deaths could have been prevented had people not been dissuaded from seeking care, because they were told by the media and the Government to stay at home and protect the NHS [National Health System]."[934] Miriam Coates similarly observed that "we suspended the precautionary principle, ignored the fact that interventions may cause harm, suspended the importance of children's education, suspended the safeguarding of children, suspended the need for medical trials, and suspended all sorts of safeguards that have stood in society."[935] In addition to these points, U.K. parliamentarians raised another important concern: access to information. This led some members of parliament to make a simple request of the government, namely, to release data "on the same anonymized basis that it was shared with the pharmaceutical groups," further stating that there "seems to be no credible reason why that should not be done immediately."[936]

Academic inquiries into excess deaths in the U.K. raised additional issues, including that the trend of growth in excess deaths has "persisted into 2023 with 8.6% or 28,024 more deaths registered in the first six months of the year than expected."[937] Pearson-Stuttard et al. has also confirmed that other institutions, such as the Continuous Mortality Investigation (CMI), which is supported by the Institute and Faculty of Actuaries in the U.K., affirmed the magnitude in the number of deaths through the use of an alternate statistical method (28,500 versus 28,024). In terms of demographic distribution, the "excess deaths for all causes were relatively greatest for 50-64 year olds (15% higher than expected), compared with 11% higher for 25-49 and < 25-year-olds, and about 9% higher for over 65 year old groups."[938] Similar dynamics were observed in the CMI analysis, which is a key observation because the risk of death from COVID-19 increases with age. In other words, younger people have lower chances of dying from COVID-19, so these excess deaths are likely attributed to reasons other than COVID-19. The leading causes of excess deaths include heart failure (20 percent increase), liver disease (19 percent), stroke (15 percent), and other cardiovascular diseases (12 percent).

However, the most worrisome excess deaths statistics pertain to middle-aged adults. For this group, "deaths involving cardiovascular diseases were 33% higher than expected, while for specific cardiovascular diseases, deaths involving ischaemic heart disease were 44% higher, cerebrovascular diseases were 40% higher and heart failure 39% higher."[939] The occurrence of poor cardiac outcomes is also confirmed by other publications. According to the British Heart Foundation in the U.K., the "latest figures show that in 2022, over 39,000 people in England died prematurely of cardiovascular conditions including heart attacks, coronary heart disease and stroke—an average of 750 people each week. It is the highest annual total since 2008."[940]

Another critical argument made by Pearson-Stuttard et al. was that "the greatest number of excess deaths in the acute phase of the pandemic were in older adults," but following this period, excess deaths affected middle-aged and younger adults.[941] The authors also observed that a significant proportion of excess deaths occurred at home (likely due to sudden adverse health events) rather than hospitals (due to COVID-19). Considering increasing evidence of non-COVID related excess deaths in the U.K., the Office of National Statistics (ONS) has recently changed its methodology for counting deaths. Under this new system, excess deaths were equal to 10,994 in 2023 in comparison to 20,448 under the old method, which represents a reduction of more than 45 percent.[942]

Excess deaths in Canada

Table 7.2 presents key mortality statistics in Canada between 2020 and 2022 (note that some data for 2023 is not available), including estimated excess deaths, COVID-19 deaths, and percentage distribution between COVID-19 and non-COVID-19 deaths.[943] At first glance, it is easy to see that the number of deaths accelerated in Canada from 285,301 in 2019 to 343,360 in 2022, which represents an increase of 20.4 percent in the number of excess deaths. The number of COVID-19-related deaths in Canada (which are recorded as a separate category) was 15,890 in 2020, declined to 14,466 in 2021, and peaked at 19,716 in 2022. This represents a percentage growth in excess mortality in Canada equal to 5.7 percent (2020), 7.5 percent (2021), and 13.5 percent (2022).[944] However, percentage growth in excess mortality also varied across provinces and over time. For example, in the early onset of the pandemic (2020), the provinces of Alberta and Quebec were most affected by excess mortality with a nearly 8 percent growth rate. According to ClubVita, a data analytics company, excess mortality accelerated in 2021 in British Columbia (17 percent) and Saskatchewan (16 percent) but declined in Quebec. Excess deaths accelerated even further across Canadian provinces, with above-average increases in Saskatchewan (20 percent) and British Columbia (19 percent). Consistent with other countries, in Canada "excess mortality concentrated at older ages, but youngest age group saw the most significant increase in excess deaths."[945] As argued above, the ages between 0 and 44 should have been less affected by COVID-19.

Table 7.2: Excess deaths in Canada between 2020 and 2023

	2020	2021	2022	2023[1]
Adjusted number of deaths	305,528	311,213	343,360	204,089
Expected number of deaths	289,088	289,511	300,268	189,065
Excess mortality estimate	16,440	21,702	43,092	15,024
COVID-19 deaths	15,890	14,466	19,716	N/A
Non-COVID deaths	550	7,236	23,376	N/A
Percentage distribution:				
COVID-19 deaths	96.7%	66.7%	45.8%	N/A
Non-COVID deaths	3.3%	33.3%	54.2%	N/A

Source: Statistics Canada.[1] Statistics only available for the first 8 months. Own compilation.

The cumulative number of COVID-19-related deaths was equal to 50,072 between 2020 and 2022 while the total number of excess deaths was equal to 81,234. It is worthwhile to remember that Neil Ferguson and colleagues from Imperial College predicted 326,000 COVID deaths in 2020 alone. Of course, he did not anticipate (or failed to disclose) any deaths not related to COVID-19. Moreover, the percentage distribution between COVID-19 deaths and non-COVID-19 deaths changed over time. At the outset of the pandemic, COVID-19 deaths accounted for 96.7 percent of excess deaths, although this percentage declined to 45.8 percent by the end of 2022. In other words, by the end of 2022, less than half of excess deaths were attributed to COVID-19. Most importantly, data from 2022 confirms that excess deaths not attributed to COVID-19 exceeded deaths from COVID-19 by 3,660.

The acceleration of excess deaths not attributed to COVID-19 in Canada is alarming, particularly those among youth.[946] Excess deaths which are not attributed to COVID-19 rose from the low number of 550 deaths in 2020 to 23,376 in 2022, which represents about a 43-fold increase, albeit from a small base figure. The levels of excess deaths not attributed to COVID-19 in 2022 also exceeded the sum of these deaths from

2020 and 2021, as well as the number of COVID-19 deaths in any of the years between 2020 and 2022. It is evident that Canadians continue to die unpredictably and perhaps surprisingly. The key causes of these excess deaths not attributed to COVID-19 are related to diseases of the heart, cancers, and accidents (i.e., unintentional injuries). Heart diseases and cancers remain the leading causes of death in Canada and account for 24.7 and 17.2 percent of deaths, respectively. Deaths resulting from unintentional injuries increased from 15,527 to 18,365 in 2022.

Furthermore, there are two intriguing categories of death in Canada that should be discussed. As noted earlier, the first is termed "other-ill-defined and unspecified causes of mortality," and excess deaths in this category rose from 3,378 in 2019 to 16,043 in 2022, an increase of 470 percent. In other words, between 2020 and 2022, about 32,355 deaths appeared to be unexplained. As noted by Statistics Canada, there was an increase in deaths among the younger population that can be attributed to substance-related overdoses, suicides, and homicides.[947] Another report, also by Statistics Canada, stated that "younger age groups made up a disproportionate number of deaths from overdose" and that "alcohol-induced mortality also increased significantly during the pandemic."[948] Researchers focusing on the province of Alberta similarly found there to be a "massive increase in non-COVID-19 related mortality among the youth."[949] Interestingly, it also appears that "accidental poisonings killed more young people than old people in 2020 and 2021," which may be related to alcohol and drug use.[950] Furthermore, about 20 percent of Canadians reported anxiety in 2020, which increased to 24 percent in 2024.[951] The levels of depression also increased from 10 to 15 percent over the same period, including in youth.

The second category of non-COVID-related excess deaths pertains to influenza and pneumonia deaths, which declined from 6,945 in 2019 to 4,115 in 2021. Deaths from influenza and pneumonia did increase to 5,985 in 2022, which represents an unprecedented 45.4 percent increase by historical standards. This raises a logical question: Where did the influenza go in 2020 and 2021?

Finally, another culprit of excess deaths in Canada may be long wait times for medical procedures. According to ClubVita, the waiting list of patients awaiting surgeries, diagnostic tests, and specialist visits was equal to 2.9 million across Canada in 2022, while the median wait time was around 7 months.[952] Based on freedom of information requests by SecondStreet.org, the number of individuals who died awaiting surgeries in Ontario since the onset of the pandemic increased steadily from 986 deaths (2019-2020), to 1,096 deaths (2020-21), to 1,417 (2021-22), and finally 2,096 (2022-23).[953] The number of individuals who died awaiting CT or MRI scans in Ontario also increased significantly from 5,534 deaths (2019-20), to 6,491 deaths (2020-21), to 7,397 (2021-22), and most recently 9,404 (2022-23).[954] These deaths reflect significant underlying problems with the Canadian healthcare system that have been further exacerbated by the COVID-19 pandemic and will require significant funding to address.[955] ClubVita has further estimated the total number of excess deaths related to delayed care in Canada as exceeding 4,000 during the pandemic.

In summary, it seems that those parts of the world that responded to the pandemic by postponing or delaying rapid treatment of the sick with COVID-19, relying on lockdowns and society-wide restrictions, and mass vaccinations have been plagued by a second epidemic of excess deaths which cannot be accounted for solely by SARS-CoV-2. These excess deaths appear because of the prescribed COVID-19 response measures, the unintended consequences of lockdowns, isolation, and potentially vaccinations.

PART IV: CONCLUSIONS

8

Public accountability and trust

In this closing chapter, it is important to turn to one of the most difficult considerations and topics pertaining to the implications of COVID-19 response. While COVID-19 and its variants continue to be present and the initial panic of the pandemic has subsided, it is vital to critically appraise public policy decisions and COVID-19 response in the context of two important components, namely public accountability and trust. This assessment is critical because these decisions not only determine people's confidence in the public sector, but they can also serve as the basis for future policy decisions. Therefore, "we owe it to ourselves to dispassionately study policy choices that were made, so that we can respond faster and better in the future."[956]

The central argument in this chapter is that if harm was caused, and it certainly was, there must be accountability as well as recognition of harm and justice. It is clear that "often, governments must respond to a crisis before its magnitude, causes, and effects are well understood."[957] and where "wait-and-see" and "do-nothing" strategies may not pay political dividends.

As argued throughout the previous chapters, the harms from COVID-19 response came in a variety of forms. In economic terms, there was damage to the economy, small business, and the middle class. Evidence confirms that public decisions forced millions of people into unemployment and, in some cases, even poverty. There were also multiple areas of negative impact on families and individual family members, including children, which has resulted in significant and long-lasting damage to mental health. Furthermore, COVID-19 response negatively impacted religious life, freedom, and liberty. On top of these impacts to nearly every aspect of individuals' lives, there were excess deaths. It turns out that, based on our analysis from previous chapters, "lockdowns may now be as dangerous as the virus, perhaps even more so, as the harms remain while any benefits are attenuated. Lockdowns ... importantly hit the working poor hardest ... and can lead to despair and self-destructive behaviour."[958]

Thus, it is essential to ask tough questions, such as whether the proverbial cure was worse than the disease. How did the state and its associated stakeholders behave? Is it possible that the "failure of authorities to act may represent the phenomenon of 'wilful blindness' to the red flags of surveillance?"[959] When "coupled with mandates and other government attitudes that have ridiculed, bullied, and coerced the vaccine injured, one arrives at a hypothesis of either negligence, or suppression driven by fear of political embarrassment."[960] So, did the state and its stakeholders create a situation of more risk out of a situation that had minimal or manageable risk? Moreover, did politicians, unelected officials, and others ask the difficult but relevant questions about policy choices, alternative modes of actions, different treatments, desired outcomes, and possible consequences? Some did, although many did not, instead choosing to stay quiet or not wishing to "touch" difficult questions for fear of political, professional, personal, and financial repercussions.

However, there are multiple notable examples of politicians who asked questions, of which two may be cited. In the first case Leslyn Lewis, Conservative Member of Parliament (MP) in Canada, for example, critically reflected on political decisions made by the state and its associated stakeholders in one statement:

> These are the same health and government officials who told us masking didn't work and then told us to mask. They assured us that the vaccines wouldn't be mandatory, and then made them so.

> They promised us the vaccines would stop transmission, and now are admitting they knew it never would. They can't be surprised that assuring us that everything is fine with absolutely no proof is not accepted by increasingly frustrated and disillusioned citizens.[961]

Another example, frequently quoted throughout this book, was Andrew Bridgen, a former MP from the United Kingdom (U.K.) who, along with a handful of colleagues, genuinely inquired about excess deaths from non-COVID-related causes. Another example is Senator Gerard Rennick from Australia. It is important that these difficult questions and concerns be asked, explored, and investigated. Hiding facts, burying information, censoring opposition and dissenting views, and engaging in name-calling only undermines public trust.

Public accountability

Public accountability is critical at any time when people's lives intersect with the public domain, political powers are delegated to the state, or when the state accepts full responsibility for effecting its powers on behalf of the public. If the state is to maintain a trustworthy relationship with its public, it must be accountable for policy orientations, decisions, and modes of execution; the allocation of public money and other resources (i.e., human, tangible, and intangible); and patterns of communication and interaction with the public.

As discussed in chapter 3, COVID-19 response does not only pertain to the actions of the state. Instead, COVID-19 response was implemented by a wide range of participants and stakeholders from various public, quasi-public, non-public, and private agencies, institutions, institutes, commissions, and offices. During the pandemic, the state and its companion stakeholders relied on a system of partnerships, structures, orders, laws, and regulations that arose from both expert and non-expert advice, but there were no society-wide public consultations. For example, nobody asked the elderly whether they wanted to be separated from their families, or children, adolescents, and young adults (and their parents) whether they wanted to spend the better part of two years learning on screens rather than in schools. It seems that the central planners knew better and did not need to ask.

Obviously, the goals and objectives pursued by the state need to balance various perspectives, circumstances, and settings as well as explore and consolidate conflicting points of view. These goals and objectives are normally reflected in the public agenda (a compendium of topics around which public policy is formulated) and public policy (a collection of principles and values that guide formal acts of the state). Public decision-making, which can be understood from different perspectives (i.e., political actions, ministerial and bureaucratic responsibilities, legal behaviours, democratic values, and so on), must also consider scope, criteria, and priorities. An important feature of public policy is accountability, as it represents a critical reflection on the attainment of the state's goals and objectives achieved through public policy, public agenda, and associated actions. Of course, it is rare that the state can achieve all its goals and objectives, so it is commonly accepted that there must be trade-offs. However, where there are decisions (including public decisions), there are also risks.

Public accountability: Key characteristics and parameters

Public accountability is not an abstract concept. It can be defined by many parameters, characteristics, conditions, and attributes such as expertise, dependability, efficiency, honesty, transparency, and legitimacy.[962] While there may be additional features of public accountability, a strong performance along these parameters can enhance public trust, instil confidence, and raise trustworthiness. Contrarily, a poor performance can destroy the public's trust, confidence, and trustworthiness in public institutions. It is important to define these key characteristics of public accountability prior to analysing their applicability to COVID-19 response.

Firstly, expertise may be viewed as a thorough and complete understanding of underlying background issues, a critical evaluation of available and possible alternatives, the quality and competence of expert advice, positive performance outcomes, the removal of underlying conflicts of interest, and a proper cost/benefit analysis. Contrarily, poor decision-making, uninformed evaluations of the available options, a lack of critical evaluation and introspection, a disregard of available information and facts, or unjust disqualification of alternative opinions cannot be viewed as demonstrating expertise.

Dependability can be defined as the ability to meet expectations by demonstrating precision, reliability, uniformity, repeatability, and certainty. Dependable public decisions set aside political calculations, external influences, and conflicts of interest in favour of fact- and evidence-based approaches. On the opposite side of the spectrum, dependability cannot include a high variability in decision-making, a lack of consultation, or flip-flopping, nor can decisions be political or ideological in nature.

Efficiency may be understood in terms of setting clear performance outcomes, communicating these targets to the public, and subsequently meeting these performance goals. Efficiency also means maintaining transparent accounting of the public purse and conducting a thorough evaluation of alternative uses of public funds. Alternatively, the improper allocation of financial resources, wasting of public funds, failure to achieve performance objectives, and poor public communication cannot be viewed as efficient public policy.

Honesty can be viewed in terms of fairness, sincerity, ethical behaviour, truthfulness, and credibility. One cannot regard as honest public actions that rely on society-wide and censorship (including academic censorship), attack of individuals advocating for alternative modes of actions or treatments, direct and indirect suppression of dissenting views through mainstream media and social media channels, persecution of physicians or religious leaders, and so on. Honest public policy also does not manipulate the public by cherry-picking information and facts to suit its desire narrative or method of communication. The act of censoring expert opinion, debate, dialogue, and alternative points of view may be regarded in itself as an act of dishonesty. As Scott Atlas, an advisor to Donald Trump on COVID-19, noted during the most recent conference at Stanford University on health policy during the COVID-19 pandemic, the act of censorship was also used to deceive the trusting, scared, vulnerable, and perhaps even naïve public into believing there was expert consensus on the subject. Censorship of subject experts during a crisis may also be viewed as an order of magnitude more egregious than under normal circumstances.

Similar to honesty is transparency, which includes the unbiased evaluation of alternative viewpoints, an openness to engage in debate, a full and complete disclosure of available information and facts, and the complete evaluation of costs and benefits. A lack of transparency in public policy is evident when facts and relevant information is hidden, information is selectively disclosed, official public business is conducted in secret, pressure is exerted on individuals and institutions, public opinion is manipulated, or when conflicts of interest are hidden.

Lastly, legitimacy pertains to the protection of basic laws of the land (i.e., constitutions, charters, declaration, etc.), human rights, and the judicial system from political interference. Legitimacy is synonymous with democratic rule, which means that public consultations and referenda should be held on important matters. Public policies and actions which violate basic human rights, suspend basic laws of the land, impede legal processes and justice, violate bodily autonomy, or use enforcement against people cannot be viewed as legitimate.

Public accountability and international perspectives

For analysis of COVID-19 response and the actions of the state and its associate stakeholders, one can focus on two analytical components that are critical for public policy, namely integrity and human consideration. The second component of public policy is especially important in times of

237

society-wide crisis that cause severe fear, stress, and anxiety, which were certainly emotions that were felt among the population since the onset of the COVID-19 pandemic. However, the first component of our analysis (i.e., integrity) may be defined as a wide-ranging concept that includes the parameters noted above, namely expertise, dependability, efficiency, honesty, transparency, and legitimacy. It is also possible to distinguish between high and low integrity levels along a spectrum. Public policy that is based on the poor disclosure of basic information and facts, the suppression of alternative views, an abstention from open public debate, the improper consideration of alternatives, and an inadequate evaluation of human and non-human costs and benefits cannot receive a high ranking for this metric.

On the other hand, "human consideration" is important for policy deliberation simply because public policy should serve the people. Therefore, key aspects to consider include human dignity and respect, values, cultures and traditions, religious practices, human relations and connections, compassion, and sympathy. In this capacity, public policy should also recognize that people have diverse needs, place different values on these needs, seek God and engage in religious faith, and value human connections. These aspects have been central to human existence and individuals' ability to flourish since the beginning of time, meaning that there is more to the human experience than physical safety. Similar to integrity, there are both high and low levels of human consideration along a spectrum. Public policy that is based on severe lockdowns, severe restrictions on movement and travel, the isolation of part of society (i.e., the elderly, the dissenters, families) from their loved ones, closing places of worship, using police forces to subdue protesters, the violation of basic human rights, and other such behaviours cannot be viewed as maintaining a high level of human consideration.

Figure 8.1 presents a graphical depiction of these two parameters (i.e., integrity and human consideration) in the context of public policies in different countries. The integrity x-axis continuum represents where the countries scored from 1 to 10 focusing on the six sub-parameters of public policy (i.e., expertise, dependability, efficiency, honesty, transparency, and legitimacy). The y-axis is related to the evaluation of human considerations in public policy and illustrates scores from 1 to 10 in five additional sub-categories (i.e., respect and dignity, values and tradition, faith, relations, and compassion and sympathy). Notably, figure 8.1 ranks the public policy considerations in the countries discussed in the previous chapter, although China is also included as a reference point since the country's COVID-19 response represents the most draconian set of lockdowns and restrictions experienced around the globe. Given that these countries were evaluated and scored along 11 sub-parameters (i.e., expertise, dependability, efficiency, honesty, legitimacy, transparency, respect and dignity, values and traditions, faith, relations, and compassion and sympathy) based solely upon available information (a detailed table with score is not included here), these scores are of course highly subjective.

Figure 8.1: A perceptual map of countries along two key parameters

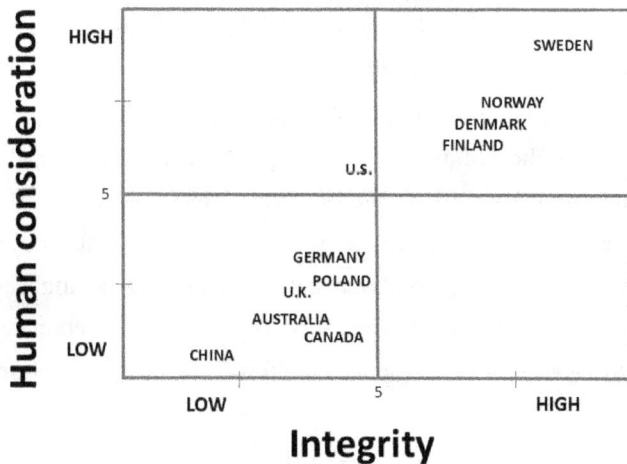

There are two main clusters visible in figure 8.1. The first cluster, located at the bottom left of the graph, includes countries which scored low in terms of both integrity and human considerations. These countries instituted severe lockdown measures and oppressive restrictions, operated a heavy-handed police state, and implemented drastic restrictions of movement and far-reaching surveillance. Furthermore, these public policies lacked human considerations, meaning that basic human rights, needs, and aspirations were outright suspended and played a subordinate role to the goals of the state. This combination of lockdowns with the inhumane treatment of individuals was allegedly for the public's physical safety, wellbeing, and common good. The leaders in the bottom-left quadrant are Australia, Canada, and the U.K., although even their restrictions and inhumane treatment of people paled in comparison to China. It would be interesting to analyse the prevailing social and political ideologies, social constructs, political structures, and other characteristics of the countries located in the bottom-left corner to establish similarities between them, as it may be no coincidence that these countries behaved in such a lockstep manner.

The second cluster, located at the top right, is the opposite of the bottom-left quadrant. It is important to note that several countries located in the top-right quadrant may have started with more severe restrictions and lockdowns, but quickly moved away from them upon a thorough evaluation of the facts, evidence, and relevant information. These countries also reflected upon people's needs beyond physical safety and re-evaluated public policy related to restrictions of movement, closures of schools, vaccination for the young, and so on. They also realized that society cannot operate with a singular and monothematic objective in mind, and that such an approach can lead to long-lasting economic, social, and mental health harms. The highest ranked country in this quadrant is Sweden, which imposed the fewest restrictions in Europe and even globally.

It is also worthwhile to note some specific distinctions in regions operated by different political parties and orientations. While provincial restrictions in Canda followed the same or similar lockstep regimes, the behaviour of specific states in the U.S. were considerably dissimilar.

On average, the states run by Democratic leaders align more with the bottom-left quadrant, while the states led by Republican leaders would more accurately fit into the middle of the graph or even the top-right quadrant.

Strategic evaluation of public decisions in the COVID-19 pandemic

The United Nations Office for Disaster Risk Reduction (UNDRR) and the World Health Organization (WHO) both define disaster as "a serious disruption of the functioning of a community or a society at any scale due to hazardous events interacting with conditions of exposure, vulnerability and capacity, leading to one or more of the following: human, material, economic and environmental losses and impacts."[963,964] The WHO also defines other disaster-adjacent terms, including disaster risk and risk assessment, disaster impact, disaster loss, and disaster risk governance, to name a few. The WHO's glossary also includes the term "disaster management," which is defined as "the organization, planning and application of measures preparing for, responding to and recovering from disasters."[965]

The standard approach to emergency management is the development of a process to deal with a disaster or emergency, including all comprehensive activities undertaken in an emergency. This standard process may contain either four or five steps (note that the first step may not be possible in all situations), including prevention (i.e., taking immediate action to avoid or reduce the chances of an incident, disaster, or emergency from occurring), mitigation (i.e., developing plans and implementing measures to prevent an emergency or moderate its impact), preparedness (i.e., building and activating capabilities to respond to a disaster, which includes organizing, planning, training, and evaluation), response (i.e., implementing actions to reduce the impact of an emergency through coordination and resource management), and recovery (i.e., employing actions aimed at normalizing conditions, restoring societal functions to a pre-emergency state, and generally recovering from an emergency). The key aim of all the stages of the standard emergency management process is to ensure that society and the people that comprise it can return to their normal functions and lives as quickly as possible. There is an implicit assumption that a return to normal is highly desirable.

In this chapter, however, a different model is used to evaluate the actions of the state and its associated stakeholders during the COVID-19 pandemic. The proposed model comes from the field of business study called strategic management. There are many advantages of employing the strategic management model in this capacity. The strategic management model relies heavily on both internal and external analysis, which is especially important in the case of the dynamic nature of the COVID-19 pandemic, due to the multiple variants with varying degrees of infection and mortality rates; availability of new information (i.e., academic studies, clinical experiences); different impact of SARS-CoV-2 upon specific age groups; effectiveness of lockdowns and other restrictive measures; and utilization of alternative methods of treatments and international experiences.

Firstly, the model also relies on an in-depth external analysis of various important forces: sociocultural (i.e., lifestyle, family, education, healthcare, population, life expectancy, age distribution, etc.), economic (i.e., growth, unemployment, inflation, family economics, etc.), legal and political (i.e., regulations, laws, trade, taxation, government spending, etc.), and technological (i.e., research and development, new products, innovation, patents, etc.). External scanning represents a comprehensive and complete analysis of the existing external environment from a wide range of perspectives, including a community analysis, from which decisions can be made. An external analysis looks at all the external forces and provides a critical evaluation which is not only based on forecasting and modelling, but also, and more importantly, based on facts and evidence, including international comparisons.

Secondly, in its focus on internal analysis, strategic management relies on a significant inward-looking analysis of underlying competencies, resource sustainability, and internal capabilities, as well as strengths and weaknesses. Thirdly, strategic management emphasizes precision in setting qualitative goals and quantifiable objectives, which are further converted into tangible plans, procedures, programs, and guidelines. The formalized goal-setting process allows for the careful evaluation of whether these goals and objectives are realistic and achievable. Fourthly, the model depends upon an iterative loop from background analysis to a thorough investigation of the analysis, to implementation and monitoring. This feedback loop is important because if used often and critically, it allows for frequent and timely adjustments to strategies, plans, programs, procedures, and executions. Thus, the loop is essential to properly addressing emergencies like the pandemic, which is not a singular event but rather a series of consecutive events. Lastly, and most importantly, the model forces one to conduct a thorough analysis before making any decisions or taking any action, therefore preventing random, ad hoc, haphazard, or capricious choices that can be driven by politics, ideology, and opinions. In essence, the feedback loop, grounded in monitoring and control, forces the state and its associated stakeholders into public accountability.

Key elements of the strategic management model

There are four steps to the strategic management process, as seen in figure 8.2. The first step involves internal and external analysis. In terms of external analysis, so-called environmental scanning is enacted and entails monitoring, evaluating, and disseminating information about the relevant environmental forces (as noted earlier) to individuals in the public sphere and its associated stakeholders. External analysis focuses on two fundamental questions with respect to the external environment: how complex is the underlying situation, and how fast is it changing? The key areas of interest in the internal scanning process pertain to an analysis of competencies, skills, processes, access to resources, procedures, assets, and so on. Another aspect of internal analysis may include value-chain analysis, which involves breaking the organizational activities of the state and its associated stakeholders into distinct elements and examining what resources the state has, how they can be utilized to achieve certain goals and objectives, and how they may be deployed effectively. A simple approach to internal analysis is a basic examination of strengths and weaknesses.

Figure 8.2: Components of the strategic management process

Strategic Management Process

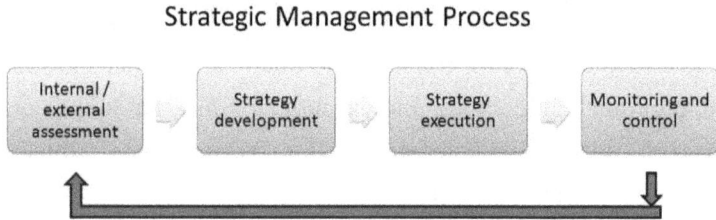

Source: Adapted from J. David Hunger and Thomas L. Wheelen, Essentials of Strategic Management (4th edition).

The second step in the strategic management process involves strategy development. This is the process of engaging in long-term planning and forecasting in the context of the performed analysis. Of course, the best results may be achieved when the analysis supports the underlying strategy. The long-term planning process involves determining what tactics and strategies can be effectively deployed and strategy development must entail the evaluation of all potential alternatives that are available on the strategic directional map. There are multiple mechanisms that allow strategies to be converted into action, although the most important objective is to choose the best strategy that will ensure sustainable, achievable, and measurable outcomes. The third step of the strategic management process is action-oriented strategy execution, which is a process through which well contemplated strategies based on a complete analysis are converted into actions with the use of detailed implementation tools such as budgets, programs, procedures, policies, processes, and mechanisms. A successful execution is dependent on people who execute the strategic plan.

The fourth and final step of the strategic management process focuses on monitoring and control. The objective of this stage of the process is to assure that goals and objectives are achieved, which can be accomplished by monitoring certain key performance measures and indicators or conducting a more comprehensive review in the form of a strategic audit. This step is critical, especially when strategic goals and objectives have not been met. If this is the case, monitoring and control serves as a trigger point to revisit the previous steps of the strategic management process and assess its individual components one-by-one.

Application of the strategic management framework to COVID-19 response

The actions, activities, and behaviours exhibited during the pandemic can be divided into the four steps of the strategic management process, which are briefly summarized in table 8.1. In terms of the background analytical component, after an initial period of fear, anxiety, and uncertainty, there were several facts about the pandemic that were ignored. It became clear early in the pandemic that lockdowns were ineffective, children and young adults were minimally impacted by SARS-CoV-2, the elderly (especially those with significant comorbidities) were disproportionately affected and at risk, physicians (out of a necessity to treat patients with SARS-CoV-2 early to avoid hospitalization) tested a number of alternative treatments with considerable success, and that there were multiple safety signals about COVID-19 vaccines not only from academia, but also from official databases and clinical practices.[966] As consistently stated throughout this book, the state and its associated stakeholders knew by August 2021 (or perhaps even earlier) that vaccination cannot prevent SARS-CoV-2 transmission. The state and its associated stakeholders therefore must have understood that the pandemic was not a "pandemic of the unvaccinated," which was an idea freely promoted by mainstream and social media.

Table 8.1: Evaluation of the state and its stakeholders in the context of the strategic management model

Internal and external analysis	• Limited focus on evidence-based assessment • Ignoring early facts about infection and fatality rates for different groups based on age, existing comorbidities, ethnic backgrounds, income levels, and so on • Lockdown and restrictions effectively aim to incentivize vaccination • No cost/benefit analysis • Society not included as a part of the consultative process • Poor assessment of risks with respect to different age groups • Censorship of doctors, academics, and the public • Silencing of physicians through local medical bodies, boards, and colleges • Mainstream and social media suppress dissident views and attack individuals, experts, and medical professionals • Adoption of a singular strategy • Suppression of early treatment aimed at avowing hospitalizations and deaths • Suppression of early warning signals related to safety and adverse events
Strategy development	• Limited strategy development beyond waiting for "safe and effective" vaccine • Ignoring facts in strategy development • Suppression of alternative strategies, including the Great Barrington Declaration • Over-reliance on epidemiological models with questionable assumptions • Reliance on uniform, one-size-fits-all strategies early in the pandemic, with limited exceptions • Some countries, local governments change strategy after initial lockdown • Using fear to drive vaccination rates

Strategy implementation	• Implementation of global one-size-fits-all strategies
	• Strategy implementation through lockstep and coordinated actions between public health officials, politicians, big pharma, medical colleges and associations, government advisors, etc.
	• Limited public communication through implementation (but also other steps of the process)
	• Massive harms to small business, families, the middle class, and religious life
Monitoring and control	• Limited evaluation of lockdowns; if held, they do not lead to public accountability and increased public trust
	• Limited or no cost/benefit analysis conducted post-mortem
	• Ignoring other key parameters of success
	• No proper account of damage and harm to selected groups, including children
	• No comprehensive review of society-wide harms
	• Vaccination numbers as the only performance criteria in the pandemic
	• Governments' general disinterest in public inquiries
	• Ignorance with respect to early warning

And yet, these realities were gravely ignored by the state, leading to the suppression of many scientists, academics, and physicians who, often at a significant personal, professional and financial expense, offered alternative views. Medical doctors who failed to support the mainstream message were deplatformed from social media and often discredited, which may have resulted in the loss of jobs or even lengthy legal proceedings with local medical boards and colleges that have continued until today. Most importantly, there was a suppression of alternative treatments such as the use of off-label medication in combination with other medicines, which has been noted in chapter 3. For example, there is evidence, which is supported by clinicians and researchers, to suggest that early treatment could significantly reduce hospitalization. How many human lives could have been saved if patients were given these off-label medications either as a treatment or prophylactically early in the pandemic? Furthermore, there was a simultaneous suppression of early safety signals about potential adverse events associated with vaccinations, warnings which are sadly becoming a visible and undeniable reality years later through confirmation by academic studies and a multitude of lawsuits. To provide just one more example of this orchestrated suppression and manipulation in the public sphere, an internal memo obtained under access to information confirmed that the Privy Council Office (PCO) in Canada, a formal administrative structure aimed to provide support to the Prime Minister and the Cabinet, "advocated downplaying COVID vaccine injuries or deaths."[967] It was also recommended that any deaths or injuries related to COVID-19 vaccines "be carefully managed with 'winning communication strategies'."[968] It is also clear that there was a multitude of lofty ideas promoted by mainstream and social media and individuals involved in the main narrative as "early slogans set the stage: 'everyone is at equal risk', 'no one is safe until everyone is safe', and 'no death from COVID is acceptable'."[969] This messaging was evidently meant to propagandise rather than to inform. In terms of strategy development, there was only a single narrative about the resolution of the pandemic: mass vaccination! Other plausible strategies, like the Great Barrington Declaration, were either suppressed or ignored. This phase of the strategic management process also ignored information and data which began to emerge. Moreover, the one-size-fits-all vaccination strategy was directed at everyone, from the young to the old, without any nuanced analysis and approach.

The strategy implementation of global mass vaccination was executed through a heavy-handed "nudge" program implemented by the state and its associated stakeholders. Many public institutions, private corporations, medical boards and colleges, universities, and schools exerted pressure to achieve an ever-increasing vaccination uptake from 50 percent of the population to 60 percent, and finally to 80 percent. Once some of these pre-determined uptake objectives were reached in the first round of vaccination, additional persuasive nudges were applied in the booster campaign. Did we really need to vaccinate healthy children, adolescents, and young adults? Was it necessary to fire unvaccinated nurses and healthcare workers? Did we have to oppress physicians? Were the unvaccinated truly such a threat if anyone, whether vaccinated or unvaccinated, was unable to prevent transmission?

Lastly, in terms of monitoring and control, it is difficult to find any analysis of the harms to the economy, education, small business, families, and most importantly children, which arose as part of COVID-19 response. It is also challenging to find any public admissions that the pandemic responses should have been more nuanced based on a proper evaluation and full disclosure to the public. There has been a similar, general disinterest in any honest evaluation of COVID-19 response by the state or its associated stakeholders.

Public trust

As noted above, public accountability is inherently connected with public trust, and the maintenance of both public trust and accountability are central features of the state's management system. This section starts with a quote from Joseph A. Ladapo, professor and State Surgeon in Florida. In his letter to the commission of the U.S. FDA and CDC dated May 10, 2023, Ladapo asserted: "Your ongoing decisions to ignore many of the risks associate with mRNA COVID-19 vaccines, alongside your efforts to manipulate the public into thinking they are harmless, have resulted in deep distrust in the American healthcare system."[970]

Ladapo further wrote in the final part of his letter, in reference to the CDC and FDA, that "your organizations are the main entities promoting vaccine hesitancy–Florida promotes the truth. It is our duty to provide all information within our power to individuals so they can make their own informed health care decisions."[971] Ladapo's commentary highlights numerous important points related to public policy, the most important of which is that truth, transparency, and openness are critical to public policy formulation and implementation. Ladapo also outlines the state's role in the provision of relevant information so people can make appropriate decisions for themselves. In this context, the access to truthful, honest, and complete information is critical. The Surgeon General has similarly summarized the importance of individual choice and decision-making, particularly in situations where the risk of adverse events exists. In short, where there is risk (whether minimal or considerable), there should be informed choice, transparency, investigation, debate, and public discussion. Otherwise, public trust is lost.

What is the existing evidence related to public trust? Let's consider a few examples from Canada and the U.S. In the case of the former, and according to StatsCan's survey conducted in the fall of 2022, Canadians have low confidence in public institutions. StatsCan specifically noted that "just under one-third of Canadians reported a good or great level of confidence in the Federal Parliament (32%) or the Canadian media (31%)."[972] The results of other research surveys confirm a general distrust of the state, such as Abacus Data, which found that "more than half of those interviewed found themselves agreeing with the statement 'official government accounts of events can't be trusted'."[973] These trends increased since the onset of the pandemic and worsened as the pandemic progressed. Proof Strategies, a PR agency in Canada, has identified that "there is a noticeable decline in how trusting Canadians are of their leaders and institutions as the pandemic drags on, and it's particularly striking among those who remain anxious or stressed about COVID-19."[974] Furthermore, a survey conducted by the PCO (Privy Council Office) in Canada found that "60 to 70 per cent of Canadians said they no longer believe many of the country's public institutions are capable of making decisions that benefit the public."[975] This evidence has led Kevin Bardosh to conclude that Canada's "approach to mandatory COVID-19 vaccine policy needlessly fomented social polarization, eroded democratic principles, harmed scientific integrity, and damaged public trust in our social institutions."[976] A more serious outcome of the aforementioned trends may be that public mistrust could also expand to universities and specialists because the government agencies may have used the "pretence of knowledge", as well as advice from some experts with multiple conflicts of interest, in their decision making. Moreover, as Thoene noted, "even though there were blatantly obvious conflicts of interest, such as vaccine producers publishing manuscripts promoting their own vaccine, articles were published in very prestigious journals."[977]

Despite a rampant emergence of so-called federal fact-checkers during the pandemic, research confirms that people are still sceptical. According to internal research by the Communications Security Establishment (CSE), a security and intelligence agency in Canada, most Canadians believed that they themselves could detect "fake news" without government interference or involvement.[978] In other words, they believed that they do not need the state to tell them what is true or false. People also distrusted the state's self-positioning as an expert on determining disinformation or misinformation because it is seen as another deceptive tool for self-expediency, self-promotion, and denigration of opposition. Moreover, according to the "2024 Edelman Trust Barometer Canada Report," 60 percent of respondents believed that the "establishment leaders were lying to them," which represented a 7-percentage point increase from 2023.[979] The mistrust of journalists and reporters was similarly high, equal to 55 percent and illustrating an increase of 5 percentage points from 2023. Additionally, 59 percent of respondents believed that "science has become politicised" in Canada.[980]

However, a general mistrust of the state, public agencies, and institutions has consequences. For example, according to Angus Reid, the proportion of parents supporting mandatory vaccination for children declined from 70 percent to 55 percent.[981] The research agency also reported that "one-in-six parents of minors (17%) say they are 'really against' vaccinating their kids, a four-fold increase from 2019" and that about one-third of parents expressed reservations about the science behind vaccinations.[982] The public has also expressed concerns related to healthcare decisions and experts as a result of their institutional scepticism. In the U.S., for instance, research from the Rasmussen Reports has found that "in the wake of the COVID-19 pandemic, a majority of Americans think it's more important to research health issues than simply trusting experts."[983]

In spite of this, "35% of American adults believe it's safe to trust advice from experts, while 58% say it's important to do your own research."[984] With respect to the "trust the science" narrative, it is important to remember President Dwight Eisenhower's farewell address wherein he noted that "in holding scientific research and discovery in respect, as we should, we must also be alert to the equal and opposite danger that public policy could itself become the captive of a scientific-technological elite."[985]

Examples of academic censorship and intimidation

In chapter 3, it was highlighted that one of the most oppressive measures implemented in the COVID-19 pandemic was censorship. The so-called "Facebook files" and "Twitter files" confirmed that "the censorship was systemic, directed, and highly effective."[986] It is worrisome that, in the U.S., issues related to censorship were only revealed when matters were pursued through court cases, legal discoveries, requests under the Freedom of Information Act (FOIA), whistleblower testimonies, individual testimonials, and various state and federal inquiries.

One of the most egregious examples of censorship is the case of Jay Bhattacharya, an accomplished academic and author of the Great Barrington Declaration (GBD). During his talk at the Massachusetts Institute of Technology (MIT) on April 4, 2024, Bhattacharya raised several thought-provoking points.[987] Firstly, Bhattacharya noted that the "vaccine establishment" sought to manufacture "unconditional scientific consensus" around a singular narrative (i.e., mass vaccinations), which resulted in any messaging that contradicted the main narrative becoming a target of attack. Bhattacharya observed that the objective was to silence any opposition, since only experts and the state were supposed to make decisions on behalf of everyone; other stakeholders were to execute. To ensure the active takedown of the GBD, Francis Collins, former director of the National Human Genome Research Institute (a separate institution that is part of the National Institute of Health [NIH]), wrote the following email to Anthony Fauci and his assistant:

> See htttps://gbdeclaration.org. This proposal from three fringe epidemiologists who met with the Secretary seems to be getting a lot of attention–and even a co-signature from Nobel Prize winner Mike Levitt at Stanford. There needs to be a quick and devastating punished takedown of its premises. I don't see anything like that online yet–is it underway?[988]

Following this call to action, Bhattacharya experienced both direct and indirect attacks on himself and the GBD. For example, he became "blacklisted" on Twitter, censored on YouTube, and Google quickly followed suit. Furthermore, a secret petition by Bhattacharya's colleagues at Stanford University was circulated for signature, asking the President of the university to silence him. As a result of his censorship, Bhattacharya has observed a close collaboration between the state, big pharma, and the media (including social media).

There have also been cases of academic censorship where academic journals either retracted an already published paper, pressured researchers to withdraw a paper after submission, rejected papers on dubious grounds, or used other intimidation tactics. While is not entirely clear how these decisions arose in the back offices of these journals, such censorious efforts may have prevented important information from getting to the public and the medical community. One could cite multiple examples here.

In one such example, an academic journal retracted an already published paper called "COVID-19 mRNA vaccines: Lessons learned from registrational trials and global vaccination campaign" in an unprecedented act of academic censorship. According to one of the article's authors Peter McCullough, who is a medical doctor and highly published academic, the paper recorded over 300,000 views, reads, or downloads in just one month, which can be compared to the standard record of less than 3,000 annual interactions for other papers published in the journal. The 38-page paper, which provided nearly 300 references, underwent a comprehensive review process lasting three months, during which the authors received comments by 8 reviewers. In broad terms, the paper focused on multiple aspects of the COVID-19 vaccines, such as potential serious harms and adverse events, control and processing issues, potential mechanisms of harms associated with the vaccine, all-cause mortality, a review of the registrational trials (i.e., omission in disclosure, methodological issues, lack of diagnostic testing), and contamination issues in some vaccine batches.

However, beyond the article's retraction, the most disturbing aspect of this act of censorship is the nature of the direct attacks on the authors. For example, one medical doctor and academic stated that the paper "is anti-vaccine gish-gallop that adds nothing useful to the literature."[989] In another instance, a professor of microbiology and immunology claimed "the authors utterly lack relevant professional qualifications that would enable them to assess the scientific publications they draw on and/or attempt to criticize ... In short, the authors cannot draw on years of training in biological science but appear to be self-taught via the 'University of Google'."[990] Such statements cannot be classified as scientific arguments or open and respectful debate and are instead attacks based on name-calling that fail to address key concerns in an attempt to discredit the authors. In response to the retraction decision, McCullough speculated that the journal was perhaps "pressured by the powerful Bio-pharmaceutical complex of coordinated public health organizations, vaccine manufacturers, and regulatory agencies to censor our paper to keep critical vaccine safety information from getting to the medical community."[991]

In a more recent case, an Indian-based company called Bharat Biotech, a manufacturer of India's first home-based COVID-19 vaccine called Covaxin, sued 11 scientists from Benaras Hindu University (BHU).[992] An academic journal also retracted their paper, which raised concerns about potential adverse events post-Covaxin vaccination, after being published for a only few months because Bharat Biotech argued that these claims were without merit and defamatory. Such actions by pharmaceutical firms are extraordinary and raise "questions regarding the balance between corporate interests and the authority of scientists to conduct and publish independent research, particularly in matters related to public health."[993] It also induces concern for academic freedom. In yet another recent case, a study called "Increased age-adjusted cancer mortality after the third mRNA-lipid nanoparticle vaccine doses during the COVID-19 pandemic in Japan" was retracted about two months after publication; the authors similarly disagreed with the retraction. In a nutshell, a wave of retractions of already published studies (which went through a thorough review process) that question the main narrative about the COVID-19 vaccines seems unprecedented. Fortunately, in many cases, the authors of these retracted studies were able to find alternative academic venues to publish their work.

McCullough and others' concerns are unfortunately not new, as similar concerns have been raised in the past and once again came to the forefront during the COVID-19 pandemic. In one instance from 2008, Marcia Agnell, Harvard University academic and former editor-in-chief of the *New England Journal of Medicine*, stated that "over the past 2 decades, the pharmaceutical industry has gained unprecedented control over the evaluation of its own products." [994] Most importantly, she reminded readers that "a study of medical school department chairs found that two-thirds received departmental income from drug companies and three-fifths received personal income," which can create significant conflicts of interest.[995] One of Agnell's key pieces of evidence was "GlaxoSmithKline's withholding of evidence that paroxetine was ineffective and possibly harmful to children and adolescents."[996] Agnell also shed light on some of the industry practices related to clinical studies, which were designed in such a way as to yield the most positive outcomes, stating that "this can be done in many ways. For example, comparator drugs may be administered at a too-low dose, so that the sponsor's drug looks more effective, or at a too-high dose, so that the sponsor's drug has relatively fewer side effects."[997] Agnell similarly exposed other potential problems, such as selectively disclosing data or downplaying adverse events.

Another editor of a prestigious medical journal (the *British Medical Journal*), Richard Smith, who served in this role for about 25 years, found that "medical journals are an extension of the marketing arm of pharmaceutical companies."[998] When reflecting on Agnell's observations, Smith observed that she "lambasted the industry for becoming 'primarily a marketing machine' and co-opting 'every institution that may stand in its way'."[999] To this end, Smith is reminded of "Jerry Kaiser, another former editor of the *New England Journal of Medicine*, [who] argues that the industry also deflected the moral compass of many physicians."[1000] Thus, Smith concluded that "the evidence is strong that companies are getting the results they want, and this is especially worrisome because between two-thirds and three-quarters of the trials published in the major journals ... are funded by the industry.[1001] Ross et al. corroborated these findings by noting that "there have been a number of recent exposés describing problems with [pharmaceutical] industry-sponsored trials, including issues related to withholding trial data, the involvement of marketing, inappropriate authorship, and lack of accountability."[1002] The corollary of these observations is that research papers presenting negative opinions of pharmaceutical products may have problems being published in top medical journals (or any journals) and the industry may have a disproportionately direct or indirect stranglehold on academic publishing.

We conclude this section with reflections from Kamran Abbasi, current editor-in-chief of the *British Medical Journal*, who stated:

> Politicians and governments are supressing science ... Science is being supressed for political and financial gains. COVID-19 has unleashed state corruption on a grand scale, and it is harmful to public health. Politicians and industry are responsible for this opportunistic embezzlement ... Importantly, supressing science, whether by delaying publication, cherry picking favourable research, or gagging scientists, is a danger to public health by exposing people to unsafe or ineffective interventions and preventing them benefiting from better ones.[1003]

Furthermore, Abbasi identified that public response to the pandemic in the U.K. "relies too heavily on scientists and other government appointees with worrying competing interests, including shareholdings in companies that manufacture COVID-19 diagnostic tests, treatments, and vaccines."[1004] One example of how COVID-19 response in the U.K. effectively suppressed scientists, cited by Abbasi, was when "the editor of the Lancet complained that an author of a research paper, a UK government scientist, was blocked by the government from speaking to media because of a 'difficult political landscape'."[1005] With respect to testing, Abbasi referred to "research published this week by the BMJ, which finds that the government procured an antibody test that in real world tests falls well short of performance claims made by its manufacturer."[1006] He also referenced the secretive and non-transparent nature of meetings by the Scientific Advisory Group for Emergencies (SAGE). As a result of a "press leak [which] forced transparency," the "inappropriate involvement of government advisers in SAGE [was revealed], while exposing under-representation from public health, clinical care, women, and ethnic minorities."[1007] Abbasi also exposed a potential financial motivation for this form of decision-making, noting that "the stakes are high for politicians, scientific advisers, and government appointees. Their careers and bank balances may hinge on the decisions that they make."[1008]

The main stakeholders in the COVID-19 pandemic

It is worth to reiterate, as discussed throughout the book, there was an overwhelming and singular focus on mass vaccination from the early onset the pandemic. This narrative was uniformly promoted by the state and its many associated stakeholders, with few notable exceptions.

Governments around the globe were not solely responsible for the implementation of lockdowns. These governments relied on a group of selected key stakeholders which behaved in lockstep to support the main narrative. Notably, these stakeholders were unelected officials who were not subjected to democratic accountability; in fact, they were accountable to no one. Instead, they were healthcare bureaucrats or public health officials with an associated healthcare apparatus who came from healthcare, academia, or clinical practice. It was the public health officials who executed restrictions, school closures, cancellations of non-essential businesses, testing requirements, capacity limitations, mask mandates, vaccination thresholds, vaccine verification cards, and various other impositions. They were also responsible for invoking public emergency orders, which were sanctioned by politicians.

Included in the unelected public health officials were those associated with various national quasi-public healthcare organizations (i.e., the Centers for Disease Control and Prevention [CDC] and the Federal Drug Administration [FDA] in the U.S.) and national medical research centres (i.e. the National Institutes of Health [NIH] and the National Institute of Allergy and Infectious Diseases [NIAID] in the U.S. and the Robert Koch Institute in Germany). These institutions provided advice and exerted disproportionate influence over the entire decision-making apparatus during the COVID-19 pandemic. They additionally maintained a significant media presence and influenced public opinions in this manner. However, there was also a wide use of experts and advisors from clinical practice, science, academia, and institutes who were instrumental in influencing public opinions by offering advice. It is unclear whether all these contributors were truly independent.

The mainstream media, and specifically social media, also played a significant role in furthering the main narrative. Sadly, as expanded upon in chapter 3, the mainstream media often perpetuated fear, anxiety, and division rather than providing calm, well-balanced, and natural views based on facts and evidence. This division was seen in Canada, for example, as "Canadians were divided into 'the virtuous' rule followers (selfless, smart) and the COVIDiot (immoral, self-centred, stupid)."[1009] Moreover, social media platforms, such as YouTube, Twitter, and Facebook, censored and de-platformed individuals, physicians, academics, and experts who questioned the narrative that vaccination was the only possible solution to the pandemic. Pharmaceutical firms, which were overwhelmingly present in mainstream media, were also influential in promoting their vaccine products and achieved robust financial benefits as a result. However, the top of this pyramid of decision-making influence was the World Health Organization (WHO), who sounded the COVID-19 pandemic alarm.

Additionally, there were other participants of impact who were less visible to the public eye, with one of the most influential being medical boards and colleges. These institutions uncompromisingly defended the main narrative and used oppressive measures towards selected physicians. They even went so far as to completely censor and threaten their own membership, which is the antithesis of what these organizations are mandated by legislation to do. As a result, physicians were pursued for utilizing alternative treatments and for vocalizing the potential adverse effects of vaccines, lockdowns, vaccination of children, and other topics. The active role of these medical bodies was unprecedented, and it is unclear why they behaved in this manner.

It is also important to consider the role of physicians, whose situations were more complex because they are subject to different forces, impacts, vulnerabilities, and dependencies. On average, physicians were timid, quiet, hesitant, and withdrawn during the pandemic, although there are examples of physicians who were outspoken. Most physicians were supportive of COVID-19 vaccine protocols while a disproportionately smaller group was hesitant. Many physicians who were initially hesitant to administer a new and experimental product often gave in pressure from the government and medical boards and colleges, or to financial incentives and other advantages, to quietly toe the line.

It was also interesting to consider why physician behaviours differed and what key drivers led to their different behavioural stances. Without formal research and multiple discussions with physicians it is difficult to generalize, but one can offer some subjective opinions. The group of physicians who firmly believed in vaccinations and supported their massive rollout acted consistently with advice from medical boards and colleges and trusted the narrative of quasi-public institutions (like the NIH, CDC, and FDA). However, it is not clear how many physicians outright rejected the possibility of adverse events even though they are well aware of the multiple side effects of medicines they prescribe every day, how many were intimidated by local medical boards and colleges, how many felt they needed to be loyal to the healthcare system, how many actually conducted their own investigations into the nature of novel COVID-19 treatments, and how many were subjected to group-think. It is also unclear how many were sceptical of the mainstream narrative but kept quiet for a combination of professional, personal, financial, and other reasons.

Of course, there was a small group of physicians that openly questioned the mainstream narrative, displayed scepticism of the medical system and the pharmaceutical industry, asked questions beyond what was presented by the state and local medical authorities, read extensively on the matter, and viewed the pandemic as an issue beyond just a health-related emergency. Some physicians from this group also saw the potential of adverse events associated with COVID-19 vaccinations and developed effective alternative ways and protocols of dealing with the pandemic, as noted in chapter 3. It is likely that many physicians switched from one group to another, but it is unclear what motivated them to change their views.

Operational functions and key stakeholders in the pandemic

Figure 8.3 presents a graphical representation of the state and its associated stakeholders in the COVID-19 pandemic along two axes. The y-axis represents a simple division into unelected and elected participants while the x-axis is complex and divides participation in the mainstream narrative in accordance with certain "functional" behaviours or functions in the pandemic. Of course, a high level of coordination and lockstep actions among these participants may be expected and even required given underlying threats in the pandemic. What is problematic is when all the stakeholders are solely engaged in pursuing a singular and monothematic public narrative that excludes other considerations and alternatives and leads to acts of intimidation, censorship, and oppression.

The graph uses different font sizes to highlight the varying levels of the stakeholders' influence in the process (i.e., bigger font sizes mean more impact, importance, influence, and decision-making power). All these participants more or less acted in lockstep, confluence, and devotion to the mainstream narrative of vaccination and lockdowns. The list of associated stakeholders is substantial, and the interconnections are complex. However, the figure does not include financial and non-financial relationships and inter-connections between the different associated stakeholders, which could have been important in motivating, eliciting, and "nudging" certain behaviours, because it would have unduly cluttered the graph. Regardless, two general observations can be made about figure 8.3, the first being that there is a disproportionate impact and influence of unelected individuals in public policy and the decisions of the state. This raises questions about who was truly running COVID-19 response and what expertise governments have if they rely extensively on unelected contributors. Secondly, different unelected stakeholders covered the entire spectrum of operational functions of the pandemic, often fulfilling multiple roles.

Figure 8.3 outlines that there were designers of the appropriate solutions and narratives regarding lockdowns, restrictive measures, and vaccination strategies. This group included various experts, scientists, advisors, academics, heads and members of health institutes, and of course, the state. It has been evident that advisors, heads of institutes, and academics such as Neil Ferguson and his colleagues from Imperial College London, Anthony Fauci, Rochelle Walensky, and Francis Collins, among many others, played key roles in developing the main narrative. The second operational function pertains to those who offered support for appropriate measures, including lockdowns and vaccinations. The associated stakeholders of the main narrative were everywhere, including in academia, the educational system, industry (in Canada, for example, this included members of healthcare, airlines, banking, transportation, etc.), trade unions, religious institutions, medical institutes, and the state. There were also designated public experts from these areas to further emphasize the main narrative; these physician-slash-expert-slash-media personalities frequently appeared on mainstream media and were active on social media. Of course, there was also the pharmaceutical firms, whose products were delivered into the marketplace for profit.

Another critical group were those, who implemented lockdowns, executed massive restrictions, and effected vaccination strategies. They predominantly included public health officers. Lastly, there were those who silenced and intimidated any counter-narratives, alternative viewpoints, or dissenting opinions. The most prominent suppressors of the free exchange of ideas, open debate, and even free speech were mainstream media and social media. However, a particularly intimidating role was played by local medical boards and colleges, which were particularly concerned with physicians prescribing alternative treatments. In one unusual case, a local medical body even pursued a retired physician for voicing raising concerns about COVID-19 vaccinations and not wearing a mask.

Figure 8.3: The state and its associated stakeholders

Pandemic functions

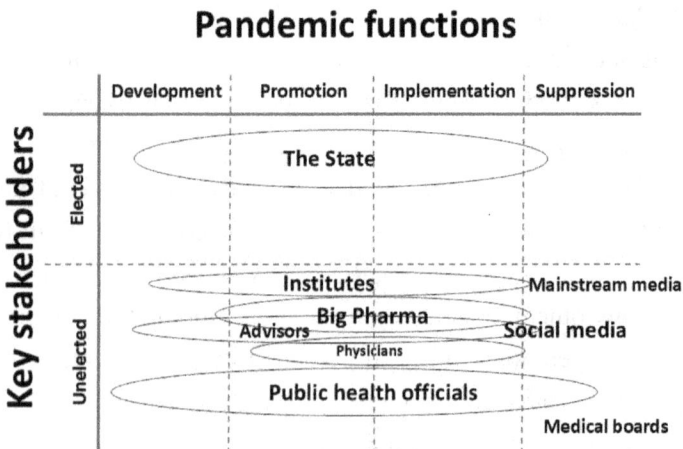

Although the influence that the pharmaceutical industry exerts upon academic publishing was already noted in this chapter, there were other groups unduly influencing academia. One of these relationships, namely the interaction between the National Institutes of Health (NIH), universities, and academics, is briefly described below.

As an example, between 2020 and the first 5 months of 2024, Harvard Medical School received $782.5 million in funding from the NIH (i.e., funding for research centres, research project grants [RPGs], training, and so on).[1010] Another key medical centre in the U.S., John Hopkins University, received $3.6 billion between 2020 and the first 5 months of 2024. The key question is: how likely is it that academics, whose careers, tenure, and advancement depend on funding from the NIH and the university at large, would publicly counter the official COVID-19 narrative promoted by the NIH?

Lastly, as noted in chapter 2, there was another important and stealth supporting "actor" in the COVID-19 pandemic, namely the problematic PCR test.

Public accountability and trust going forward

It is not an ambition of this book to be prescriptive with respect to public policy or alternative modes of action, as this requires much more reflection, investigation, and contemplations from multi-disciplinary perspectives, including health, economics, family, and religion, among others. However, an article from Kamran Abbasi in the *British Medical Journal* offers a simple but elegant solution:

> The first step is full disclosure of competing interests from government, politicians, scientific advisers, and appointees, such as the heads of test and trace, diagnostic test procurement, and vaccine delivery. The next step is full transparency about decision making systems, processes, and knowing who is accountable for what.[1011]

It is critical to address the two points mentioned above to move forward with any proper evaluation of COVID-19 response. There is also a need for full disclosure of the conflicts of interest of medical professionals and scientists, especially in relation to financial matters.

If this is not the case, we will surely have to revisit the Langstaff report (discussed in chapter 1) although this time it may be in the context of the COVID-19 pandemic. If we do not learn, we will experience another round of similar behaviours when the next Disease X or SPARS (St. Paul Acute Respiratory Syndrome coronavirus),[1012] already envisaged, comes around. Also, we will surely have to revisit the COVID-19 pandemic yet again, the legacy of which can be summarized in the following paragraph:

> Families and parishes at loggerheads. Education and healthcare on hold. Young people with heart damage and fertility issues. Livelihoods, reputations, and economies destroyed. The poor getting poorer and hungrier (something that began before the war in Ukraine). The unvaccinated ostracized, cut off, blamed for the sins of others or for a modicum of once-common sense. The vaccinated dying inexplicably. Ubiquitous, unrelenting propaganda; furious censorship of every reasoned argument. Constitutional rights and freedoms shredded. Protesters bludgeoned, fined, incarcerated. And, all the whole, children in anti-social isolation and soul-destroying masks–children still subject, despite everything we know, to experimental treatments they do not need that lay then open to any number of unexamined hazards.[1013]

Endnotes

Preface

1   Robert F. Kennedy Jr., *The Real Anthony Fauci: Bill Gates, Big Pharma, and the Global War on Democracy and Public Health*, New York, 2021, p. xix.

2   Ibid., p. xviii.

Chapter 1

3   Michael Palmer, Sucharit Bhakdi, and Stefan Hockertz, "Expert statement regarding Comirnaty–COVID-19-mRNA-Vaccine for children," Doctors for COVID Ethics, 3 July 2021, p. 2.

4   Edouard Mathieu et al., "Mortality risk of COVID-19", Our World in Data, August 2024.

5   The CMR is calculated by dividing the total number of deaths by the total population and expresses the proportion of death in the entire population exposed to the risk of death. The CMR illuminates the overall population impact. This is a less commonly used measure compared to the CFR and IFR statistics.

6   "Covid Statistics Canada", Justice Centre for Constitutional Freedom (JCCF), 10 February 2022.

7   Ibid.

8   "Leading causes of death, total population, age group", Statistics Canada, 27 November 2023.

9   Isaac Sasson, "Age and COVID-19 mortality: A comparison of Gompertz doubling time across countries and causes of death", *Demographic Research*, February 2021, pp. 379-396.

10   Mathieu, E. et al., op. cit.

11   JCCF (Canada), op. cit.

12   "Covid Statistics Manitoba", JCCF, 10 February 2022.

13   Ibid.

14   Note that the IFR and the CFR are similar statistics, but the CFR is higher since the number of infections is likely higher than the number of confirmed cases.

15   Cathrine Axfors and John P.A. Ioannidis, "Infection fatality rate of COVID-19 in community-dwelling populations with emphasis on the elderly", *European Journal of Epidemiology*, March 2022, pp. 235-249.

16   John P.A. Ioannidis, Cathrine Axfors, and Despina G. Contopoulos-Ioannidis, "Population level COVID-19 mortality risk for non-elderly individuals overall and for non-elderly individuals without underlying diseases in pandemic epicentres", *Environmental Research*, September 2020, p. 1.

17   Eisuke Nakazawa, Hiroyasu Ino, and Akira Akabayashi, "Chronology

of COVID-19 cases on the Diamond Princess cruise ship and ethical considerations: A report from Japan", *Disaster Medicine and Public Preparedness*, 2020, pp. 1-8.

18 Nina Dragicevic, "What we learned about COVID-19 from the Diamond Princess: Lessons learned from the once-biggest outbreak outside of China", *CBC*, 24 November 2020.

19 Note that another publication by Chris Baraniuk from April 2020 quotes 721 confirmed cases, resulting in the CFR of 0.42 percent.

20 Matthew R. Kasper et al., "An outbreak of COVID-19 on an American carrier", *New England Journal of Medicine*, November 2020, pp. 2417-2426.

21 Note that deaths on cruise ships are not uncommon, with about 200 deaths per year.

22 Kasper, M. et al., op. cit., p. 2417.

23 Kasper, M. et al., op. cit., p. 2417.

24 Nakazawa, E., Ino, H., and Akabayashi, A., op. cit., p. 2.

25 "Report 9: Impact of non-pharmaceutical interventions (NPIs) to reduce COVID-19 mortality and healthcare demand", Imperial College COVID-19 Response Team, 16 March 2020, p. 3.

26 "21 U.S. Code § 60bbb-3–Authorization for medical products for use in emergencies", *Chapter 9–Federal Food, Drug, and Cosmetic Act, Subchapter V–Drugs and Devices*, Food and Drug Administration, March 2018.

27 Regina Watteel, *Fisman's Fraud: The Rise of Canadian Hate Science,* Canada, pp. 55-56.

28 "Coronavirus (COVID-19) Vaccinations", Our World in Data.

29 Carlo Brogna et al., "Detection of recombinant spike protein in the blood of individuals vaccinated against SARS-CoV-2: Possible molecular mechanisms", *Proteomics Clinical Applications*, August 2023, p. 2.

30 Kellie D. Nance and Jordan L. Meier, "Modifications in an emergency: The role of N1-methylpseudouridine in COVID-19 vaccines", *ASC Central Science*, April 2021, pp. 748-756.

31 Franz X. Heinz and Karin Stiasny, "Distinguishing features of current COVID-19 vaccines: Knowns and unknowns of antigen presentation and modes of action", *NPJ Vaccines*, August 2021, pp. 1-13.

32 Alberto Rubio-Casillas et al., "Review: N1-methyl-pseudouridine (m1Ψ): Friend or foe of cancer?", *International Journal of Biological Macromolecules*, May 2024, pp. 1-12.

33 "Fact Sheet for Healthcare Providers Administering Vaccine", Pfizer-BioNTech, 6 April 2021.

34 "Fact Sheet for Recipients and Caregivers", Pfizer-BioNTech, 6 April 2021.

35 "Advance Purchase Agreement", European Commission, 20 November 2020 (redacted version).

36 "Advance Purchase Agreement", European Commission, 20 November 2020 (unredacted version).

37 Nadia Kounang, "Pfizer says early analysis shows its COVID-19 vaccine is more than 90% effective", *CNN*, 9 November 2020.

38   Maggie Fox, "Pfizer and BioNTech say final analysis shows coronavirus vaccine is 95% effective with no safety concerns", *CNN*, 18 November 2020.

39   Ibid.

40   "BioNTech SE–Depository Receipt", Securities and Exchange Commission, Form 20-F, 31 December 2021.

41   Kounang, N., op, cit. (see video).

42   Robert Hart, "Pfizer-BioNTech says COVID-19 vaccine is 95% effective, will seek emergency approval on Friday", *Forbes*, 8 November 2020.

43   Fox, M., op. cit.

44   Holly Yan, "10 reasons why young, healthy people should get vaccinated against Covid-19", *CNN*, 5 May 2021.

45   Bruce Stadel, Eric Colman, and Todd Sahlroot, "Misleading use of risk ratios", *Lancet*, April 2005, pp. 1306-1307.

46   Baruch Fischhoff, Noel Brewer, and Julie Downs (eds.), "Communicating risks and benefits: An evidence-based user's guide", FDA, August 2011.

47   Peter Doshi, "Pfizer and Moderna's '95% effective' vaccines–We need more details and the raw data", *British Journal of Medicine*, 4 January 2021.

48   Ibid.

49   Ibid.

50   "Connecticut pathologist offers to verify Pfizer vaccine efficacy for FDA evaluation if Pfizer is unable to perform the necessary tests: FDA petition filed seeking halt to vaccine approval until efficacy confirmed", *Business Wire*, 7 December 2020.

51   Piero Olliaro, Els Toreele, and Michel Vaillant, "COVID-19 vaccine efficacy", *Lancet Microbe*, July 2021, p. 279.

52   "Pfizer-BioNTech announces positive topline results of pivotal COVID-19 vaccine study in adolescents", Pfizer, 21 March 2021.

53   Kevin Bardosh et al., "COVID-19 vaccine boosters for young adults: A risk benefit assessment and ethical analysis of mandate policies at universities", *Journal of Medical Ethics*, January 2024, pp. 135-136.

54   "JCVI joint statement on vaccination of children 5 to 11 years old", Joint Committee on Vaccination and Immunization, 16 February 2022.

55   Harriet Alexander, "CDC is refusing to publish data it has collected on booster effectiveness for 333 million Americans aged 18-49 over fears it might show the vaccines as ineffective: FDA expert tells CDC to 'tell the truth'", *Daily Mail*, 21 February 2021.

56   Ibid.

57   Doshi, P., op. cit.

58   Camilla Turner, "Pfizer accused of 'bringing discredit' on pharmaceutical industry after Covid social media posts", *Telegraph*, 6 April 2024.

59   Ibid.

60   "ABPI Code of Practice for the Pharmaceutical Industry", Prescription Medicines Code of Practice Authority (PMCPA), 2021.

61   *CASE AUTH/3741/2/23–Complainant v Pfizer: Promotional use of Twitter,*

PMCPA, 1 March 2024.

62 Turner, C., op. cit.

63 Turner, C., op. cit.

64 PMCPA (1 March 2024), op. cit., p. 6.

65 *CASE AUTH/3591/12/21–Complainant v Pfizer: Concerns about a Pfizer BBC news article*, PMCPA, 6 December 2022, p. 40.

66 Ibid., p. 46.

67 Ibid., p. 46.

68 Sarah Knapton, "Moderna under fire at the children offered cash to test Covid vaccines", *Telegraph*, 2 October 2024.

69 Ibid.

70 *CASE AUTH/3886/3/24–A Complaint of Children's COVID Vaccine Advisory Council v Moderna*, PMCPA, 6 August 2024, p. 10.

71 Ibid., p. 12.

72 Esther McVey, "Corporate interests vs the public right to know", *Telegraph*, 2 October 2024.

73 Ibid.

74 *CASE AUTH/3746/2/23–Complainant v MODERNA: Allegations regarding promotion of Spikevax*, PMCPA, 9 August 2024, p. 1

75 Ibid., p. 7.

76 Sivan Gazit et al., "Severe Respiratory Syndrome Coronavirus 2 (SARS-CoV-2) naturally acquired immunity versus vaccine-induced immunity, reinfections versus breakthrough infections: A retrospective cohort study", *Clinical Infectious Disease,* August 2022, p. 1.

77 Ibid., p. 1.

78 Nabin K. Shrestha et al., "Effectiveness of the coronavirus disease 2019 bivalent vaccine", *Open Forum Infectious Disease*, April 2024, p. 1.

79 Hiam Chemaitelly et al., "Duration of immune protection of SARS-CoV-2 natural infection against reinfection in Qatar", *Journal of Travel Medicine*, December 2022, p. 2.

80 Nabin K. Shrestha et al., "Necessity of COVID-19 vaccination in previously infected individuals", *Clinical Infectious Diseases*, August 2022, p. 2.

81 Abdelilah Majdoubi et al., "A majority of uninfected adults show preexisting antibody reactivity against SARS-CoV-2", *JCI Insights*, March 2021, p. 1.

82 Colleen Shalby et al., "Healthcare workers refuse Covid-19 vaccine, even in priority access", *Los Angeles Times*, 31 December 2020.

83 Doha Madani, "Many front-line workers refuse Covid vaccines as distribution rollout struggles", *NBC News*, 31 December 2020.

84 Christopher J. Peterson, Benjamin Lee, and Kenneth Nugent, "COVID-19 vaccine hesitancy among healthcare workers–A review", *Vaccines*, June 2022, p. 1.

85 "WHO warns number of deaths surging–as it happened", *Guardian*, 12 December 2020.

86   Michael A. Thoene, "Changing views toward mRNA based covid vaccines in the scientific literature", *Polish Annals of Medicine*, July 2024, p. 152.

87   Ibid., p. 155.

88   Ibid., p. 153.

89   Ibid., p. 155.

90   Ibid., p. 153.

91   "COVID-19 viral vector vaccines and rare blood clots–Vaccine safety surveillance in action", Public Health Ontario (post deleted).

92   "Myocarditis and pericarditis after COVID-19 mRNA vaccines", Public Health Ontario, March 2022.

93   "Surveillance report: Adverse events following immunization (AEFIs) for COVID-19 in Ontario: December 13, 2020 to May 19, 2024", Public Health Ontario, 2024.

94   Ildus Pateev, Kristina Seregina, Roman Ivanov, and Vasiliy Reshetnikov, "Biodistribution of RNA vaccines and of their products: Evidence from human and animal studies", *Biomedicines*, December 2023, pp. 1-15.

95   Marco Cosentino and Franca Marino, "Understanding the pharmacology of COVID-19 mRNA vaccines: Playing dice with the spike?", *International Journal of Molecular Science*, September 2022, pp. 10-11.

96   Pateev, I. et al., op. cit., p. 1.

97   Elizabeth C. Bryda, "The mighty mouse: The impact of rodents on advances in biomedical research", *Missouri Medicine*, May-June 2013, pp. 207-208.

98   P. Mukherjee et al., "Role of animal models in biomedical research: A review", *Laboratory Animal Research*, 2022, p. 4.

99   "Pfizer enters into agreement with Acuitas Therapeutics for lipid nanoparticle delivery system or use in mRNA vaccines and therapeutics", Pfizer, 10 January 2022.

100   Kimberly J. Hassett et al., "mRNA vaccine trafficking and resulting protein expression after intramuscular administration", *Molecular Therapy*, March 2024, p. 1.

101   "4.2 Nonclinical Overview", Pfizer, 8 February 2021, obtained by Judicial Watch, Inc. from the U.S. Department of Health and Human Services on 28 February 2022.

102   Ioannis P. Trougakos et al., "Adverse effects of COVID-19 mRNA vaccines: The spike hypothesis", *Trends in Molecular Medicine*, July 2022, p. 551.

103   Wided Najahi-Missaoui, Robert D. Arnold, and Brian Cummings, "Safe nanoparticles: Are we there yet?", *International Journal of Molecular Sciences*, January 2021, p. 4.

104   Ibid., p. 1.

105   Nicolas Hulscher et al., "Autopsy findings in cases of fatal COVID-19 vaccine-induced myocarditis", *ESC Heart Failure*, January 2024, p. 1.

106   Peter I. Parry et al., "'Spikeopathy': COVID-19 spike protein is pathogenetic, from both virus and vaccine mRNA", *Biomedicines*, August 2023, p. 1.

107   Ibid., p. 1.

108   Marco Cosentino and Franca Marino, "The spike hypothesis in vaccine-

induced adverse effects: Questions and answers", *Trends in Molecular Medicine*, October 2022, p. 798.

109   Robert Tindle, "Long COVID: Sufferers take heart", *Australian Journal of General Practice*, April 2024, p. 239.

110   Cosentino, M. and Marino, F., op. cit. (October 2022), p. 797.

111   Marco Cosentino and Franca Marino, "Understanding the pharmacology of COVID-19 mRNA vaccines", *International Journal of Molecular Sciences*, September 2022, p. 1.

112   Pateev, I. et al., op. cit., p. 1.

113   Alana F. Ogata et al., "Circulating Severe Acute Respiratory Coronavirus 2 (SARS-CoV-2) vaccine antigen detected in the plasma of mRNA-1237 vaccine recipients", *Clinical Infectious Diseases*, March 2022, pp. 715-718.

114   Pateev, I. et al., op. cit., p. 1.

115   Pateev, I. et al., op. cit., p. 4.

116   Aram J, Krauson et al., "Duration of SARS-CoV-2 mRNA vaccine persistence and factors associated with cardiac involvement in recently vaccinated patients", *Vaccines*, September 2023, p. 1.

117   Jose S.A. Castruita et al., "SARS-CoV-2 spike mRNA vaccines sequences circulate in blood up to 28 days after COVID-19 vaccination", *Journal of Pathology, Microbiology, and Immunology*, March 2023, p. 128.

118   Krauson, A. et al., op. cit., p. 1.

119   Brogna, C., et al., op. cit., p. 1.

120   K. Dhuli et al., "Presence of viral spike protein and vaccinal spike protein in the blood serum of patients with long-COVID syndrome", *European Review for Medical and Pharmacological Sciences*, December 2023, pp. 13-19.

121   Nazeeh Hanna et al., "Detection of messenger RNA COVID-19 vaccines in human breast milk", *JAMA Pediatrics*, September 2022, pp. 1268-1270.

122   Ibid., pp. 1268-1270.

123   Note that expressed breast milk (EBM) refers to milk that is removed from breast prior to infant having access to it.

124   Nazeeh Hanna et al., "Distribution of mRNA COVID-19 vaccines in human breast milk", *Lancet*, October 2023, p. 1.

125   Ibid., pp. 1, 7.

126   Marco Cosentino, "COVID-19 vaccines mRNA detected into breast milk– now what?", *Substack*, 29 September 2022.

127   Xinhua Lin et al., "Transplacental transmission of the COVID-19 vaccine messenger RNA: Evidence from placental, maternal, and cord blood analyses postvaccination", *American Journal of Obstetrics and Gynecology*, June 2024, p. 1.

128   "5.3.6 Cumulative Analysis of Post-authorization Adverse Event Reports", Pfizer, 30 April 2021, pp. 12-15.

129   "ARCHIVE: Information for Healthcare professionals on COVID-19 vaccines Pfizer/BioNTech" (Regulation 174), Medicines and Healthcare Products Regulatory Agency, December 2021.

130 Dong Hyuk Kim et al., "Adverse events following COVID-19 vaccination in adolescents: Insights from pharmacovigilance study of VigiBase", *Journal of Korean Medicine Science*, March 2024, p. 1.

131 Palmer, M., Bhakdi, S. and S. Hockertz, op. cit., p. 18.

132 Palmer, M., Bhakdi, S. and S. Hockertz, op. cit., p. 19.

133 Palmer, M., Bhakdi, S. and S. Hockertz, op. cit., p. 19.

134 Timothy Cardozo and Ronald Veazey, "Informed consent disclosure to vaccine trial subjects of risks of COVID-19 vaccines worsening clinical disease", *International Journal of Clinical Practice*, March 2021, pp. 1-3.

135 Chien-Te Tseng et al., "Immunization with SARS coronavirus vaccines leads to pulmonary immunopathology on challenge with SARS virus", *PLoS One*, April 2012, p. 11.

136 Pfizer (30 April 2021), op. cit., pp. 7-12.

137 Christopher Nowinski et al., "Applying the Branford Hill criteria for causations to repetitive impacts and chronic traumatic encephalopathy", *Frontier of Neurology*, July 2022, pp. 1-19.

138 David Fredricks and David Relman, "Sequence-based identification of microbial pathogens: A reconsideration of Koch's postulates", *Clinical Microbiology Reviews*, January 1996, p. 18.

139 "About the Vaccine Adverse Event Reporting System (VAERS)", CDC, 7 August 2024.

140 Ibid.

141 "Electronic support for public health–Vaccine Adverse Event Reporting System (ESP: VAERS)–Final report", Harvard Pilgrim Health Care, Inc., 2010.

142 Jessica Rose, "Critical appraisal of VAERS pharmacovigilance: Is the U.S. Vaccine Adverse Events Reporting System (VAERS) a functioning pharmacovigilance system?", *Science, Public Health Policy, and the Law*, October 2021, pp, 100-129.

143 G.S. Goldman and N.Z. Miller, "Relative trends in hospitalizations and mortality among infants by the number of vaccine doses and age, based on the Vaccine Adverse Event Reporting System (VAERS), 1990-2010", *Human and Experimental Toxicology*, November 2012, p. 1112.

144 Ibid., p. 1112.

145 https://openvaers.com/covid-data.

146 Joseph A. Ladapo, "Drs. Callif and Walensky" (letter), Florida Health, 10 May 2023, p 1.

147 "Canadian COVID-19 vaccination safety report", Ottawa: Public Health Agency of Canada, 19 January 2024.

148 Ibid.

149 Ibid.

150 *Budget 2024*, Government of Canada, p. 135.

151 "COVID-19 vaccines safety update", European Medicines Agency, 17 February 2022.

152 "About V-safe", CDC, 8 August 2024.

153 *Informed Consent Action Network v Centers for Disease Control and Prevention and Health and Human Services, Civil Action No. 1:22-cv-481-RP*, 8 September 2022.

154 Sir & Glimstad LLP, "CDC's Covid-19 vaccine v-safe data released pursuant to court order", *PR Newswire*, 3 October 2022.

155 "Vaccines and Related Biological Products Advisory Committee", U.S. Food and Drug Administration (FDA), 22 October 2020.

156 Imran Rizvi et al., "Acute hemorrhagic leukoencephalitis after administration of the first dose of ChAdO1 nCoV-19 SARS-CoV-2 (COVISHELD) vaccine", *Neuroimmunology Reports*, March 2022, pp. 1-3.

157 Ahmed S. Aly et al., "Guillain-Barre syndrome following COVID-19 vaccination: A case report and an updated review", *Neuroimmunology Reports*, February 2022, pp. 1-6.

158 Giuseppe Carli et al., "Deep vein thrombosis (DVT) occurring shortly after the second dose of mRNA SARS-CoV-2 vaccine", *Internal and Emergency Medicine*, February 2021, pp. 803-804.

159 Isabel Garrido et al., "Autoimmune hepatitis after COVID-19 vaccine–more than a coincidence", *Journal of Autoimmunity*, October 2021, pp. 1-3.

160 Abdallah D. Abukhalil et al., "Side effects of Pfizer/BioNTech (BNT162b2) COVID-19 vaccine reported by the Birzeit University community", *BMC Infectious Diseases*, January 2023, pp. 1-15.

161 Valerio Liguori et al., "Multisystem inflammatory syndrome in children following COVID-19 vaccination: A sex-stratified analysis of the VAERS database using Brighton collaboration criteria", *Pharmaceuticals*, August 2023, pp. 1-14.

162 Ahmed N. Alghamdi et al., "BNT162b2 and ChAdOx1 SARS-Cov-2 post vaccination side-effects among Saudi vaccinees", *Frontiers in Medicine*, October 2021, pp. 1-10.

163 Maryam Kakovan et al., "Stroke associated with COVID-19 vaccine", *Journal of Stroke and Cerebrovascular Disease*, June 2022, pp. 1-23.

164 Nadia McMillian et al., "Fatal post COVID mRNA-vaccine associated cerebral ischemia", *Neurohospitalist*, April 2023, p. 156.

165 Ibid., p. 156.

166 Itai Gat et al., "COVID-19 vaccination BNT162b2 temporarily impairs semen concentration and total motile count among semen donors", *Andrology*, June 2022, p. 1.

167 Jing-Xing Li et al., "Risk assessment of retinal vascular occlusion after COVID-19 vaccination", *NPJ Vaccines*, May 2022, p. 1.

168 Joseph Fraiman et al., "Serious adverse events of special interest following mRNA COVID-19 vaccination in randomized trials in adults", *Vaccine*, September 2022, pp. 5798-5805.

169 Hui-Lee Wong et al., "Surveillance of COVID-19 vaccine safety among elderly persons aged 65 years and older", *Vaccine*, January 2022, pp. 532-539.

170 Tindle, R., op. cit., p. 239.

171 Nicolas Hulscher et al., "Clinical approach to post-acute sequelae after

COVID-19 infection and vaccination", *Cureus*, November 2023, p. 1.

172   Vladimir N. Uversky et al., "IgG4 antibodies induced by repeated vaccination may generate immune tolerance to the SARS-Cov-2 spike protein", *Vaccines*, May 2023, p. 1.

173   Ibid., p. 1.

174   Max Schmeling, Vibeke Manniche, and Peter Riis Hansen, "Batch-dependent safety of the BNT182b2 mRNA COVID-19 vaccine", *European Journal of Clinical Investigation*, March 2023, pp. 1-3.

175   Ibid., 2.

176   Hulscher, N. et al. (January 2024), op. cit., p. 11.

177   Kevin McKernan et al., "Sequencing of bivalent Moderna and Pfizer mRNA vaccines reveals nanogram to microgram quantities of expression vector dsDNA per dose", *OSF Preprints*, April 2023.

178   David J. Speicher et al., "DNA fragments detected in monovalent and bivalent Pfizer/BioNTech and Moderna modRNA COVID-19 vaccines from Ontario, Canada: Exploratory dose response relationship with serious adverse events", *OSF Preprints*, October 2023.

179   Rocky Swift, "Japan suspends 1.6 mln doses of Moderna shot after contamination reports", *Reuters*, 26 August 2021.

180   Tindle, R., op. cit., p. 239.

181   "Coronavirus (COVID-19) update", FDA News Release, 25 June 2021.

182   Jason P. Block, "Cardiac complications after SARS-CoV-2 infection and mRNA COVID-19 vaccination–PCORnet, United States, January 2021–January 2022", *Morbidity and Mortality Weekly Report*, April 2022.

183   Constantin Schwab et al., "Autopsy-based histopathological characterization of myocarditis after anti-SARS-CoV-2-vaccination", *Clinical Research in Cardiology*, March 2023, p. 431.

184   Bardosh et al., op. cit., p. 126.

185   Jessica Rose, Nicolas Hulscher, and Peter A. McCullough, "Determinants of COVID-19 vaccine-induced myocarditis requiring hospitalization", *Therapeutic Advances in Drug Safety*, January 2024, pp. 1-15.

186   Christian Baumeier et al., "Intramyocardial inflammation after COVID-19 vaccination: An endomyocardial biopsy-proven case series", *International Journal of Molecular Sciences*, June 2022, p. 1.

187   Sangjoon Choi et al., "Myocarditis-induced sudden death after BNT162b2 mRNA COVID-19 vaccination in Korea: Case report focusing on histopathological findings", *Journal of Korean Medical Science*, October 2021, p. 1.

188   Anis Barmada et al., "Cytokinopathy with aberrant cytoxic lymphocytes and profibrotic myeloid response in SARS-CoV-2 mRNA vaccine-associated myocarditis", *Science Immunology*, May 2023, p. 2.

189   Dimitrios Tsilingiris et al., "Potential implications of lipid nanoparticles in the pathogenesis of myocarditis associated with the use of mRNA vaccines against SARS-CoV-2", *Metabolism Open*, March 2022, p. 1.

190   Allison Krug, Josh Stevenson, and Tracy B. Høeg, "BNT162b2 vaccine-

associated myo/pericarditis in adolescents: A stratified risk-benefit analysis", *European Journal of Clinical Investigation*, February 2022, pp. 1-16.

191   Muazzam M. Sherrif et al., "A study on the self-reported physician-diagnosed cardiac complications post mRNA vaccination in Saudi Arabia", *Cureus*, January 2024, pp. 1-12.

192   Suyanee Mansanguan et al., "Cardiovascular manifestations of the BNT162b2 mRNA COVID-19 vaccine in adolescents", *Tropical Medicine and Infectious Disease*, August 2022, p. 1.

193   Ibid., p. 1.

194   Takehiro Nakahara, "Assessment of myocardial F-FDG uptake at PET/ CT in asymptomatic SARS-CoV-2 vaccinated and nonvaccinated patients", *Radiology*, September 2023, p. 1.

195   Investigations Team and Robert Mendick, "AstraZeneca admits its Covid vaccine can cause rare side effects in court documents for first time", *Telegraph*, 28 April 2024.

196   Ibid.

197   "AstraZeneca/Oxford vaccine approval is a 'triumph of British science': Johnson", *Reuters*, 30 December 2020.

198   Investigations Team and Mendick, R., op. cit.

199   "Scientists may have solved an important part of the mystery of ultra-rare blood clots linked to adenovirus COVID-19 vaccines", Cardiff University, 2 December 2021.

200   Clare Dyer, "Patients launch legal action against AstraZeneca over its COVID-19 vaccine", *British Medical Journal*, March 2023, p. 1.

201   "Ontario confirms first case of rare AstraZeneca-linked blood clotting", *Ontario News*, 23 April 2021.

202   Andreas Greinacher et al., "Pathogenesis of vaccine-induced immune thrombotic thrombocytopenia (VITT)", *Seminars in Hematology*, April 2022, pp. 97-107.

203   "AstraZeneca withdraws its COVID-19 vaccine worldwide", *CBC News*, 8 May 2024.

204   Ingunn Skjesol and Jonathan Q. Tritter, "The Norwegian way: COVID-19 vaccination policy and practice", *Health Policy and Technology*, June 2022, pp. 1, 7.

205   Ibid., p. 2.

206   Ibid., p. 3.

207   Ibid., p. 3.

208   "AstraZeneca withdraws its COVID-19 vaccine worldwide", *CBC News*, 8 May 2024.

209   Ibid.

210   Lara Keay, "Infected blood scandal 'not an accident' with catalogue of failures' and 'downright deception' by NHS and governments", *Sky News*, 20 May 2024.

211   Ibid.

212 "The Report", Infected Blood Inquiry, 20 May 2024.

213 Neil Johnston, "'Children treated as guinea pigs'–Five damning findings from infected blood report", *Telegraph*, 20 May 2024.

214 Ibid.

215 Ibid.

216 Ibid.

217 Infected Blood Inquiry (volume 7), p. 189.

218 Ibid., p. 286.

219 Infected Blood Inquiry (volume 1), p. 6.

Chapter 2

220 Emma Farge and John Revill, "'Test, test, test': WHO's chief coronavirus message to the world", *Reuters*, 16 March 2020.

221 "The Noble Prize in Chemistry 1993. Kary B. Mullis: Facts", The Nobel Prize, 1993.

222 Michael Palmer, Sucharit Bhakdi, and Stefan Hockertz, "Expert statement regarding Comirnaty–COVID-19-mRNA vaccine for children", Doctors for COVID Ethics, 4 October 2021, p. 5.

223 Byram Bridle, Expert testimony (letter to Mr. James Kitchen), 23 April 2021, p. 4.

224 Ibid., p. 4.

225 Jared Bullard et al., "Predicting infectious Severe Acute Respiratory Syndrome Coronavirus 2 from diagnostic samples", *Clinical Infectious Diseases*, December 2020, pp. 2663-2666.

226 Victor M. Corman et al., "Detection of 2019 novel coronavirus (2019-nCoV) by real-time RT-PCR", *Eurosurveillance*, January 2020, pp. 1-8.

227 Rogier R. Jansen et al., "Frequent detection of respiratory viruses without symptoms: Toward defining clinically relevant cut-off values", *Journal of Clinical Microbiology*, July 2011, pp. 2631-2636.

228 *Gateway Bible Baptist Church et al. v Manitoba et al.*, 21 October 2021, pp. 1-156.

229 "Manitoba chief microbiologist and laboratory specialist: 56% of positive 'cases' are not infectious", Justice Centre for Constitutional Freedom (JCCF), 11 May 2021.

230 Ibid.

231 *Gateway Bible Baptist Church et al. v Manitoba et al.*, op. cit., p. 71.

232 *Gateway Bible Baptist Church et al. v Manitoba et al.*, op. cit., p. 72.

233 Bullard, J. et al., op. cit., p. 3.

234 *Gateway Bible Baptist Church et al. v Manitoba et al.*, op. cit., p. 57.

235 JCCF, op. cit.

236 Rita Jafaar et al., "Correlation between 3790 qPCR positives samples and positive cell cultures including 1941 SARS-CoV-2 isolates", *Clinical Infectious Diseases*, September 2020, pp. 2-3.

237 Nandinin Sethuraman, Sundararaj S. Jeremiah, and Akihide Ryo, "Interpreting

diagnostic tests for SARS-CoV-2", *JAMA*, 6 May 2020, p. 1.

238 Apoorva Mandavilli, "Your coronavirus test is positive. Maybe it shouldn't be", *New York Times*, 15 September 2020.

239 Ibid.

240 Ibid.

241 Elena Surkova, Vladyslav Nikolayevsky, and Francis Drobniewski, "False-positive COVID-19 results: Hidden problems and costs", *Lancet*, September 2020, p. 1168.

242 "International guidelines for certification and classification (coding) of COVID-19 cause of death", World Health Organization (WHO), 20 April 2020, pp. 1-14.

243 "Communicable disease management protocol: Coronavirus-COVID-19", Manitoba Public Health Branch, November 2023, p. 11.

244 Ibid., p. 3.

245 Ibid., p. 3.

246 "COVID-19 specific disease protocol (provincial)–Acute and community health-care settings", Manitoba Shared Health, 25 October 2024, p. 9.

247 See, for example, the affidavit from medical doctor and former chief medical officer of health and chief public health officer in the province of Manitoba Joel Kettner posted on the JCCF's website, which is also available elsewhere. https://www.jccf.ca/wp-content/uploads/2021/10/08-Affidavit-of-Joel-Kettner-sw-Apr1-21.pdf

248 Surkova, H., Nikolayevsky, V. and F. Drobniewski, op. cit., p. 1167.

249 Shiyi Cao et al., "Post-lockdown SARS-CoV-2 nucleic acid screening in nearly ten million residents of Wuhan, China", *Nature*, November 2020, p. 1.

250 Ibid., p. 2.

251 Józef Białek, *COVID-19: Globalna mistyfikacja*, Wrocław, 2021, p. 172.

252 "Covid PCR test reliability doubtful–Portugal judges", *Portugal News*, 27 November 2020.

253 Ibid.

254 Pieter Borger et al., "External review of the RT-PCR test to detect SARS-CoV-2 results reveals 10 major scientific flaws at the molecular and methodological level: Consequences for false positive results", *ResearchGate*, November 2020, p. 2.

255 Ibid., p. 2.

256 Corman, V. M. et al., op. cit., p. 1.

257 Trestan Pillonel et al., "Letter to the editor: SARS-CoV-2 detection by real-time RT-PCR", *Eurosurveillance*, May 2020, p. 1.

258 "CDC 2019-Novel Coronavirus (2019-nCoV) Real-Time RT-PCR Diagnostic Panel", FDA, 21 July 2021, p. 40.

259 Jessica Watson et al., "Interpreting a COVID-19 test result", *British Medical Journal*, March 2020, p. 1.

260 Borger, P. et al., op. cit., p. 17.

261 Corman, V. M. et al., op. cit., p. 4.

262   Borger, P. et al., op. cit., p. 17.

263   Pillonel, P. et al., op. cit., p. 1.

264   Borger, P. et al., op. cit., pp. 1-29.

265   Corman, V. M. et al., op. cit., p. 1.

266   Edward Hadas, "The assault on humanity", Together for the Common Good.

267   Kevin Bardosh et al., "Was lockdown worth it? Community perspectives and experiences of the Covid-19 pandemic in remote southwestern Haiti", *Social Sciences & Medicine*, August 2023, p. 1.

268   Seth Flaxman et al., "Estimating the effects of non-pharmaceutical interventions on COVID-19 in Europe", *Nature*, August 2020, p. 257.

269   Linda Thunstrom et al., "The benefits and costs of using social distancing to flatten the curve for COVID-19", *Journal of Benefit-Cost Analysis*, May 2020, pp. 179-195.

270   Rabail Chaudhry et al., "A country analysis measuring the impact of government actions, country preparedness and socioeconomic factors on COVID-19 mortality and related health outcomes", *Lancet*, July 2020, p. 7.

271   Ibid., p. 7.

272   Douglas W. Allen, "Covid-19 lockdown cost/benefits: A critical assessment of the literature", Simon Fraser University, April 2021, p. 1.

273   Ibid., p. 4.

274   Casey Mulligan, Kevin Murphy, and Robert Topel, "Some basic economics of Covid-19 policy", *Chicago Booth Review*, 27 April 2020.

275   Ibid.

276   Andrew Atkenson et al., "Four stylized facts about Covid-19", NBER, August 2020.

277   Christian Bjornskov, "Did lockdowns work? An economist's cross-country comparison", SSRN, August 2020, p. 7.

278   Hunt Allcott et al., "What explains temporal and geographic variations in the early US coronavirus pandemic", NBER, December 2020.

279   Thomas Meunier, "Full lockdown policies in Western Europe countries have no evident impacts on the COVID-19 pandemic", *MedRxiv*, May 2020.

280   John Gibson, "Government mandated lockdowns do not reduce Covid deaths: Implications for evaluating the stringent New Zealand response", University of Waikato, June 2020.

281   Allen, D., op. cit., p. 1.

282   Jonas Herby, Lars Jonung, and Steve H. Henke, "Did Lockdowns Work? The Verdict on Covid Restrictions", IEA Perspective, June 2023, p. 20.

283   "Lockdowns were a costly failure, finds new IEA book", Institute of Economic Affairs, 5 June 2023.

284   Ibid.

285   Allen, D., op. cit., p. 33.

286   Jonas Herby, Lars Jonung, and Steve H. Hanke, "A systematic literature review and meta-analysis of the effects of lockdowns on COVID-19 mortality", Johns Hopkins University, May 2021, p. 30.

287 Ibid., p. 2.

288 John Gibson, "Government mandated lockdowns do not reduce Covid-19 deaths: Implications for evaluating the stringent New Zealand response", *New Zealand Economic Papers*, November 2020, pp. 17-28.

289 Ibid., pp. 17-28.

290 Martin Lally, "The costs and benefits of COVID-19 lockdowns in New Zealand", Capital Financial Consultants, July 2021, p. 23.

291 Christopher R. Berry et al., "Evaluating the effects of shelter-in-place policies during the COVID-19 pandemic", *PNAS*, April 2021, p. 3.

292 Benjamin Cooper, "Lockdown backlog feared to be killing more than Covid", *Independent*, August 2022.

293 Allen, D. op. cit., p. 37.

294 Per Engzell et al., "Learning loss due to school closures during the COVID-19 pandemic", *PNAS*, April 2021, pp. 1-7.

295 Susan Rose et al., "Impact of school closures and subsequent support strategies on attainment and socio-emotional wellbeing in key stage 1. Research report", Education Endowment Foundation, December 2021.

296 Tomasz Gajdorowicz et al., "Capturing the educational and economic impacts of school closures in Poland", IZA Institute of Labor Economics, December 2022.

297 Josh Christenson, "The key moments when Dr. Anthony Fauci contradicted himself during heated Covid hearing", *New York Post*, 3 June 2024.

298 "Top Vancouver doc caught admitting vax passports are merely 'incentive' program", *Daily*, 23 October 2021.

299 "Provincial health officer rescinds orders for COVID-19", Office of the Provincial Health Minister, 26 July 2024.

300 "COVID-19 public-health emergency ends, new vaccine registry will keep people safe", Office of the Provincial Health Minister, 26 July 2024.

301 Ibid.

302 Regina Watteel, *Fisman's Fraud: The Rise of Canadian Hate Science,* Canada, 2023, p. 88.

303 Thomas V. Ingelsby et al., "Disease mitigation measures in the control of pandemic influenza", *Biosecurity and Bioterrorism*, December 2006, p. 373.

304 Allen, D., op. cit., p. 44.

305 Ingrid Sperre Saunes et al., "Nordic response to COVID-19: Governance and policy measures in the early phase of the pandemic", *Health Policy*, May 2022, p. 420.

306 Ibid., p. 420.

307 Jostein Askim and Tomas Bergstrom, "Between lockdown and calm down. Comparing the COVID-19 responses of Norway and Sweden", *Local Government Studies*, August 2021, p. 304.

308 Ibid., p. 298.

309 Johan Norberg, "Sweden during the pandemic: Pariah or paragon?", Cato Institute, August 2023, p. 3.

310   Ibid., p. 3.

311   Ibid., p. 3.

312   Ibid., pp. 3-4.

313   Ibid., p. 4.

314   Lise M. Helsingen et al., "The COVID-19 pandemic in Norway and Sweden–threats, trust, and impact on daily life: A comparative survey", *Biomed Central,* October 2020, p. 7.

315   Ibid., p. 7.

316   Norberg, J., op. cit., p. 4.

317   Norberg, J., op. cit., p. 3.

318   Kelly Bjorklund and Andrew Ewing, "The Swedish COVID-19 response is a disaster. It shouldn't be a model for the rest of the world", *Time*, 27 July 2020.

319   Derek Robertson, "'They are leading us to catastrophe': Sweden's coronavirus stoicism begins to jar", *Guardian*, 30 March 2020.

320   Peter S. Goodman, "Sweden has become the world's cautionary tale", *New York Times*, 8 July 2020.

321   Norberg, J., op. cit., p. 6.

322   Norberg, J., op. cit., p. 10.

323   Helsingen, L. et al., op. cit., p. 7.

324   Goril Ursin, Ingunn Skjesol, and Jonathan Tritter, "The COVID-19 pandemic in Norway: The dominance of social implications in framing the policy response", *Health Policy and Technology*, December 2020, p. 671.

325   Ibid., p. 663.

326   Askim, J. and T. Bergstrom, op. cit., p. 291.

327   Saunes, I. et al., op. cit., p. 419.

328   Ingunn Skjesol and Jonathan Q. Tritter, "The Norwegian way: COVID-19 vaccination policy and practice", *Health Policy and Technology*, June 2022, p. 1.

329   Helsingen, L. et al., op. cit., p. 5.

330   Helsingen, L. et al., op. cit., p. 5.

331   Saunes, I. et al., op. cit., pp. 418-426.

332   Askim, J. and T. Bergstrom, op. cit., pp. 291-311.

333   Tom Christensen and Per Laegrid, "Balancing governance capacity and legitimacy: How the Norwegian government handled the COVID-19 crisis as a high performer", *Public Administration Review*, October 2020, p. 775.

334   Helsingen, L. et al., op. cit., p. 1.

335   Helsingen, L. et al., op. cit., p. 3.

336   Saunes, I. et al., op. cit., p. 420.

337   Christensen, T. and P. Laegrid, op. cit., p. 775.

338   Askim, J. and T. Bergstrom, op. cit., p. 296.

339   Skjesol, I. and J. Tritter, op. cit., p. 1.

340   Skjesol, I. and J. Tritter, op. cit., p. 7.

341   Danuta A. Tomczyk, "Norway's strategy to cope with Corona pandemics",

Zdrowie Publiczne i Zarządzanie, 2020, p. 60.

342   Helsingen, L. et al., op. cit., p. 1.

343   Helsingen, L. et al., op. cit., p. 3.

344   Helsingen, L. et al., op. cit., p. 5.

345   Helsingen, L. et al., op. cit., pp. 3-4.

346   Christensen, T. and P. Laegrid, op. cit., p. 778.

347   David Olagnier and Trine H. Mogensen, "The COVID-19 pandemic in Denmark: Big lessons from a small country", *Cytokine and Growth Factor Reviews*, 2020, p. 10.

348   Saunes, I. et al., op. cit., p. 422.

349   Saunes, I. et al., op. cit., p. 422.

350   Saunes, I. et al., op. cit., p. 422.

351   Ursin, G., Skjesol, I. and J. Tritter, op. cit., p. 668.

352   Saunes, I. et al., op. cit., p. 422.

353   Saunes, I. et al., op. cit., p. 422.

354   Saunes, I. et al., op. cit., p. 424.

355   Christensen, T. and P. Laegrid, op. cit., p. 776.

356   Tomczyk, D., op. cit., p. 61.

357   Hanna Tiirinki et al., "COVID-19 in Finland: Vaccination strategy as part of the wider governing of the pandemic", *Health Policy and Technology*, June 2022, p. 4.

358   Saunes, I. et al., op. cit., p. 426.

359   "Fauci's controversial '60 Minutes' interview about mask-wearing was one year ago", *CBS*, 8 March 2020.

360   Ibid.

361   "CDC does not currently recommend the use of facemasks to help prevent novel coronavirus", CDC (X post), 27 February 2020.

362   Angel Desai, "Medical masks", *Journal of the American Medical Association*, March 2020, p. 1517.

363   Jingyi Xiao et al., "Nonpharmaceutical measures for pandemic influenza in nonhealthcare settings–Personal protective and environmental measures", *Emerging Infectious Diseases*, May 2020, p. 967.

364   M. Joshua Hendrix et al., "Absence of apparent transmission of SARS-CoV-2 from two stylists after exposure at a hair salon with a universal face covering policy–Springfield, Missouri, May 2020", *Morbidity and Mortality Weekly Report*, 17 July 2020, pp. 1-3.

365   Cory Stieg, "Dr. Fauci: Double-masking makes 'common sense' and is likely more effective", *CNBC*, 25 January 2021.

366   "Mask use in the context of COVID-19", World Health Organization, 1 December 2020.

367   Deborah Netburn, "A timeline of the CDC's advice on face masks, *Los Angeles Times*, 27 July 2021.

368   Ibid.

369 Natalie Wolfe, "Coronavirus Sweden: Mask evidence 'astonishingly weak', health boss claims", *News*, 12 August 2020.

370 Byram Bridle, "A year of COVID-19 lockdown is putting kids at risk of allergies, asthma, and autoimmune disease", *Conversation*, 9 March 2021.

371 Ibid.

372 Faisal bin-Reze et al., "The use of masks and respirators to prevent transmission of influenza: A systematic review of the scientific evidence", *Influenza and Other Respiratory Diseases*, July 2012, p. 257.

373 Jeffrey D. Smith et al., "Effectiveness of N95 respirators versus surgical masks in protecting health care workers from acute respiratory infection: A systematic review and meta-analysis", *Canadian Medical Association Journal*, May 2016, p. 567.

374 Charlie Da Zhou, Pamela Sivathondan, and Ashok Handa, "Unmasking the surgeons: The evidence base behind the use of facemasks in surgery", *Journal of the Royal Society of Medicine*, June 2015, p. 223.

375 A. Beder et al., "Preliminary report on surgical masks induced deoxygenation during major surgery", *Neurocirugia*, April 2008, pp. 121-126.

376 Xioa, J. et al., op. cit., pp. 967-975.

377 Joshua L. Jacobs et al., "Use of surgical face masks to reduce the incidence of the common cold among health care workers in Japan: A randomized controlled trial", *American Journal of Infectious Control*, June 2009, pp. 417-419.

378 Cowling et al., "Face masks to prevent transmission of influenza virus: A systematic review", *Epidemiology and Injection*, January 2010, p. 455.

379 Nicolas Dugre et al., "Masks for prevention of viral respiratory infections among health care workers and the public", *Canadian Family Physician*, July 2020, pp. 509-517.

380 C. Raina MacIntyre et al., "A cluster randomized trial of cloth masks compared with medical masks in healthcare workers", *British Medical Journal*, April 2015, p. 1.

381 Tara Oberg and Lisa Brousseau, "Surgical mask filter and fit performance", *American Journal of Infection Control*, January 2008, p. 276.

382 Lewis J. Radonovich et al., "N95 respirators vs medical masks for preventing influenza among health care personnel: A randomized clinical trial", *JAMA*, September 2019, pp. 824-833.

383 Youlin Long et al., "Effectiveness of N95 respirators versus surgical masks against influenza: A systematic review and metal-analysis", *Journal of Evidence-Based Medicine*, May 2020, pp. 93-101.

384 *St. Michael's Hospital and the Ontario Hospital Association v Ontario Nurses' Association*, 2016, p. 47.

385 "Union says Ontario nurses can't be forced to wear masks in flu season. Union head says policy 'shamed, coerced' nurses into getting flu vaccine", *Canadian Press*, 10 September 2015.

386 *Sault Area Hospital v Ontario Nurses' Association*, 2015, p. 113.

387 Henning Bundgaard et al., "Effectiveness of adding a mask recommendation

to other public health measures to prevent SARS-CoV-2 infection in Danish mask wearers: A randomized controlled trial", *Annals of Internal Medicine*, March 2021, p. 5.

388   Tom Jefferson et al., "Physical interventions to interrupt or reduce the spread of respiratory viruses (Review)", Cochrane Library, January 2023, p. 2.

389   Jefferson, T. et al., op. cit., p. 35.

390   Fernando Pifarre et al., "COVID-19 and mask in sports", *Apunts Sport Medicine*, October–December 2020, pp. 143-145.

391   Edward A. Laferty and Ray McKay, "Physiologic effects and measurement of carbon dioxide and oxygen levels during qualitative respirator fit testing", *Journal of Chemical Health and Safety*, September–October 2006, pp. 22-28.

392   Nigel J. Langford, "Carbon dioxide poisoning", *Toxicological Reviews*, 2005, pp. 229-235.

393   Tai Kisielinski et al., "Possible toxicity of chronic carbon dioxide exposure associated with face mask use, particularly in pregnant women, children and adolescents–A scoping review", *Heliyon*, June 2022, pp. 1-18.

394   Ibid., pp. 6-8.

395   Ibid., p. 1.

396   Ibid., p. 13.

397   Ibid., p. 10.

398   Ibid., p. 11.

399   Harald Walach et al., "Carbon dioxide rises beyond acceptable safety levels in children under nose and mouth covering: Results of an experimental study in healthy children", *Environmental Research*, September 2022, p. 1.

400   S. Marina Cosalino-Matsuda et al., "Hypercapnia alters expression of immune response, nucleosome assembly and lipid metabolism genes in differentiated human bronchial cells", *Nature*, September 2018, p. 1.

401   Astrid M. Westerndorf et al., "Hypoxia enhances immunosuppression by inhibiting CD4+ effector T cell function and promoting treg activity", *Cellular Physiology and Biochemistry*, March 2017, pp. 1271-1284.

402   Hussein Shehade et al., "Cutting edge: Hypoxia-inducible factor 1 negatively regulates Th1 function", *Journal of Immunology*, August 2015, pp. 1372-1376.

403   Jaclyn Sceneay et al., "Hypoxia-driven immunosuppression contributes to the premetastatic niche", *OncoImmunology*, January 2014, pp. 1-2.

404   Ji-Won Lee et al., "Hypoxia-inducible factor (HIF-1) alpha: its protein stability and biological functions", *Experimental and Molecular Medicine*, February 2004, p. 1.

405   Aldo Pezzuto and Elisabetta Carico, "Role of HIF-1 in cancer progression: Novel insights. A review", *Current Molecular Medicine*, 2018, pp. 343-351.

406   Yuhui Liu et al., "Non-targeted analysis of unknown volatile chemicals in medical masks", *Environmental International*, March 2022, pp. 1-10.

407   Kisielinski, T. et al., op. cit., p. 12.

408   Dyani Lewis, "Is the coronavirus airborne? Experts can't agree", *Nature*, 2

April 2020, p. 175.

409   "COVID-19 transmission through short and long-range respiratory particles", Public Health Ontario, February 2022, p. 5.

410   Henry P. Oswin et al., "The dynamics of SARS-CoV-2 infectivity with changes in aerosol environment", *PNAS*, June 2022, p. 1.

411   Graison Dangor, "CDC's six-foot social distancing rule was 'arbitrary', says former FDA commissioner", *Forbes*, 10 December 2021.

412   Editorial Board, "Anthony Fauci fesses up: It turns out that the six-feet social-distancing rule had no scientific basis", *Wall Street Journal*, 11 January 2024.

413   Tomczyk, D., op. cit., p. 60.

Chapter 3

414   Coronavirus Resource Center, Johns Hopkins University of Medicine.

415   "The Great Barrington Declaration", https://gbdeclaration.org/.

416   Ibid.

417   "US state governors impose tighter restrictions to slow coronavirus spread", *Guardian*, 21 March 2020.

418   Christy Samos, "Growing list of Canadian politicians caught travelling abroad despite pandemic", *CTV News*, 1 January 2021.

419   Slawomir A. Danilczuk, *Globalny bunt elit*, Łaskarzew, 2020, p. 72.

420   Ibid., p. 17.

421   Marek A. Zamorski, Krzysztof Komenda, and Renata Przekora, *Wielki Reset: Jaka przyszłość planuje nam globalna władza*, Wrocław, 2021, p. 99.

422   Danilczuk, S., op. cit., p. 17.

423   Douglas Farrow, "A new Catholicism? On the eugenic health tyranny as a test of fidelity", In *Politics, Law, & Religion in Times of Covid*, Jane Adolphe, Fulvio di Blasi, and Robert Fastiggi (eds.), 2024, pp. 323-362.

424   Ibid., pp. 323-362.

425   Kevin Bardosh, "Commentary: COVID vaccines mandates in Canada were a mistake: Are we ready to learn the right lessons?", Macdonald-Laurier Institute, November 2022, p. 5.

426   Murray Brewster and Ashley Burke, "Military campaign to influence public opinion continued after defence chief shut it down", *CBC News*, 24 June 2021.

427   "3 tactics to overcome COVID-19 hesitancy", World Economic Forum (WEF), 28 June 2021.

428   Aidan Macnab, "Manitoba churches and individuals suing over COVID-19 restrictions lose at Court Appeal", *Canadian Lawyer*, 7 July 2023.

429   Zamorski, M., Komenda, K. and R. Przekora, op. cit., p. 58.

430   Dalvin Brown, "Cash can carry coronavirus? World Health Organization says use digital payments when possible", *USA Today*, 6 March 2020.

431   Danilczuk, S., op. cit., pp. 63, 89.

432   Paul Daly, "Judicial review and the COVID-19 pandemic", *Administrative Law Matters*, 20 December 2020.

433 "Judge ignores evidence of lockdown harms when justifying Charter violations", Justice Center for Constitutional Freedoms (JCCF), 27 November 2023.

434 Phil Tank, "Saskatoon surgery professor suspended, terminated from key roles", *Saskatoon Star Phoenix*, 23 June 2021.

435 "Saskatchewan surgeon sues Health Authority and College of Medicine after being terminated and defamed for questioning covid vaccines for children", JCCF, 23 June 2022.

436 "Notice to Defendant: Statement of Claim", JCCF, October 2022.

437 Tyler Dawson, "Ontario professor on paid leave after refusing to get vaccinated or wear a mask", *National Post*, 9 September 2021.

438 Hillary Vaughn, "Facebook suppressed information on vaccines to avoid 'vaccine negative environment', files show", *Fox News*, 3 August 2023.

439 Robby Soave, "Inside the Facebook files: Emails reveal the CDC's role in silencing COVID-19 dissent", *Reason*, 19 January 2023.

440 Robert Cuffe and Rachel Schraer, "Excess deaths in 2022 among worst in 50 years", *BBC News*, 10 January 2023.

441 "Excess death trends, volume 743", UK Parliament, 16 January 2024.

442 Madeline Holcombe and Christina Maxouris, "Fully vaccinated people who get a COVID-19 breakthrough infection can transmit the virus, CDC chief says", *CNN*, 6 August 2021.

443 "Pfizer did not know whether Covid vaccine stopped transmission before rollout", *Daily Telegraph* (post on YouTube.com and its own transcription), 12 October 2022.

444 Ibid.

445 "Fact Check: Preventing transmission never required for COVID vaccines' initial approval; Pfizer vax did reduce transmission of early variant", *Reuters*, 12 February 2024 (updated).

446 "Posts mislead on Pfizer COVID vaccine's impact on transmission", *AP News*, 13 October 2022.

447 "FDA Briefing Document: Application for licensure of a booster dose for COMIRNATY (COVID-19 Vaccine, mRNA), Vaccine and Related Biological Products Advisory Committee Meeting", FDA, 17 September 2021, p. 22.

448 Anika Singanayagam et al., "Community transmission and viral load kinetics of the SARS-CoV-2 delta (B.1.167.2) variant in vaccinated and unvaccinated individuals in the UK: A prospective, longitudinal, cohort study", *Lancet Infectious Diseases*, February 2022, pp. 183-195.

449 Han Zhang, "How Shanghai residents endured the COVID lockdown", *New Yorker*, 7 June 2022.

450 Danilczuk, S., op. cit., p. 61.

451 Farrow, D. op. cit., pp. 323-362.

452 "COVID-19: Stringency Index", Our World in Data.

453 Ibid.

454 Caitlin Cassidy, "Victoria Covid update: police arrest 44 people and fire rubber

pellets during Melbourne construction protests", *Guardian*, 21 September 2021.

455 Rachel Gilmore, "'Fringe minority' in truck convoy with 'unacceptable views' don't represent Canadians: Trudeau", *Global News*, 26 January 2022.

456 Christopher Nardi and Catherine Levesque, "Bureaucrats who froze bank accounts of Freedom Convoy leaders weren't trying to 'get at the family'", *National Post*, 17 November 2022.

457 *The Emergencies Act*, Government of Canada.

458 "Major Canadian bank apologizes to trucker convoy for freezing accounts", *Natural News*, 1 June 2022.

459 "Federal court decision", JCCF, 23 January 2024.

460 Jacob Sullum, "Justice Samuel Alito highlights the legal issues raised by 'previously unimaginable' COVID-19 restrictions", *Reason*, 13 November 2020.

461 Samuel Alito, "Remarks to the 2020 Federalist Society", National Lawyers Convention, 2020, p. 87.

462 Ibid., p. 89.

463 Ibid., p. 94.

464 Francisco H.G. Ferreira, "Inequality in the time of COVID-19 pandemic", International Monetary Fund, Summer 2021.

465 John Williams, Shadow government statistics, www.shadowstats.com.

466 "US Aggregate Inflation Index", Truflation.

467 Ferreira, F., op. cit.

468 "Ten richest men double their fortunes in pandemic while income of 99 percent of humanity fall", Oxfam International, 17 January 2022.

469 Danilczuk, S., op. cit., p. 25.

470 Danilczuk, S., op. cit., p. 26.

471 Ryan Tumilty, "Canada spent $147M on a public health surveillance system that isn't being used during Covid pandemic", *National Post*, 12 September 2020.

472 Catharine Tunney, "Trudeau leaves door open to use smartphone data to track Canadians' compliance with pandemic rules", *CBC News*, 4 March 2020.

473 Sarah Villeneuve and Darren Elias, "Surveillance creep: Data collection and privacy in Canada during COVID-19", Brookfield Institute for Innovation and Entrepreneurship, 2 September 2020.

474 Swikar Oli, "Canada's public health agency admits it tracked 3 million mobile devices during lockdown", *National Post*, 24 December 2021.

475 Alfred Ng, "How China uses facial recognition to control human behavior", Cnet, 11 August 2020.

476 Shawn Yuan, "How China is using AI, big data to fight COVID", *Asean Post*, 31 March 2022.

477 *Public Health and Medical Professional for Transparency v US Food and Drug Administration, Case 4:21-cv-01058-p*, document 22 filed 6 December 2021.

478 Ibid.

479 Aaron Siri, "Why a judge ordered FDA to release Covid-19 vaccine data pronto", *Bloomberg Law*, 18 January 2022.

480 Michael Nevradakis, "FDA releases 10,000 more Pfizer vaccine documents. What will they reveal?", *Defender*, 4 March 2022.

481 Michelle Maluske, "'Data is power': Experts weigh-in on court-ordered release of Pfizer vaccine documents", *CTV News*, 11 March 2022.

482 "Cumulative analysis of post-authorization adverse event reports of PF-072048 (BNT162B2) made public through 28-Feb-2021", Pfizer-BioNTech, 30 April 2021.

483 Ibid., p. 5.

484 "FDA approved first COVID-19 vaccine", FDA, 23 August 2021.

485 Darius Tahir, "Medical boards get pushback as they try to punish doctors for Covid misinformation", *Politico*, 2 January 2022.

486 Roland Derwand, Martin Scholz, and Vladimir Zelenko, "COVID-19 outpatients: Early risk-stratified treatment with zinc plus low-dose hydroxychloroquine and azithromycin: A retrospective case series study", *International Journal of Antimicrobial Agents*, December 2020, pp. 1-10.

487 Peter A. McCullough et al., "Pathophysiological basis and rationale for early outpatient treatment of SARS-CoV-2 (COVID-19) infection", *American Journal of Medicine*, January 2021, pp. 16-22.

488 A.D. Santin et al., "Ivermectin: A multifaceted drug of Nobel price-honored distinction with indicated efficacy against a new global scourge, COVID-19", *New Microbes and New Infections*, September 2021, pp. 1-6.

489 Lucy Kerr et al., "Regular use of ivermectin as prophylaxis for COVID-19 led up to a 92% reduction in COVID-19 mortality rate in a dose-response manner: Results of a prospective observational study of a strictly controlled population of 88,012 subjects", *Cureus*, August 2022, pp. 1-37.

490 Charles Piller and Kelly Servick, "Two elite medical journals retract coronavirus papers over data integrity questions", *Science*, 4 June 2020.

491 Sarah Boseley and Melissa Davey, "COVID-19: Lancet retracts paper that halted hydroxychloroquine trials", *Guardian*, 4 June 2020.

492 *Robert L. Apter, Mary Talley Bowden, and Paul E. Marik v Department of Health and Human Services et al.* (Filed September 1, 2023), p. 5.

493 Ibid., p. 5.

494 Susan Shelley, "FDA overstepped against ivermectin", *Los Angeles Daily News*, 30 March 2024.

495 Paul Bond, "FDA settles lawsuit over ivermectin social media posts", *Newsweek*, 22 March 2024.

496 Jen Christensen, "FDA settles lawsuit over ivermectin content doctors claimed harmed their practice," *CNN*, 27 March 2024.

497 *Apter, Bowden, and Marik v Department of Health and Human Services et al.*, op, cit., p. 24.

498 Ibid., p. 25.

499 Ashleigh Stewart, "40 Ontario physicians currently being investigated for COVID-19 issues: College", *Global News*, 19 January 2022.

500 Wallis Snowdon, "Alberta doctors accused of spreading COVID-19 misinformation face unannounced inspections", *CBC News*, 5 November 2021.

501 "College drops charges against Alberta doctor who granted Covid vaccine exemptions", JCCF, 18 January 2024.

502 Ashleigh Stewart, "Revealed: How a web of Canadian doctors are undermining the fight against COVID-19", *Global News*, 18 January 2022.

503 Ibid.

504 Marlene Lenthang, "Texas doctor who promoted ivermectin as Covid treatment suspended by the hospital", *NBC News*, 15 November 2021.

505 Ibid.

506 Karen Brooks Harper, "Texas House approves ban on COVID-19 vaccine mandates by private employers", *Texas Tribune*, 26 October 2023.

507 Brandon Waltens, "Texas Medical Board suspends license after doctor defied mask mandates", *Texas Scorecard*, 28 March 2023.

508 "Ontario doctor accused of spreading COVID-19 misinformation barred from providing vaccine, mask exemptions", *CBC News*, 28 September 2022.

509 Adrian Humphreys, "Ontario doctors critical of COVID measures fail to stop medical college's disciplinary hearings", *North Bay Nugget*, 19 January 2023.

510 Ibid.

511 Justin Zadorsky, "Ontario doctor suspended after being banned from giving exemptions to COVID-19 vaccine", *CTV News*, 28 October 2021.

512 Carlie Porterfield, "Dr. Fauci on GOP criticism: 'Attacks on me, quite frankly, are attacks on science'", *Forbes*, 10 December 2021.

513 Józef Białek, *COVID-19: Globalna mistyfikacja*, Wrocław, 2021, p. 35.

514 Ibid., p. 35.

515 Marek A. Zamorski, "Przedmowa." In *COVID-19: Globalna mistyfikacja*, Wrocław, Białek, p. 11.

516 David N. Fisman, Afia Amoako, and Ashleigh R. Tuite, "Impact of population mixing between vaccinated and unvaccinated subpopulations on infectious disease dynamics: Implications for SARS-CoV-2 transmission", *Canadian Medical Association Journal*, April 2022, pp. 577-578.

517 Regina Watteel, *Fisman's Fraud: The Rise of Canadian Hate Science*, Canada, 2023, p. 6.

518 Ibid., p. 6.

519 Ibid., p. 2.

520 "Province slams doctor on Covid advisory table over paid work", *CBC News*, 27 January 2021.

521 Kamran Abbasi, "Covid-19: politicization, 'corruption,' and suppression of science", *British Journal of Medicine*, November 2020, p. 2.

522 Ibid., p. 1.

523 Białek, J., op. cit., pp. 104-105.

524 Białek, J., op. cit., pp. 106-107.

525 "Report 12: The global impact of COVID-19 and strategies for mitigation and suppression", Imperial College COVID-19 Response Team, 26 March 2020, p. 1.

526 "Report 9: Impact of non-pharmaceutical interventions (NPIs) to reduce COVID-19 mortality and healthcare demand", Imperial College COVID-19 Response Team, 16 March 2020, p. 3.

527 Peter St. Onge and Gael Campan, "The flawed COVID-19 model that locked down Canada", Montreal Economic Institute (MEI), 4 June 2020.

528 Farrow, D. op. cit., pp. 323-362.

529 Imperial College COVID-19 Response Team (26 March 2020), op. cit., p. 2.

530 St. Onge, P. and G. Campan, op. cit.

531 UK Parliament, op. cit.

532 John P.A. Ioannidis, Sally Cripps and Martin A. Tanner, "Forecasting for COVID-19 has failed", *International Journal of Forecasting*, August 2020, p. 423.

533 Brian Lilley, "Ontario doing well on COVID despite what some 'experts' say", *Toronto Sun*, 17 November 2020.

534 Clare E. Craig, *Expired: Covid the Untold Story*, London, 2023, p. 4.

535 Ferreira, F., op. cit.

536 Bruce Haring, "Toronto Star backs down from article headlines that slammed the unvaccinated", *Deadline*, 29 August 2021.

537 Bruce C. Smith, "Toronto Star front-page design exacerbated division between readers. Greater care should have been taken", *Toronto Star*, 28 August 2021.

538 Ibid.

539 Białek, J., op. cit., p. 144.

540 Białek, J., op. cit., p. 143.

541 Paige Parsons, "Why are COVID-19 vaccine rates lower in some parts of rural Alberta", *CBC News*, 20 May 2021.

542 Nicholas Frew, "Time for Alberta to target COVID-19 vaccine uptake in rural, remote areas: health experts", *CBC News*, 1 September 2021.

543 Verity Stevenson and Isaac Olson, "Unvaccinated Quebecers will have to pay a health tax, Legault says", *CBC News*, 11 January 2022.

544 Emily Mertz, "Danielle Smith addresses comments about unvaccinated being 'most discriminated against group'", *Global News*, 12 October 2022.

545 Gabriela Capurro et al., "Moral panic about 'covidiots' in Canadian newspaper coverage of COVID-19", *PLoS One*, January 2022, p. 1.

546 Fabienne Labbe et al., "Stigma and blame related to COVID-19 pandemic: A case study of editorial cartoons in Canada", *Social Science and Medicine*, March 2022, pp. 1-12.

547 Anja Karadeglija, "More than one in four Canadians support jail time for the unvaccinated, poll finds", *National Post*, 19 January 2022.

548 "COVID-19: Democratic voters support harsh measures against unvaccinated", Rasmussen Reports, 13 January 2022.

549 Ibid.

550 "Alberta woman who was denied organ transplant after refusing COVID vaccine dies", *Global News*, 25 August 2023.

551 Paige Parson, "Charter not violated in denying transplant to patient who refused COVID-19 vaccine, court rules", *CBC News*, 12 July 2022.

552 Ibid.

553 Kelly Geraldine Malone, "Supreme Court won't hear case of Alberta patient denied transplant for refusing COVID vaccine", *CBC News*, 9 June 2023.

554 Andrew Joseph, "Hospitals are denying transplants for patients who aren't vaccinated against Covid, with backing from ethicists", *Stat News*, 16 January 2022.

555 "Patient who refused COVID vaccine was denied a heart transplant", *Associated Press*, 26 January 2022.

556 Jacob Serebrin, "Some–not all–Canadian hospitals require COVID-19 vaccination for organ transplant patients", *Canadian Press*, 4 August 2023.

557 Lanie Friedman Ross, "COVID-19 vaccine refusal and organ transplantation", *American Journal of Kidney Diseases*, June 2022, pp. 771-773.

Chapter 4

558 Józef Białek, *COVID-19: Globalna mistyfikacja*, Wrocław, 2021, p. 211.

559 Ibid., p. 212.

560 Kevin Bardosh, "Covid vaccine mandates in Canada were a mistake: Are we ready to learn the right lessons?", Macdonald Laurier Institute, 24 November 2022.

561 Rachel Gilmore, "'Fringe minority' in truck convoy with 'unacceptable views' don't represent Canadians: Trudeau", *Global News*, 26 January 2022.

562 Fred Cooper, Luna Dolezal, and Arthur Rose, *COVID-19 and Shame: Political Emotions and Public Health in the UK*, London, 2023.

563 Amanda Connolly, "Spot a COVIDIOT? Here's how to report coronavirus rule-brakers", *Global News*, 30 March 2020.

564 "How to report someone breaking COVID-19 rules?", Covidtests.

565 "Province slams doctor on Covid advisory table over paid work for teacher's union", *CBC News*, 27 January 2021.

566 Sarah Petz, "How do you report COVID-19 rule breakers without causing a fight? Two experts weigh in", *CBC News*, 22 May 2021.

567 Tyler Dawson, "Majority of Canadians unwilling to let unvaccinated friend, family member into their home: poll", *National Post*, 2 December 2021.

568 "78% of Canadians support COVID-19 passports for public places: Poll", *Global News*, 2 October 2021.

569 "Stress and decision-making during the pandemic", *American Psychological Association*, 26 October 2021.

570 Białek, J., op. cit., p. 317.

571 Samantha Brown et al., "Stress and parenting during the global COVID-19 pandemic", *Child Abuse and Neglect*, December 2020, pp. 1-14.

572 Brittaney Chain, "Divorce rate jumps to an eight-year high with rise of nearly 10% between 2020 and 2021 as 'lockdown put even the strongest relationships to the test'", *Daily Mail*, 2 November 2022.

573 Mark Czeisler et al., "Mental health, substance abuse, and suicide ideation during the COVID-19 pandemic–United States, June 24-30, 2020", *Morbidity and Mortality Weekly Report*, August 2020, p. 1049.

574 Białek, J., op. cit., p. 213.

575 Aditi Shrinkat, "Youth suicide rates rose 62% from 2007 to 2021: 'People feel hopeless' one recent grad says", *CNBC*, 5 December 2023.

576 Białek, J., op. cit., p. 326.

577 Clare Halloran et al., "Pandemic schooling mode and student test scores: Evidence from US states", NBER working paper 29497, p. 1.

578 Ibid., p. 1.

579 Ibid., p. 12.

580 Megan Kuhfeld, James Soland, and Karyn Lewis, "Test score patterns across three COVID-impacted school years", Working paper no. 22-521, Annenberg Institute, January 2022, p. 1.

581 Santiago Pinto, "The pandemic's effects on children's education", Federal Reserve of Richmond, Economic brief no. 23-29, August 2023.

582 Ibid.

583 Russell Viner et al., "School closures during social lockdown and mental health, health behaviors, and well-being among children and adolescents during the first COVID-19 wave: A systematic review", *JAMA,* January 2022, pp. 400-409.

584 Czeisler, M. et al., op. cit., p. 1049.

585 Leo Sher, "The impact of the COVID-19 pandemic on suicide rates", *QJM: An International Journal of Medicine*, October 2020, pp. 1-17.

586 Louisa Clarence-Smith, "Ministers were warned that suicide would kill more children than Covid", *Telegraph*, 3 July 2023.

587 "Excess deaths debate", volume 743, UK Parliament, 16 January 2024.

588 Emily Alpert Reyes, "Suicides in U.S. hit historic high in 2022, driven by increase among older adults", *Los Angeles Times*, 19 November 2023.

589 Kanishka Sing, "US suicide deaths reached record high in 2022, CDC data shows", *Reuters*, 10 August 2023.

590 Emily K. Jenkins et al., "A portrait of early and differential of mental health impacts of COVID-19 pandemic in Canada: Findings from the first wave of a nationally representative cross-sectional survey", *Preventive Medicine*, January 2021, pp. 1-12

591 Lisa A. Best et al., "The psychological impact of COVID-19 in Canada: Effects of social isolation during the initial response", *Canadian Psychology*, February 2021, pp. 143-154.

592 "Mental health among healthcare workers in Canada during the COVID-19 pandemic", StatsCan, 2 February 2021.

593 Sher, L., op. cit., p. 2.

594   Chris Harmon, "Suicide rates for 2023 at an all-time high for the United States", *NBC 15 News*, 3 January 2024.

595   UK Parliament, op. cit.

596   Ellen Badone, "From Cruddiness to catastrophe: COVID-19 and long-term care in Ontario", *Medical Anthropology*, May 2021, pp. 389-403.

597   Lucia Ann Silecchia, "COVID-19, visitation, and spiritual care: Responding to the silent suffering of the isolated in the time of crisis", Catholic University of America, May 2023, p. 639.

598   Ibid., p. 647.

599   Ibid., p. 648.

600   Ibid., p. 672.

601   Lisa Marshall, "Suicide rates in the US are on the rise. A new study offers a surprising reason why", Phys.org, 15 February 12024.

602   Robin Foster, "As suicide rates climb, older men are more vulnerable", *US News*, 15 November 2023.

603   Clancy Martin, "The pandemic's surprising effect on suicide rates", *Atlantic*, 23 April 2023.

604   Czeisler, M. et al., op. cit., p. 1049.

605   Jane Pirkis et al., "Suicide numbers during the first 9-15 months of the COVID-19 pandemic compared with pre-existing trends: An interrupted time series analysis in 33 countries", *Lancet*, August 2022, pp. 1-19.

606   Karen Blum, "Suicide rates in Black populations during COVID-19 pandemic", Johns Hopkins Medicine, 20 April 2021.

607   Mark Moran, "Suicides drop during past year of pandemic, study finds", *Psychiatric News*, 20 May 2021.

608   Ibid.

609   Kevin Bardosh (Affidavit), *Randy Hillier v Her Majesty the Queen, Court File No. CV-22-00682682-0000*, 14 September 2022.

610   Li Liu et al., "Prevalence of suicidal ideation among adults in Canada: Results of the second survey COVID-19 and mental health", *Health Reports*, May 2022, pp. 13-21.

611   Lisa T. Ying, Mark C. Yarema, and Chad Bousman, "Dispending patterns of mental health medications before and during the COVID-19 pandemic in Alberta, Canada: An interrupted time series analysis", *International Journal of Psychiatry in Medicine*, March 2023, pp. 172-184.

612   Nathan King et al., "The impact of COVID-19 pandemic on the mental health of the first-year undergraduate students studying at a major university in Canada: A successive cohort study", *Canadian Journal of Psychiatry*, July 2023, pp. 499-509.

613   Anne Gadermann et al., "Early adolescents' experiences during the COVID-19 pandemic and changes in their wellbeing", *Frontiers in Public Health*, May 2022, pp. 1-14.

614   Natasha R. Saunders et al., "Changes in hospital-based care seeking for acute mental health concerns among children and adolescents during the COVID-19 pandemic in Ontario, Canada, through September 2021", *JAMA*, July 2022,

pp. 1-4.

615   Gabrielle Beaudry et al., "A comparative analysis of pediatric mental health-related emergency department utilization in Montreal, Canada, before and during the COVID-19 pandemic", *Annals of General Psychiatry*, June 2022, pp. 1-10.

616   Samantha Salmon et al., "Pandemic-related experiences, mental health symptoms, substance use, and relationship conflict among older adolescents and young adults in Manitoba, Canada", *Psychiatry Research*, May 2022, pp. 1-9.

617   Anne Gadermann et al., "Examining the impacts of the COVID-19 pandemic on family mental health in Canada: Findings from a national cross-sectional study", *BMJ Open*, January 2021, pp. 1-11.

618   Jesse Newman, "It's been 30 years since food ate up to this much of your income", *Wall Street Journal*, 21 February 2024.

619   "Household debt", OECD.

620   "Risks to Canada economy remain high as household debt levels continue to grow", Canada Mortgage and Housing Corporation (CMHC), May 2023.

621   "Canadian households now the third most indebted in the world", Better Dwelling, 3 July 2024.

622   Pamela Heaven, "Posthaste: More borrowers struggle as IMF warns Canada at highest risk of mortgage defaults", *Financial Post*, 6 June 2023.

623   Matt Lundy, "Canadians are paying highest portion of disposable income toward debt on record", *Globe and Mail*, 13 December 2023.

624   Craig Lord, "2.2M mortgage holders will face 'interest rate shock' in next 2 years: CMHC", *Global News*, 9 November 2023.

625   Ibid.

626   "Renewal jitters: Canadians concerned about upcoming mortgage renewals consider extending their amortization periods, switching lenders", Royal LePage Real Estate Services, 25 October 2023.

627   "Mortgage rate history", Super Brokers.

628   Maria teNyenhuis and Adam Su, "The impact of higher interest rates on mortgage payments", Bank of Canada, December 2023.

629   Ibid.

630   "MNP consumer debt index dips to second-lowest level in last 5 years, Canadians' debt perception reaches all-time high", *Financial Post*, 8 January 2024.

631   Michelle Zadikian, "More Canadians turning to reverse mortgages amid savings crunch", *Yahoo Finance*, 18 January 2023.

632   Alicja Siekierska, "More Canadians worried about debt levels, dipping into savings: MNP survey", *Yahoo Finance*, 8 January 2024.

633   John MacFarlane, "Investors have pulled billions from Canadian mutual funds in the high interest rate era", *Yahoo Finance*, 26 March 2024.

634   Pamela Heaven, "Canadians are showing the strain of their historically high debt", *Financial Post*, 22 January 2024.

635 Alicja Siekierska, "One-third of Canadians considering alternative home ownership model among low affordability", *Yahoo Finance*, 27 February 2024.

636 Alicja Siekierska, "Consumer insolvencies hit 4-year high in Canada as interest rates weigh on households", *Yahoo Finance*, 2 August 2024.

637 "Credit card and auto loan delinquencies continue rising, notably among young borrowers", Federal Reserve Bank of New York, 6 February 2024.

638 Ibid.

639 "US personal saving rate", Y Charts.

640 Alicia Wallace, "Credit card delinquencies surpass pre-pandemic levels", *CNN*, 11 January 2024.

641 Andrew Haughwout et al., "Credit card delinquencies continue to rise–who is missing payments?", Federal Reserve Bank of New York, 7 November 2023.

642 Gabriella Cruz-Martinez, "Millennials are struggling under mounting credit card debt, NY Fed finds", *Yahoo Finance*, 6 February 2024.

643 Robert F. Kennedy Jr., *The Real Anthony Fauci: Bill Gates, Big Pharma, and the Global War on Democracy and Public Health*, New York, 2021, p. xix.

644 "Global poverty", World Vision.

645 "Poverty rate", OECD.

646 "Uncovering poverty's complexities", UK Collaborative on Development Research (UKCDR).

647 "Blueprint for transformation: The 2023 report of the National Advisory Council on Poverty", Employment and Social Development Canada, 2023.

648 Emily A. Shrider and John Creamer, "Poverty in the United States: 2022", United States Census Bureau, September 2023.

649 Matthew Hanick, "One in four Canadians live in poverty, new report says", *National Post*, 19 June 2024.

650 Ibid.

651 Michael Mendelson et al., "Poverty in Canada: through a deprivation lens", Food Banks Canada, May 2024, p. 3.

652 Jessica Dickler, "Amid inflation, more middle-class Americans struggle to make ends meet", *CNBC*, 18 January 2023.

653 Rakesh Kochhar and Stella Sechopoulos, "How the American middle class has changed in the past five decades", Pew Research Center, 20 April 2022.

654 Dickler, J., op. cit.

655 Alyssa Fowers, Emily Guskin, and Scott Clement, "How American defined a middle-class lifestyle–and why they can't reach it", *Washington Post*, 15 February 2024.

656 Natalie Lin, "Fidelity sees quarter-on-quarter decline in retirement balances", *Plan Adviser*, 20 November 2023.

657 Alex Tanzi, "Only richest 20% of Americans still have excess pandemic savings", *Bloomberg*, 25 September 2023.

Chapter 5

658 Józef Białek, *COVID-19: Globalna mistyfikacja*, Wrocław, 2021, p. 20.

659 Ibid., p. 21.

660 Ibid., p. 47.

661 Ibid., p. 47.

662 Ibid., p. 23.

663 Ivan Illich, *Limits to Medicine: Medical Nemesis: The Expropriation of Health*, London, pp. 14-15.

664 Ibid., p. 22.

665 Rafał Boguszewski, Marta Makowska, and Monika Podkowińska, "Changes in intensification of religious involvement during the COVID-19 pandemic in Poland", *PloS One*, June 2022, pp. 1-15.

666 Tracy Munsil, "New post-pandemic research shows how COVID rocked American's faith", *Arizona Christian*, 14 June 2023.

667 Philippa Martyr, "Factors affecting Australian Catholics' return to Mass after COVID-19 church closures", *Journal of Religion and Health*, July 2022, pp. 4245–4259.

668 Białek, J., op. cit., p. 28.

669 Białek, J., op. cit., p. 28.

670 Białek, J., op. cit., p. 19.

671 Bimbo Stanley Omopo, "Impact of COVID-19 on religious practices and religious conviviality in Ibadan: The place of religious leaders in maintaining close-knit religious communities", *Hal Open Science*, 5 November 2021.

672 Misha Boutilier, "Limiting freedom of religion in a pandemic: The constitutionality of restrictions on religious gatherings in a response to COVID-19", *Alberta Law Review*, July 2022, p. 955.

673 Ibid., p. 956.

674 "Religious people coped better with Covid-19 pandemic, research suggests", Cambridge University Research, 30 January 2024.

675 Kate Blackwood, "Religion follows patterns of politicization during COVID-19", *Cornell Chronicle*, 7 April 2021.

676 Ibid.

677 Christine Rousselle, "Maine Diocese frozen out of Covid restrictions discussion", *National Catholic Register*, 1 November 2020.

678 Lucia Ann Silecchia, "COVID-19, visitation, and spiritual care: Responding to the silent suffering of the isolated in the time of crisis", Catholic University of America, 22 May 2023, p. 642.

679 Edward Hadas, "The assault on humanity", Together for the Common Good.

680 "Archdiocese of Vancouver to assess impact of pandemic restrictions", *Canadian Catholic News*, 1 April 2022.

681 Tom Hellman, "In a season of faith, new COVID-19 restrictions impact the Catholic Church in Portland, Oregon", *Oregonline*, 16 November 2020.

682 Sriya Iyer, Shaun Larcom, and Po-Wen She, "Do religious people cope better

in crisis? Evidence from the UK pandemic lockdowns", Cambridge working papers in economics, January 2024, p. 1.

683   Sergey Budeav, "Safety and reverence: How Roman Catholic liturgy can respond to the COVID-19 pandemic", *Journal of Religion and Health*, May 2021, p. 2341.

684   *Catechism of the Catholic Church*, Vatican, November 2019, par. 1324.

685   Ibid., par. 1362.

686   Budeav, S., op. cit., p. 2341.

687   "Memoriale Domini, the Instruction on the Manner of Administering Holy Communion", Congregation of Divine Worship, 29 May 1969.

688   Father Paul J. Keller, "Receiving Holy Communion on the tongue", *Catholic Times Columbus*, 7 February 2024.

689   Congregation of Divine Worship, op. cit.

690   Congregation of Divine Worship, op. cit.

691   *The General Instruction of the Roman Missal*, Vatican City State, 2008, p. 44.

692   "The executive summary of the Real Presence Coalition's survey of U.S. lay Catholics", Real Presence Coalition (RPC), September 2024.

693   Budeav, S., op. cit., p. 2342.

694   "How the pandemic has affected attendance at U.S. religious services", Pew Research Center, 28 March 2023.

695   Boguszewski, R., Makowska, M., and M. Podkowińska, op. cit., pp. 1-15.

696   Iyer, S., Larcom, S., and P. She, op. cit., pp. 1-28.

697   Daniel Payne, "Catholic survey shows 'shocking' impact of church closures during COVID pandemic", *Catholic News Agency*, 12 December 2023.

698   Harriet Sherwood, "Catholic church leader criticizes worship restrictions in England", *Guardian*, 1 November 2020.

699   Martyr, P. (2022), op. cit., p. 4247.

700   Simon Caldwell, "Survey: Pandemic lockdown of churches causes widespread mental, physical suffering", *Diocese of Tucson Online News*, 18 December 2023.

701   Boguszewski, R., Makowska, M., and M. Podkowińska, op. cit., pp. 1-15.

702   Philippa Martyr, "Australian Catholics' Lived experiences of COVID-19 church closures", *Journal of Religion and Health*, April 2023, p. 2885.

703   Daniel Arasa et al., "The response of Roman Catholic priests to Covid-19: A case study of the pastoral and communication activities of nine dioceses worldwide during the first months of the pandemic", *Church, Communication and Culture*, November 2021, p. 251.

704   John Longhurst, "Common themes emerge on pandemic's impact on religion", *Winnipeg Free Press*, 15 May 2021.

705   Ibid.

706   "What is the COVID-19 report on Catholics?", Vinea Research.

707   Giuseppe Crea, Lorenzo Filosa, and Guido Alessandri, "Emotional distress in Catholic priests and religious sisters during COVID-19: The mediational role

of trait positivity", *Mental Health, Religion and Culture*, September 2021, pp. 728-744.

708   Stephan Kappler et al., "The impact of the COVID-19 pandemic on the psychological well-being of Catholic priests in Canada", *Religions*, August 2022, pp. 1-19.

709   Ibid., pp. 1-19.

710   Joshua Raimundo, "Citing COVID-19, Canada cracks down on churches", *World*, 22 February 2021.

711   Matthew F. Manion, "Study of COVID-19 impact on U.S. Catholic parish giving", Villanova University Center for Church Management, 1 February 2023.

712   Brendan Hodge, "Special report: The Covid Mass effect", *Pillar*, 11 November 2021.

713   Marcel LeJeune, "The long-term impact of coronavirus on the Catholic Church", Catholic Missionary Disciples, 2021.

714   Vinea Research, op. cit.

715   Manion, M., op. cit.

716   Frank Newport, "Religion and the COVID-19 virus in the U.S.", *Gallup*, 6 April 2020.

717   Ashleigh Stewart, "How COVID could change religion in Canada forever: 'There is no going back'", *Global News*, 16 January 2022.

718   Brian Dryden, "Going online may have a lasting impact on the Catholic Church in Canada", *Catholic Saskatoon News*, 5 May 2020.

719   Martyr, P. (2023), op. cit., p. 2881.

720   Longhurst, J., op. cit.

721   Stewart, A., op. cit.

722   Pew Research (2023), op. cit.

723   Stewart, A., op. cit.

724   Vinea Research, op. cit.

725   Martyr, P. (2022), op. cit., p. 2893.

726   *Roman Catholic Archbishop of Washington v Muriel Bowser, Civil Action No. 1:20-cv-3625*, District of Columbia, 11 December 2020, p. 2.

727   "Supreme Court will not hear case about government's violations of rights and freedoms", Justice Center for Constitutional Freedoms (JCCF), 14 March 2024.

728   *Ingram v Alberta (Chief Medical Officer of Health), 2023 ABKB 453*, 1 July 2023.

729   "Challenging the constitutionality of Alberta's public health measures", JCCF, 9 December 2020.

730   Ibid.

731   Ibid.

732   Aidan Macnab, "Manitoba churches and individuals over Covid restrictions lose at Court of Appeal", *Canadian Lawyer*, 7 July 2023.

733 Ibid.

734 Vinea Research, op. cit.

735 "Most Americans who go to religious services say they would trust their clergy's advice on COVID-19 vaccines", Pew Research Center, 15 October 2021.

736 Christine Rousselle, "Canadian diocese requires COVID-19 vaccination to attend Mass", *Catholic Business Journal*, 26 October 2021.

737 "Statement of the Catholic Bishops of Wisconsin on COVID-19 vaccination and the protection of conscience", Wisconsin Catholic Conference, 20 August 2021.

738 Ibid.

739 Ibid.

740 "A letter from the bishops of Colorado on COVID-19 vaccine mandates", Colorado Catholic Conference, 6 August 2021.

741 Most Reverand Joseph E. Strickland, "Dear Flock of East Texas" (pastoral letter), Office of the Bishop, 8 December 2020.

742 Colorado Catholic Conference, op. cit.

743 Most Reverand Mark A. Hagemoen, "Update re: Ongoing concerns about the COVID-19 pandemic and government mandates", Roman Catholic Diocese of Saskatoon, 2 November 2021.

744 Most Reverand Marcel Damphousse, "Vaccination: yes or no?", Archbishop's Message, Archdiocese of Ottawa-Cornwall, 29 January 2021.

745 Most Reverand William T. McGrattan, "Bishop's pastoral letter re: Exemption from COVID-19 vaccination", Roman Catholic Diocese of Calgary, 22 September 2021.

746 Ibid.

747 "Note on the morality of using some anti-Covid-19 vaccines", Congregation for the Doctrine of the Faith, Vatican, 21 December 2020.

748 Ibid.

749 *Catechism of the Catholic Church*, Vatican, November 2019, par. 2295.

750 "Pope urges people to receive COVID-19 vaccine", *Vatican News*, 18 August 2021.

751 Douglas Farrow, "A new Catholicism? On the eugenic health tyranny as a test of fidelity", In *Politics, Law, & Religion in Times of Covid*, Jane Adolphe, Fulvio di Blasi, and Robert Fastiggi (eds.), St. Louis, pp. 323-362.

752 Ibid., pp. 323-362.

753 Ibid., pp. 323-362.

754 Ibid., pp. 323-362.

755 Ibid., pp. 323-362.

756 Ibid., pp. 323-362.

Chapter 6

757 "CFIB urges permanent end to small business lockdowns", Canadian Federation of Independent Business (CFIB), 15 March 2021.

758   Eric Van Nostrand, "Small business and entrepreneurship in the post-COVID expansion", U.S. Department of the Treasury, 3 September 2024.

759   "Impact of COVID-19 on small businesses in Canada, second quarter of 2021", Statistics Canada, June 2021.

760   Van Nostrand, op. cit.

761   Patricia Greene, "How small business owners are leading the country in innovation", *Inc.*, 15 November 2016.

762   Judith Magyar, "Technology and the power of small business to drive innovation and jobs", *Forbes*, 10 April 2012.

763   Briana Radicioni, "New research: The real impacts of COVID-19 on small business", Babson College, 29 September 2020.

764   Dimitri Akhrin, "Three business realities post COVID-19", *Forbes*, 14 April 2022.

765   Dylan Balla-Elliot et al., "Determinants of small business reopening decision after Covid restrictions were lifted", *Journal of Policy Analysis and Management*, January 2022, p. 279.

766   Simon Gaudreault, "One year of COVID-19: 7 ways the world has changed for small business", CFIB, March 2021, p. 8.

767   Maria Nicola et al., "The socio-economic implications of the coronavirus pandemic (COVID-19): A review", *International Journal of Surgery*, April 2020, pp. 185-193.

768   Andrew J. Patterson et al., "Estimating the impact of the COVID-19 shock", Vanguard, June 2020.

769   Falk Brauning, Jose L. Fillat, and J. Christina Wang, "Did high leverage render small business vulnerable to the COVID-19 shock?", Boston Federal Reserve, 2022.

770   Józef Białek, *COVID-19: Globalna mistyfikacja*, Wrocław, 2021, p. 255.

771   Matt Dodge, "How COVID-19 is affecting small business", *Jobillico*, 8 October 2020.

772   Białek, J., op. cit., p. 266.

773   "Pandemic threatens to deepen divide between big and small business", CFIB, 21 October 2020.

774   "No rest for the leveraged", Allianz Trade, 11 April 2023.

775   Alexander W. Bartik et al., "The impact of COVID-19 on small business outcomes and expectations", *PNAS*, July 2020, pp. 17656-17666.

776   "Small businesses feel biggest impact of coronavirus pandemic", *Business Wire*, 8 October 2020.

777   "COVID-19 impact felt by 81 percent of Canadian small business owners: CIBC poll", Canadian Imperial Bank of Commerce (CIBC), 4 May 2020.

778   Wulong Gu, "Economic impact of the COVID-19 pandemic on Canadian businesses across firm size classes", Statistics Canada, 19 August 2020.

779   James Hurley, Sarah Venables, and Danny Walker, "How has COVID-19 affected small UK companies", Bank of England, 27 October 2020.

780   Gaudreault, S., op. cit., p. 4.

781 Gaudreault, S., op. cit., p. 6.

782 Myint M. Chit, Richard Croucher, and Marian Rizov, "Surviving the COVID-19 pandemic: The antecedents of success among European SMEs", *European Management Review*, May 2022, pp. 113-127.

783 Robert Fairlie, "The impact of COVID-19 on small business owners: Evidence from the first three months after widespread social-distancing restrictions", *Journal of Economics and Management Strategy*, August 2020, p. 727.

784 "Two years of COVID-19 for Canada's small businesses", CFIB, March 2022.

785 Lydia DePillis, "After enduring a pandemic, small businesses face new worries", *New York Times*, 26 July 2022.

786 "Small businesses in Canada hit hard: The big financial toll of labour shortages", CFIB, November 2023.

787 "Canadian business insolvencies up 37.2 per cent in 2022, consumer insolvencies up 11.2 per cent", *Ottawa Business Journal*, 7 February 2023.

788 David Parkinson, "Three years after COVID-19, Amanda Munday and other small-business owners face debt hangover", *Globe and Mail*, 13 March 2023.

789 Ibid.

790 Marvin Cruz, "'Your voice' omnibus survey on small business issues", CFIB, April 2024.

791 Jenna Benchetrit, "Business insolvencies shot up by more than 41% last year, as pandemic debt mount", *CBC News*, 2 February 2024.

792 "Back in business? Spring update on small business debt and CEBA", CFIB, 6 June 2023.

793 "2023 Annual & Q4 Canadian insolvency statistics", Canadian Association of Insolvency and Restructuring Professionals (CAIRP), 5 February 2024.

794 Ibid.

795 Gigi Suhamic, "90% of small businesses have yet to pay COVID loans as deadline looms", *Financial Post*, 11 May 2023.

796 Jake Link, "How COVID-19 is impacting small businesses and what you can do about it", *Constant Contact*, 3 June 2024.

797 "Entrepreneurs' mental health has decreased significantly compared to last year, warns new survey results from BDC", Business Development Bank of Canada (BDC), 9 May 2023.

798 Gaudreault, S., op. cit., p. 12.

799 "Survey on SME owners mental health and support: 5th survey wave", BDC, May 2023.

800 Edward Segal, "Covid-related burnout is having a big impact on small business owners: Survey", *Forbes*, 18 January 2022.

801 Bianca Bharti, "Small business owners' poor mental health has gotten even worse, BDC says", *Financial Post*, 10 May 2023.

802 Sherry Walling and Chelsea Brown, "Entrepreneurs could be at a higher risk of suicide: A psychologist explains why", *Entrepreneur*, 4 September 2022.

803 Tom Woods, *Your Facebook Friends are Wrong About the Lockdown: A Non-Hysteric's Guide to COVID-19*, Harmony, 2020, p. 4.

804   V. Narayan and Malathy Iyer, "Suicides up 30% among small business owners", *Times of India*, 10 November 2021.

805   Ibid.

806   "COVID-19 impact: More businessmen committed suicide in 2021 than farmer", *Business Today*, 21 August 2021.

807   Peter St. Onge and Gael Campan, "The flawed COVID-19 model that locked down Canada", Montreal Economic Institute, June 2020.

808   John P.A. Ioannidis, Sally Cripps and Martin A. Tanner, "Forecasting for COVID-19 has failed*", International Journal of Forecasting*, August 2020, p. 423.

809   CIBC, op. cit.

810   Etan Rotberg, "3 months later: How the pandemic is impacting Canadian businesses", Charter Professional Accountants Canada, 29 June 2020.

811   "Guidance on essential services and functions in Canada during the COVID-19 pandemic", Public Safety Canada, 14 October 2021.

812   "Uncovering the hidden iceberg: Why the human impact of COVID-19 could be a third crisis", Deloitte, August 2020.

813   John Haltiwanger, "Entrepreneurship during the COVID-19 pandemic: Evidence from the business formation statistics", *Entrepreneurship and Innovation Policy and the Economy*, 2022, p. 1.

814   Ibid., p. 1.

815   "Small Business Index, Q2", MetLife and U.S. Chamber of Commerce, 2024.

816   Heide Pearson, "COVID-19: Questions raised after Kenney, cabinet ministers dine on 'Sky Palace' balcony in Edmonton", *Global News*, 2 June 2021.

817   "Class action lawsuit launched against Alberta provincial government over COVID-19 restrictions", Police on Guard for Thee, 18 November 2023.

818   Meghan Grant, "'You're free to go': Alberta judge acquits restaurant owner on trial for breaking law during pandemic", *CBC News*, 28 August 2023.

819   "Rath and company files class action suit against Alberta for illegal health orders", *Rebel News*, 9 February 2024.

820   Ibid.

821   Isaac Lamoureux, "Alberta government faces class action for unlawful health orders", TNC, 9 February 2024.

822   Ibid.

823   "Small businesses feel biggest impact of coronavirus pandemic", *Business Wire*, 8 October 2020.

824   Chad Otar, "The impact of the coronavirus on small business", *Forbes*, 29 May 2020.

825   "Key small business statistics", Government of Canada, 2023, pp. 1-42.

826   Daniel Wong, "Canadian business closures surge, fewest business openings since lockdown", Better Dwelling, 25 September 2023.

827   Thibaut Duprey et al., "Business closures and (re)openings in real time using Google Places", Bank of Canada, January 2022, pp. 1-24.

828   *Ottawa Business Journal*, op. cit.

829 "COVID killing off Canada's small businesses: Report", *Toronto Sun*, 24 December 2021.

830 CAIRP, op. cit.

831 "Business bankruptcies are on the rise, but account for only 10% of looming business closures", CFIB, 18 August 2022.

832 Sudesh Baniya, "Business bankruptcy in EU surges to the highest levels since 2023", *Euro News*, 26 August 2023.

833 "European Union: Sectoral variations in business bankruptcies", BNP Paribas, 22 February 2023.

834 Indrabati Lahiri, "2023: The year of big bankruptcies", *Euro News*, 12 December 2023.

835 "Two sectors are driving the wave of bankruptcies in Europe", Lamond Group, 3 June 2023.

836 "Impact of COVID-19 on selected sectors of Canada's economy", *Hill Notes*, 8 April 2020.

837 Theo Bourgery-Gonse, "Business bankruptcies up 35% in France, 55,000 jobs on the line", *Euractiv*, 11 July 2023.

838 Martin Banks, "Business Europe: Rapidly increasing numbers of bankruptcies are alarming", *European Business Review*, 20 February 2023.

839 Danie Di Santo, "Will 2023 bankrupt Europe's businesses?", *Trumpet*, 2 March 2023.

Chapter 7

840 John P.A. Ioannidis, "Over- and under-estimation of COVID-19 deaths", *European Journal of Epidemiology*, June 2021, p. 581.

841 Ibid., p. 585.

842 Ibid., p. 581.

843 Ibid., p. 584.

844 Carlos Alegria and Yuri Nunes, "Estimate of the COVID-19 over-reporting bias as underlying cause of death in the USA", ResearchGate, p. 12.

845 Rob Arnott, Vitali Kalesnik, and Lilian Wu, "Collateral damage from Covid", Reason Foundation, October 2021, p. 1-11.

846 Casey B. Mulligan, "Deaths of despair and the incidence of excess mortality in 2020", NBER working paper 2803, December 2020, p. 6.

847 "Value-for-money audit: COVID-19 vaccination program", Office of the Auditor General of Ontario, November 2022, p. 31.

848 Ibid., p. 31.

849 Kayla Rosen, "New Manitoba program to have doctors, pharmacists encourage COVID-19 vaccination", *CTV News*, 21 September 2021.

850 "COVID-19 vaccine provider incentive program", Anthem Medicaid, October 2021.

851 Enrique Acosta, "Global estimates of excess deaths from COVID-19", *Nature*, 5 January 2023, pp. 31-33.

852   Patrick Beane, "Insurance executive says deaths rates among working-age people up 40 percent", *Indiana Public Media*, 3 January 2022.

853   "Powerful warning in connection with the reporting of COVID-19 vaccination side-effects and the importance attached to the vaccination strategy relative to support for therapeutics", European Parliament, 25 February 2022.

854   Karolina Klaskova, "Large German health insurer says up to 3 million people potentially suffered Covid-19 side effects", *ReMix*, 25 February 2022.

855   Tadhg Pidgeon, "German Health Minister admits 'disturbing' vaccine side-effects", *European Conservative*, 15 March 2023.

856   "The future of excess mortality after COVID-19", Swiss Re Institute, September 2024, p. 2.

857   Ibid., p. 2.

858   "The emergence of Sudden Adult Death Syndrome: What you need to know", Tampa Cardiovascular Associates, 1 January 2024.

859   "Sudden Arrhythmic Death Syndrome", Cleveland Clinic, 6 June 2022.

860   Jonathan Bradley, "Lewis demands answers on Sudden Adult Death Syndrome", *Western Standard*, 3 August 2022.

861   Andre Picard, "Life expectancy is falling in Canada. It's not all COVID's fault", *Globe and Mail*, 5 December 2023.

862   Maria Polyakova et al., "Initial economic damage from the COVID-19 pandemic in the United States is more widespread across ages and geographies than initial mortality impacts", *PNAS*, November 2020, p. 27934.

863   "The rise of excess deaths and unexplained deaths in Canada", Justice Center for Constitutional Freedoms, 25 August 2023.

864   Casey B. Mulligan and Robert D. Arnott, "Non-Covid excess deaths, 2020-21: Collateral damage of policy choices?", NBER working paper, June 2022, p. 1.

865   Wency Leung, "More people than expected are dying in Canada in 2023 for reasons that are not yet clear", *Globe and Mail*, 15 August 2023.

866   Mulligan, C. and R. Arnott, op. cit., p. 12.

867   Mulligan, C. and R. Arnott, op. cit., p. 1.

868   Arnott, R., Kalesnik, V. and L. Wu, op. cit., p. 4.

869   Arnott, R., Kalesnik, V. and L. Wu, op. cit., p. 16.

870   Arnott, R., Kalesnik, V. and L. Wu, op. cit., p. 16.

871   Arnott, R., Kalesnik, V. and L. Wu, op. cit., p. 17.

872   Arnott, R., Kalesnik, V. and L. Wu, op. cit., p. 17.

873   Christopher J. Ruhm, "Excess deaths in the United States during the first year of COVID-19", *Preventive Medicine*, July 2022, pp. 1-10.

874   Mulligan, C., op. cit., p. 13.

875   Arnott, R., Kalesnik, V. and L. Wu, op. cit., pp. 5-6.

876   Christopher J. Cronin and William N. Evans, "Excess mortality from COVID and non-COVID causes in minority populations", *PNAS*, September 2021, p. 1.

877   Peter Rhodes and Peter Parry, "Gene-based COVID-19 vaccines: Australian

perspectives in a corporate and global context", *Pathology–Research and Practice*, January 2024, p. 4.

878 Jonathan Pearson-Stuttard et al., "Excess mortality in England post COVID-19 pandemic: implications for secondary prevention", *Lancet*, January 2024, p. 1.

879 Leung, W., op. cit.

880 Mulligan, C. and R. Arnott, op. cit., p. 8.

881 Megan E. Patrick et al., "Using substances to cope with the COVID-19 pandemic: U.S. national data at age 19 years", *Journal of Adolescents Health*, February 2022, p. 340.

882 Richard Woodbury, "Why StatsCan says Nova Scotia is seeing 'significant' excess mortality", *CBC News*, 20 June 2023.

883 "A province-by-province look at excess deaths in Canada during the pandemic", UBC Faculty of Medicine, 30 May 2022.

884 Arnott, R., Kalesnik, V. and L. Wu, op. cit., p. 13.

885 Ruhm, C., op. cit., p. 6.

886 Mary G. Fidling, Robert J. Blendon, and John M. Benson, "Delayed care with harmful health consequences–Reported experienced from national surveys during coronavirus disease 2019", *JAMA*, August 2020, p. 1.

887 Ruhm, C., op. cit., p. 6.

888 Mulligan, C. and R. Arnott, op. cit., p. 11.

889 Saskia Mostert et al., "Excess mortality across countries in the Western World since the COVID-19 pandemic: 'Our World in Data' estimates of January 2020 to December 2022", *BMJ Public Health*, June 2024, p. 8.

890 Anthony Lin et al., "Body weight changes during pandemic-related shelter-in-place in a longitudinal cohort study", *JAMA*, March 2022, pp. 1-4.

891 Surabhi Bhutani et al., "Longitudinal weight gain and related risk behaviors during the COVID-19 pandemic in adults in the US", *Nutrients*, February 2021, pp. 1-13.

892 Tu-Hasan Chang et al., "Weight gain associated with COVID-19 lockdowns in children and adolescents", *Nutrients*, October 2021, pp. 1-10.

893 Eugenio Paglino et al., "Excess natural-cause mortality in US counties and its association with reported COVID-19 deaths", *PNAS*, February 2024, p. 1.

894 Ibid., p. 1.

895 Sam Peltzman, "The effects of automobile safety regulations", *Journal of Political Economy*, August 1975, pp. 677-726.

896 Leo S. Robertson, "A critical analysis of Peltzman's 'The effects of automobile safety regulation'", *Journal of Economic Issues*, September 1977, pp. 587-600.

897 Deepak Juyal et al., "COVID-19: The vaccination drive in India and the Peltzman effect", *Journal of Family Medicine and Primary Care*, November 2021, p. 3946.

898 Ibid., pp. 3945–3947.

899 Karthikeyan P. Iyengar et al., "Influence of the Peltzman effect on the recurrent COVID-19 waves in Europe", *Postgraduate Medical Journal*, March 2022,

pp. 110-111.

900   Casey B. Mulligan, "Peltzman revisited: Quantifying 21st century opportunity costs of FDA regulation", NBER working paper 29574, December 2021.

901   Sam Williams et al., "COVID-19 mortalities in England and Wales and the Peltzman offsetting effect", *Applied Economics*, August 2021, pp. 6982-6998.

902   Mostert, S. et al., op. cit., p. 8.

903   Rhodes, P. and P. Parry, op. cit., p. 1.

904   Mostert, S. et al., op. cit., p. 2.

905   Bruce K. Patterson et al., "Persistence of S1 spike protein in CD16+ monocytes up to 245 days in SARS-CoV-2 negative post COVID-19 vaccination individuals with Post-Acute Sequalae of COVID-19 (PASC)-like symptoms", *medRxiv Preprint*, March 2024, p. 3.

906   Mostert, S. et al., op. cit., p. 2.

907   Jarle Aarstad and Andreas Kvitastein, "Is there a link between the 2021 COVID-19 vaccination uptake in Europe and 2022 excess all-cause mortality?", *Asian Pacific Journal of Health Sciences*, January-March 2023, p. 25.

908   Ibid., p. 25.

909   Marco Alessandria et al., "A critical analysis of all-cause deaths during COVID-19 vaccination in an Italian province", *Microorganisms*, June 2024, p. 13.

910   Ibid., p. 13.

911   Nicolas Hulscher et al., "Autopsy findings in cases of fatal COVID-19 vaccine-induced myocarditis", *ESC Heart Failure*, January 2024, p. 12.

912   Hannah Van Wyk et al., "Letter to the editor regarding 'Autopsy findings in cases of fatal COVID-19 vaccine-induced myocarditis'", *ESC Heart Failure*, August 2024, pp. 2467-2468.

913   Mark Skidmore, "COVID-19 illness and vaccination experiences in social circles affect COVID-19 vaccination decisions", *Science, Public Health Policy, and the Law*, October 2023, pp. 208-226.

914   Spiro Pantazatos and Herve Seligman, "COVID vaccination and age-stratified all-cause mortality risk", ResearchGate, October 2022, pp. 1-52.

915   Denis Rancourt, Joseph Hickey, and Christian Linard, "Spatiotemporal variation of excess all-cause mortality in the world (125 countries) during the Covid period 2020-2023 regarding socio-economic factors and public-health and medical interventions", Correlation, July 2024.

916   Hui-Lee Wong et al., "Surveillance of COVID-19 vaccine safety among elderly persons aged 65 years and older", *Vaccine*, January 2023, p. 532.

917   Ron Johnson, "Vaccine side effects censorship drove vaccine hesitancy", *News Nation*, 4 May 2024.

918   Ibid.

919   Apoorva Mandavilli, "Thousands believe Covid vaccines harmed them. Is anyone listening?", *New York Times*, 3 May 2024.

920   Ibid.

921   "Countermeasures Compensation Injury Program", U.S. Human Resources and Services Administration, 1 April 2024.

922   Mandavilli, A., op. cit.

923   Mostert, S. et al., op. cit., p. 1.

924   "OECD data explorer", OECD.

925   "Excess mortality rose sharply to 19% in December 2022", *Eurostat*, 17 February 2023.

926   Pearson-Stuttard, J. et al., op. cit., pp. 1-2.

927   Mulligan, C. and R. Arnott, op. cit., p. 5.

928   Mulligan, C. and R. Arnott, op. cit., p. 8.

929   "Investigation into spikes in newborn baby deaths in Scotland", *BBC News*, 30 September 2022.

930   "Excess death trends, volume 743", UK Parliament, 16 January 2024.

931   Ibid.

932   Ibid.

933   Ibid.

934   Ibid.

935   Ibid.

936   Camilla Turner, "Health Secretary urged to release data that 'may link Covid vaccine to excess deaths'", *Telegraph*, 2 March 2024.

937   Pearson-Stuttard, J. et al., op. cit., p. 1.

938   Pearson-Stuttard, J. et al., op. cit., p. 1.

939   Pearson-Stuttard, J. et al., op. cit., p. 1.

940   "Early heart disease deaths rise to 14-year highs", *British Heart Foundation*, 22 January 2024.

941   Pearson-Stuttard, J. et al., op. cit., p. 1.

942   "Estimating excess deaths in the UK, methodology changes: February 2024", Office of National Statistics (ONS), 20 February 2024.

943   "Deaths, 2022", Statistics Canada, 27 November 2023.

944   Alexandra Sonnenwirth et al., "What happened in 2022? The Canadian excess mortality conundrum, what caused it and will it continue?", ClubVita, 19 October 2023, pp. 1-48.

945   Ibid., p. 16.

946   Sanjay Beesoon et al., "Excess deaths during COVID-19 pandemic in Alberta, Canada", *International Journal of Infectious Diseases*, December 2022, pp. 62-67.

947   Statistics Canada (2023), op. cit.

948   "Provisional death counts and excess mortality, January 2020 to October 2022", Statistics Canada, 12 January 2023.

949   Beesoon, S. et al., op. cit., p. 62.

950   Craig Gilbert, "Alcohol, drugs helped drive excess mortality during pandemic: Statistics Canada", *Edmonton Journal*, 15 January 2023.

951   Anthony Vasquez-Peddie, "Delayed health care during pandemic may have led to thousands of excess deaths: study", *CTV News*, 30 November 2021.

952   Sonnenwirth, A. et al., op. cit., pp. 36-43.

953   "Ontario waiting list deaths jump", *Second Street*, 15 August 2023.

954   Ibid.

955   Hana Mae Nassar, "Pandemic may have contributed to thousands of 'excess deaths' in Canada: report", *CityNews Toronto*, 30 November 2021.

Chapter 8

956   Rob Arnott, Vitali Kalesnik, and Lilian Wu, "Collateral damage from Covid", Reason Foundation, October 2021, p. 2.

957   Jostein Askim and Tomas Bergstrom, "Between lockdown and calm down. Comparing the COVID-19 responses of Norway and Sweden", *Local Government Studies*, August 2021, p. 304.

958   Arnott, R., Kalesnik, V. and L. Wu, op. cit., pp. 24-25.

959   Peter Rhodes and Peter Parry, "Gene-based COVID-19 vaccines: Australian perspectives in a corporate and global context", *Pathology–Research and Practice*, January 2024, p. 4.

960   Ibid., p. 4.

961   Drea Humphrey, "Leslyn Lewis sounds the alarm over Sudden Adult Death Syndrome", *Rebel News*, 5 August 2022.

962   "Public accountability: A matter of trust and confidence. Discussion paper", Controller and Auditor General New Zealand, 3 September 2019, pp. 1-64.

963   "Disaster" (definition), United Nations Office for Disaster Risk Reduction.

964   "Glossary of health emergency and disaster risk management terminology", World Health Organization (WHO), 2020, p. 13.

965   Ibid., p. 14.

966   Kevin Bardosh, "Commentary: COVID vaccines mandates in Canada were a mistake: Are we ready to learn the right lessons?", Macdonald-Laurier Institute, November 2022, p. 1.

967   "Privy Council advocated downplaying COVID vaccine injuries or deaths", *Toronto Sun*, 6 June 2023.

968   Ibid.

969   Bardosh, K., op. cit., p. 2.

970   Joseph A. Ladapo, "Drs. Callif and Walensky" (letter), Florida Health, 10 May 2023, p. 1.

971   Ibid., p. 3.

972   "Do Canadians have confidence in their public institutions?", StatsCan, 23 November 2023.

973   Michael Monopoli, "Millions of Canadians lack trust in government and news media", Abacus, 8 June 2022.

974   Mia Rabson, "Canadians less trusting of governments as COVID wear on for second year: Poll", *Global News*, 9 February 2022.

975   John Miller, "Federal poll suggests declining confidence in government and media", *Rabble*, 17 January 2024.

976   Bardosh, K., op. cit., p. 6.

977   Michael A. Thoene, "Changing views toward mRNA based COVID vaccines in the scientific literature", *Polish Annals of Medicine*, July 2024, p. 152.

978   "Don't trust fed fact checker", Blacklocks, 19 March 2024.

979   "2024 Edelman Trust Barometer Canada Report", Edelman Trust Institute, 2024, p. 10,

980   Ibid., p. 15.

981   "Parental opposition to childhood vaccination grows as Canadians worry about harms of anti-vax movement", Angus Reid Institute, 19 May 2024.

982   Ibid.

983   "Democrats trust heath experts more", Rasmussen Reports, 31 January 2024.

984   Ibid.

985   Dwight Eisenhower, "Farewell Address", 1961.

986   Jeffrey A. Tucker, "The proof of censorship is … censored", Brownstone Institute, 7 May 2024.

987   Jay Bhattacharya, "The US Government censored dissident scientists to protect it from criticism of its own misinformation", MIT Free Speech Alliance, March 2024.

988   Ibid.

989   "Paper claiming 'extensive' harms of COVID-19 vaccines to be retracted", Retraction Watch, 19 February 2024.

990   Ibid.

991   Brenda Baletti, "'Stunning act of scientific censorship': Journal retracts peer-reviewed study critiquing COVID-19 vaccine", *Defender*, 28 February 2024.

992   Swati Bharadwaj, "Bharat Biotech sues BHU researchers over Covaxin study", *Times of India*, 13 September 2024.

993   Shuriah Niazi, "Company's defamation suit raises research freedom concerns", *University World News*, 4 October 2024.

994   Marcia Agnell, "Industry-sponsored clinical research: A broken system", *Journal of American Medical Association*, 3 September 2008, p. 1069.

995   Ibid., p. 1070.

996   Ibid., p. 1070.

997   Ibid., p. 1070.

998   Richard Smith, "Medical journals are an extension of the marketing arm of pharmaceutical companies", *PLoS Medicine*, May 2005, p. 0364.

999   Ibid., p. 0364.

1000   Ibid., p. 0364.

1001   Ibid., p. 0365.

1002   Joseph S. Ross et al., "Promoting transparency in pharmaceutical industry-sponsored research", *American Journal of Public Health*, January 2012, p. 72.

1003   Kamran Abbasi, "COVID-19: Politicization, 'corruption,' and suppression of science", *British Journal of Medicine*, November 2020, p. 2.

1004 Ibid., pp. 1-2.

1005 Ibid., p. 1.

1006 Ibid., p. 1.

1007 Ibid., p. 1.

1008 Ibid., p. 2.

1009 Bardosh, K., op. cit., p. 4.

1010 "NIH awards by organization and location", National Institute of Health (NIH).

1011 Abbasi, K., op. cit., p. 1.

1012 Monica Schoch-Spana et al., "The SPARS pandemic 2025-2028: A futuristic scenario for public health risk communicators", Johns Hopkins University, pp. 1-89.

1013 Douglas Farrow, "A new Catholicism? On the eugenic health tyranny as a test of fidelity", In *Politics, Law, & Religion in Times of Covid*, Jane Adolphe, Fulvio di Blasi, and Robert Fastiggi (eds.), St. Louis, pp. 323-362.

www.ingramcontent.com/pod-product-compliance
Lightning Source LLC
Chambersburg PA
CBHW050336270326
41926CB00016B/3485